Colonial fantasies investigates the intersection between post-colonial theory and feminist criticism, focusing on the persistent Western fascination with the veiled women of the Orient. In her original and compelling book, Meyda Yeğenoğlu examines the veil both as a site of fantasy and of nationalist ideologies and discourses of gender identity. Through her analysis of travel literature and anthropological and literary texts, she demonstrates that the very desire to penetrate the veiled surface of "otherness" is constitutive of hegemonic, colonial identity. She also shows how representations of cultural difference are inextricably linked to representations of sexual difference. Recognizing that the figure of the Oriental woman has functioned as the veiled interior of Western identity, she calls into question dualistic conceptions of identity and difference, and of West and East. She draws on recent critical theory to challenge both traditional masculinist assumptions of Orientalism and those Western feminist discourses which seek to "liberate" the veiled woman in the name of progress. Meyda Yeğenoğlu is Associate Professor in the Department of Sociology, at the Middle East Technical University, Ankara. She has also taught in North America and published in Turkish and English on Orientalism, and cultural and women's studies. She is the co-editor, with Mahmut Mutman, of *Orientalism and Cultural Differences*, a special issue of the journal *Inscriptions*.

Colonial fantasies

Cambridge Cultural Social Studies

Series editors: JEFFREY C. ALEXANDER, *Department of Sociology, University of California, Los Angeles, and* STEVEN SEIDMAN, *Department of Sociology, University at Albany, State University of New York.*

Titles in the series

Colonial fantasies

Towards a feminist reading of Orientalism

Meyda Yeğenoğlu

CAMBRIDGE
UNIVERSITY PRESS

CAMBRIDGE UNIVERSITY PRESS
Cambridge, New York, Melbourne, Madrid, Cape Town,
Singapore, São Paulo, Delhi, Mexico City

Cambridge University Press
The Edinburgh Building, Cambridge CB2 8RU, UK

Published in the United States of America by Cambridge University Press, New York

www.cambridge.org
Information on this title: www.cambridge.org/9780521482332

© Cambridge University Press 1998

First published 1998
Reprinted 1999

A catalogue record for this publication is available from the British Library

Library of Congress Cataloguing in Publication Data
Yeğenoğlu, Meyda.
    Colonial fantasies: towards a feminist reading of Orientalism /
Meyda Yeğenoğlu.
        p.   cm. – (Cambridge cultural social studies)
    Includes bibliographical references (p. 167) and index.
    ISBN 0 521 48233 X. – ISBN 0 521 62658 7 (pbk.)
    1. Feminist literary criticism.   2. East and West in literature.
3. Exoticism in literature.   I. Title.   II. Series.
PN98.W64Y45   1998
809´.89287 – dc21   97-25638 CIP

ISBN 978-0-521-48233-2 Hardback
ISBN 978-0-521-62658-3 Paperback

Contents

Acknowledgment

This book owes much to many people who directly or indirectly assisted with their suggestions, encouragement, and support. My heart-felt gratitude must certainly go to those who generously took the time to read it while it was still in its formative stages; I owe special thanks to Elizabeth Grosz and Stephen Heath who read early versions of the manuscript, made probing suggestions and helped me to sharpen the text in many ways. I thank Wendy Brown, Victor Burgin, John Brown Childs, James Clifford, and Donna Haraway for reading and commenting on various chapters. The Center for Cultural Studies at the University of California Santa Cruz has contributed in a vital way to the intellectual and social milieu in which the ideas of this book have originated. I have been enriched and challenged by the discussions with friends and colleagues in the Postcolonial Representations Group. I would like to thank especially Gordon Bigelow, Gabe Brahm Jr., Mark Driscoll, Christoph Cox, and Molly Whalen for their stimulation. I have been greatly inspired by my friend and colleague Vicki Kirby. I will always remember the pleasures of thought-provoking discussions with her and the joyous support she gave on numerous occasions which helped me to survive the uncertainties of institutional life. Many thanks go to Donna Landry and Gerald MacLean for cheerful conversations, meals and all-purpose support. My gratitude to Sharon Baṣtuǧ for friendship, support, and stimulation of all kinds. I thank my series editors Jeffrey Alexander and Steven Seidman. I am indebted to Jeffrey Alexander for showing interest in my work and for approaching me with the idea of publishing it and to Steven Seidman for offering valuable criticism as well as editorial guidance and support. I am grateful to Catherine Max for her patience, supervision and advice at all stages in the publication of this work. Sheila Kane's copyediting was a gift. She has my gratitude for her careful and close reading. The person to whom I owe most in the writing of this book is Mahmut Mutman who suffered my disappointments and excitements but has always been there with encouragement, care, and support. The insightful comments, suggestions, and criticisms he generously offered are the real source of all that is noteworthy and stimulating here. Finally, this book is dedicated to the memory of my parents Saliha Yeğenoğlu and Kasım Yeğenoğlu, who taught me the importance of persistence and commitment, with love. The study of patriarchal and colonial discourse has its own vicissitudes, from which one nevertheless benefits. So I offer my peculiar thanks to some of my colleagues in the Department of Sociology, Middle East Technical University, where I am currently employed, for providing me with, to borrow an expression from another author, "the neurotic intellectual and political energy" which culminated in this book.

This work was made possible by financial support from several institutions. Many thanks to the Center for Cultural Studies, Feminist Research Activities Center and Social Sciences Division of the University of California, Santa Cruz which have provided much-needed financial assistance. I am also very grateful for the financial support provided by the Fullbright Commission and the American Association of University Women.

Introduction

This book explores the discursive dynamics that secure a sovereign subject status for the West. It is about the cultural representation of the West to *itself* by way of a detour through the other. With the proliferation of post-colonial studies, we are witnessing a number of studies investigating the operating principles of Orientalism. Moreover, studies that explicate the articulation of gender with Orientalism are also flourishing. Part of the reason that motivates me to write this book is to provide an analysis of Orientalism that does not relegate the question of sexual difference to a sub-field in the analysis of colonial discourse and this study focuses on the unique articulation of sexual and cultural difference as they are produced and signified in the discourse of Orientalism. I have found that investigations into the question of gender in Orientalism often fall short in recognizing how representations of cultural and sexual difference are constitutive of each other and thus risk reproducing the categorical distinction between the two that feminist theory attempts to combat. With a few exceptions, questions of sexual difference in the discourse of Orientalism are either ignored or, if recognized, understood as an issue which belongs to a different field, namely gender or feminist studies. My decision to explore this question came with an awareness that the critiques of Orientalism and colonial discourse manifest a persistent reluctance to examine the unique nature of the articulation of cultural and sexual difference in the case of Orientalism. Hence the writing of this book grew out of a concern that the gendered categories of Orientalism warrant a more complicated analysis than what is available; it requires a reformulation of the nature of Orientalist discourse itself. By intervening in such debates, my aim is to call into question the usefulness of simply adding the gender "variable" to the accounts of Orientalism. It is the contention of this book that if we are to engage the complex significations that constitute

Orientalism we need to examine closely how the discursive constitution of Otherness is achieved simultaneously through sexual as well as cultural modes of differentiation. A more sexualized reading of Orientalism reveals that representations of sexual difference cannot be treated as its sub-domain; it is of fundamental importance in the formation of a colonial subject position.

Understanding the sexualized nature of Orientalism requires an examination of its unconscious structure. It has been demonstrated time and again that colonialism was and is an economic as well as a political and cultural phenomenon. That colonialism is also structured by unconscious processes, however, is rarely discussed. In addressing the question of sexual difference, it needs to be recognized that fantasy and desire, as unconscious processes, play a fundamental role in the colonial relation that is established with the colonized. In introducing the concepts of fantasy and desire I am fully aware of the risk of psychologizing structural processes by reducing them to individual psychological motivations. I use these concepts to refer to a historically specific construction and to a collective process. In other words, by colonial or Orientalist fantasy I refer not to biologically or psychologically innate individual characteristics, but to a set of discursive effects that constitute the subject.

This book engages with otherness but it is not an ethnography of the other. Although the necessity of recognizing the self's indebtedness to the other and the need to establish a non-dominating relation with the other are always in between the lines of this study, I remain convinced that such a relation can be established only when the hegemonic position of the Western subject is deconstructed. Therefore, an inquiry into Orientalism cannot afford to ignore the constitution of the Western subject. As I am aware of the metaphysical, ontological, and essentialist connotations of the term "Western subject," I feel the need to make some cautionary remarks about the way in which I use the term in this book.

The Western subject should not be thought of as an essence. There are many lines of fractures, rifts, discontinuities, and divisions that crisscross the Western subject. The use of such a term carries the risk of disregarding its diversity and the variety of class, gendered, national, ethnic, and other differences that permeate and impregnate it. It is true that there has never been *one* Western subject; it covers a great variety of differences. The process of *becoming-a-Western-subject* is not a process that simply homogenizes and makes uniform but that also *differentiates*. Hence it implies neither an essential unity nor homogeneity. This subject is working class, English, female, male, French, upper class and so on. The intricate processes at work that influence this differentiation require a sophisticated analysis beyond the scope and aim of this book. Although the word covers a great variety of other determinants, the traces and effects of the location I call "Western" nevertheless wait to be accounted for. Despite the difficulties in attributing unity to this subject (as the differentiations are great and there are contradictory, discordant, and disharmonious positions), it is nevertheless not easy to claim that there is no validity or justified ground in the usage of such a term. The task that awaits us is to affirm the validity of the term "Western subject" while at the same time complicating and revisiting the modernist, humanist, and metaphysical bind in which such a term is caught up; we should be wary of the risk of "re-introducing precisely what is in question."[1] Should I be using the term Western subject without problematizing this humanist bind, I would be betraying the whole mission upon which this book is based. The critique of the fundamental categories of humanism and metaphysics is of central importance for post-colonial criticism as these categories (especially the illusory self-certainty and the Western bind apparent in Enlightenment notions of the human and the individual) are constitutive of Western modernity and colonialism. Thus, my use of the term does not imply returning to the humanist notion of subjectivity or assuming it is present to itself. On the contrary, a critique of the Western subject implies critiquing its self-certainty, authority, and value. Such a critique, in other words, relies on deconstructing the very metaphysical gesture upon which it is based, yet it is far from indicating the dissolution or annihilation of the subject. The well-celebrated gesture of the "death of the subject" or the "decentring of the subject" does not imply its final annihilation. The presumptions that celebrate this dissolution are themselves part of the metaphysical gesture that such a celebration aims to criticize.[2]

Accordingly, in this work the category Western subject does not refer to an essence or uniformity nor to a metaphysical self-presence. The connotation is not essence but the process of constitution of identity; it thus refers to a position or positioning, to a place, or placing, that is, to a specific inhabiting of a place. It refers to a process of generation, to a process of coming into being, of invention and of fashioning of a place called "Western". The peculiarity of a colonial discourse such as Orientalism may be said to reside precisely in the Westernizing (as well as Orientalizing) operation itself. This is a process by which members are instituted as Western subjects. The operation I call "Westernizing" consists in the fashioning of a historically specific *fantasy* whereby members imagine themselves as Western. This engendering and fashioning of the Western subject thus has a fictive character. But the fictive character of this position does not mean that it is not *real*; on the contrary, it produces material effects by constituting the very bodies of the subjects that it subjects. It refers to the historical inscription of a particular identity. To put it in different terms, the process of "becoming" a Western subject refers to its members becoming ontologized.[3] One is not a Western subject because there exists a pregiven structure called the Western culture which imposes itself upon its members. The transformation of individuals into Western subjects is not accomplished by issuing Western identity cards.[4] One "becomes" and is made Western by being subjected to a process called Westernizing and by imagining oneself in the fantasy frame of belonging to a specific culture called the "West." This imaginary, however, is not a private or an individual undertaking. It is a process that exists externally and objectively. The Lacanian formulation of fantasy and the desire that induces it is central to my discussion of the Orientalist discourse in the following pages, but my use of the psychoanalytic notion of "fantasy" and the associated term "object petit a" should not be considered as an individual matter, but rather something conditioned by objective and structural processes.

However, the process that constitutes subjects as Western is not identical in each individual instance; it is subject to differential articulation at every specific historical moment and in different cases. Therefore, I do not claim that the analysis I offer here is valid for every specific instance of Orientalist discourse. What I do here is to chart the unconscious of Orientalism that needs to be rethought and reconfigured at every different instance. The specific instance I address in this book is veiling.

The modern subject

This modern idea of the subject has been severely criticized in the last two decades. Indeed, as these criticisms and deconstructions have pointed out, the subject itself is a modern idea that came with Enlightenment and humanism. The thinking and conscious "subject" finds its most elaborate articulation in Descartes' well-known philosophical statement, "I think therefore I am." Epistemologically the subject is constructed as a knowing subject, in opposition to or before an "object" that is to be known and controlled. The subject is also considered to be a causal and responsible agent, the "ego" or "self" that is supposed to be the center and source of the world and his/her actions. Post-structuralist and post-modern criticism has declared that the end of the subject signifies the end or perhaps the closure of the modern era, and the end of the category "Man," taken as a neutral term synonymous with the subject in this humanist discourse. Hence the attraction of post-structuralist criticism or deconstruction of the subject for feminist and post-colonial theory, because the social reference of the philosophical category of "Man" has been the European white male subject constructed as hegemonic by these discourses. But such deconstruction has also generated the feeling of unease and hesitancy because it also seems to undermine philosophically the notion of agency that is implied in the concept of subject and that political discourses require. The challenges and criticisms directed to the category of subject by recent deconstruction and psychoanalysis expose the subject as a historical construction – European, male, and bourgeois. One can not develop an ethical, political, and theoretical position on the subject without questioning the often abstract – though historical – and complicated mechanisms which produce it. However, a deconstruction of the subject is not sufficient if it is merely limited to exposing it as a "Western white male." The abstract moment which constitutes this historical subject as "sovereign" and "universal" should not be missed. A different sense of subjectivity, especially from the point of view of the notion of agency that an ethical position requires, can only be developed if we take the notion of otherness as constitutive.

What underlies this modern idea of subject? Emerging out of the religious symbolic and ideological universe of the feudal Middle Ages, the modern notion of the subject is the result of a fundamental reversal and dislocation. It does not simply replace the notion of God, but signifies a transformation of the very coordinates which organized the symbolic universe of European societies for centuries. Such a transformation, closely related with the transformation in the structure of production relations, has produced the secular notion of an individual "I" as an abstract and universal consciousness free of all embodiment and locality. At once a legal, philosophical, and psychic conceptual unity, the ego or subject finds its full meaning in this assumption of *autonomy*. It is the assumption of autonomy which gives the subject a universal status. Such a universal status is produced in a complex discursive strategy. The construction of the subject requires another term or condition from which the subject distinguishes itself. This "other" term remains repressed, and its "forgotten" or repressed presence is the very condition of the autonomy and universality of the subject. This is why a critique of the subject can only be conducted from the point of view of this other term.

For instance, from the point of view of feminist discourse, modern humanism appears to be a mode of patriarchal discourse (or patriarchy to be a mode of humanist discourse). How is "human" signified in the grammar of Western metaphysics? We might read humanism as a discourse which marks *woman* rather than man. The place of the subject is emptied out by marking the other – woman – as different (emotional, weak, irrational, dependent, etc.). "Man" thus becomes the universal norm occupying that "empty" place and constituting the universal being of the "human" – from which woman is a "natural" deviation. In this structure, that which is marked as other is attributed the opposite characteristics of the subject. Thus, on the one hand, the other is made an element of comparison with the subject; on the other hand, she is and remains radically different from the subject. In this humanist trial in which the judge is also the prosecutor, the "other" is born accused: she is made lacking what the subject has and yet is threatening to the stable world of the subject by her radical difference. This structure of the subject is equally valid for colonial or imperial discourse. For instance, Edward Said defines Orientalism as an "epistemological and ontological distinction between the West and East." This distinction is achieved by marking the East as lacking "civil society," "individuality" or "secondary structures" – all the sociological and anthropological properties that the West is naturally assumed to have. By a rhetorical strategy, the Oriental or non-Western societies are pushed back in time and constructed as primitive or backward. The Western subject thus constitutes the universal norm by occupying that empty, abstract place reached by a "natural" and "normal" evolution. The subject is thus produced by a linguistic/discursive strategy in which the denial of dependence on the other guarantees an illusion of autonomy and freedom.

Hegelian philosophy can be seen as the main theoretical text that constituted the fiction of autonomy and sovereignty of the subject. The modern philosopher *par excellence*, Hegel, provided the highest articulation of this dialectic of subject in his *Phenomenology of Spirit*.[5] In the Hegelian text, the subject is constructed by a mediation through the other. The subject represents itself to itself through the other and constitutes itself as universal, abstract subject (the I or ego) by signifying the other as a categorical opposite, a radical denial or negation of itself. In this operation of *aufhebung*, the different loses its difference, its incommensurability and its singularity and becomes the subject's other – a moment of identity. The problem with this account is that, by conceiving difference in the form of a contradiction that will be resolved in a higher synthesis, the Hegelian text produces the effect of a final closure. While negativity is regarded as essential in the movement which produces the subject, such negativity is always turned into an internal moment of the dialectic of the subject. This is then a denial of difference; all difference is turned into sameness; the production of the subject as abstract and universal consciousness is this very movement of transforming difference into sameness. The Hegelian assumption is that *the other shares the same universe with the subject*. Hegel's text can be read therefore as the subject's necessary forgetting of its dependence on the other, who is different, elsewhere, as its very sign. This Hegelian dialectical economy of subject-constitution cannot accept that the other is differently constituted. The other's difference can only be recognized comparatively, that is to say, in terms of the same. While the other is necessary to the subject's constitution, the subject can constitute itself only on the basis of a denial of the other's difference.

Deconstructing the subject

Hegelian subjectivity has been deconstructed by discourses of psycho-analysis and post-structuralism. Lacan traces the presence of the other in the absences and lacunae of the discourse of the subject, and splits the subject between his conscious and unconscious discourses while showing his dependency on language on the basis of a model of the primacy of the signifier. In the Lacanian approach, the subject is not seen as identical to self-consciousness as in Hegel, but as an effect of language, of the move-ment of the signifier. In his deconstruction of Western metaphysics, Derrida identifies what he calls a *binary structure* that characterizes the dis-course of metaphysics. This is indeed the very structure that I have described above, but Derrida provides us with an argument that recognizes the other as different. According to him, a binary structure constructs an "other" as a privileged term, against which the latter can distinguish itself. One term is taken out of a system of terms and is given a positive value, which thus constructs an "other" or negative of itself which signifies every-thing that it does not accept. There can be no third term in a binary struc-ture, and no mediation between the two terms. One of them is given a logical priority and a positive value, while the other is characterized as the absence of the positive attributes of the first. The second term is thus denied an existence of its own; it is merely a negation of the first term. Derrida proposes a two-step strategy to deconstruct the binary structure. The first moment is to reverse the hierarchy by re-valuing the de-valued or subordinate "other" term. However, this is not sufficient, because reversal in itself does not come to terms with the domination of the first term and it leaves the binary structure unquestioned. A second step is necessary to break the structure apart: this is the procedure of displacement. Displacement is the operation of locating the subordinate term into the heart of the dominant one. It is through displacement that the dependence of the subject on the other is made explicit.

Post-structuralism and psychoanalysis thus expose the subject as a Western and male constitution. However, what is at stake is not merely an unveiling of the subject's abstract universal pretensions, but also a demonstration of the fact that its illusory self-production is a denial of relationality, complexity and dependence on the other. As I have noted above, theoretical discourses of post-structuralism and psychoanalysis are often criticized for leaving no space for a concept of agency. The implicit argument here is that when the subject is deconstructed, there is no ground left for action, and therefore no possibility of changing the existing order of things. By deconstructing the subject but offering no alternative in its place, post-structuralism is considered to be somehow complicit with the existing order of things. I would like to argue that this widespread criticism misses the point, not so much because it insists on the necessity of agency but rather because it risks leaving the very structure of the subject intact. The dangerous result of this attitude is to reverse the structure and to enact the same subject, to repeat the same desire for a sovereign, autonomous position on the side of the subordinate, hegemonized, second term. The very structure of the production of subject implies that the subordinate term can not be a subject in the way that the dominant term is. How do we account for this different sense of the subject where embodiment, relationality, difference, and otherness are not denied but are turned into a productive moment?

Obviously this is not simply a question of giving a subject his or her right. How could one (who?) give his or her right to the oppressed subject while his/her subjectivity/subject-ness carries a sense and a force that always remains different? How could the oppressed be the same as or equal to the subject whose presence and rationality always requires an "other"? Derrida's strategy of deconstruction is essential here. To many, deconstruction seems to be an overly theoretical reading of texts or an obsessive calculation of minute details. But this too-careful reading, "an analysis of all possible givens in a situation," in Derrida's words, which so often bores his readers and frustrates his political critics, is *not* without an aim. The fact that deconstruction is a two-step "operation" or strategy of reversal *and displacement* puts it in a different position *vis-à-vis* the question of the subject. Rather than continuing a certain economy of the subject, deconstruction interrupts it. Such an interruption would be a merely negative operation if it were limited to demonstrating the presence of a hegemonic structure. The genuine aim of deconstruction is *not yet* realized by this demonstration which implies a reversal of terms. The aim of shaking the structure itself is possible only when the other and otherness is located in the heart of the subject. In other words, displacement is the move by which the desire for a sovereign, possessive, and unitary position is itself interrupted. The binary structure is the very structure which produces the *desire for sovereign subjectivity*, i.e. the economy of the subject. The sovereign subject is based on the fiction of an absolute limit by which he excludes others and recognizes himself as autonomous. A reversal of terms is not sufficient precisely because it maintains the economy by which the same absolute limit is sustained, whereas the whole point of deconstruction is to turn that limit into a passage (hence its difference from relativism). If the Hegelian economy works by making the subject recognize himself in the other, Derridean deconstruction makes the subject recognize the other in himself or herself.

Such a recognition implies a different concept of the subject, one that is not fixed but open and changing. An identity politics based on reversal is limited to changing the cultural or subjective contents of identity. The identity of the subject changes in such politics, but the subject continues to be constituted in the same essentialist form. Therefore it does not actually make the subject an agent, but reproduces the same form of the subject as fixed and fixing. The constitution of the oppressed or subordinate subject implies the "in-between" or "passage" to which I have referred above. It implies a subjectivity where embodiment and relationality are not denied but become the constitutive moment of subjectivity, challenging and subverting the Western form of sovereign subject. Luce Irigaray's feminist deconstruction of Western phallocentrism shows how woman can not be a subject in the sense Man is. Irigaray's effort to construct an imaginary for women is rooted in the embodiment of women: a kind of subjectivity in which the other is recognized rather than denied, in which "the two lips communicate with each other." Homi Bhabha's critique of colonial and racist discourse also evokes a sense of the subject as "in-between" or "passage" especially in his concept of the colonized as "mimic men."[6] The mimicry of the colonized is not a repetition of the same but the opening of *difference and otherness within* the subject, making a return to the self-same impossible.

Although these arguments share a common thread, I do not claim that they can be brought together in an easy way. A new sense of the subject cannot be produced by a simple addition of different arguments, but by keeping the difference and tension between them alive. Only such an approach can develop a notion of agency as an active and transformative principle. This sense of agency is not active in the sense of dominating and controlling the others and the world as nature; but it is active in the sense of a receptivity and openness to others and otherness. The "other" is not what the subject distinguishes itself from, nor the beyond of an absolute limit which the subject cannot pass, but the necessary possibility that makes the subject possible, again and again, each time anew. Unless this sense of otherness and limitlessness is conceived as a condition of subject, we are bound to repeat the same dominating and possessive form of subjectivity.

Chapter 1 offers a discussion of the issues and concerns that Edward Said's *Orientalism* opens up. Throughout the project I acknowledge his major theoretical achievement: establishing a field of study which has today come to be called "colonial discourse studies" and which has become one of the most contested fields in cultural studies. Focusing on the epistemological dualism Said sets between the "real" Orient versus its representation, I suggest that although Said refutes an appeal to a notion of "real" or "true" Orient as preceding its discursive constitution, his analysis is nevertheless bound to remain dualistic as he does not go beyond conceptualizing discourse as a linguistic activity. Said's important proposition regarding the "Orientalization of the Orient" can be further deepened by acknowledging the involuted relationship of the referent with discourse or textuality. To be able to overcome this epistemological dualism, the Orient needs to be conceptualized as a material effect of Orientalist signification. Rather than simply giving up the referentiality of the Orient, I suggest that it be seen as an embodiment of a certain discursive production. Although I follow in many ways the path Said has opened up, I critically engage with his relegation of the questions of gender and of sexuality to a sub-domain of Orientalism. I suggest that the distinction Said makes between the *manifest* and *latent* content of Orientalism can be utilized as a useful guide for this purpose and can enable us to formulate the articulation of sexuality with Orientalism. I then turn to Homi Bhabha's psychoanalytic theory of colonial discourse and acknowledge his attempt to integrate the question of sexual difference with the theories of colonial discourse. However, the psychoanalytic formula of fetishism that Bhabha employs for this purpose is fraught with difficulties as it is formulated to understand the representation of sexual difference and therefore cannot be easily translated to comprehend the specificity of the representation of cultural difference. Criticisms directed at the usefulness of the concept of colonial discourse as a unified category are the subject of the last section of this chapter. Focusing on criticisms about undoing colonial discourse as a homogenizing category, I suggest that the totalizing notion of colonialism cannot be called into question by focusing on particularity or by an uncritical celebration of colonialism*s* instead of colonialism. I do advocate retaining the general category of colonial discourse without seeing its unity as a simple harmonious totality, but by recognizing the complexity within such a unity.

In chapter 2, I examine the homology between the structures of patriarchal/sexist and colonial/imperial discourses. For instance, in the case of Orientalism, the discourses of cultural and sexual difference are powerfully mapped onto each other. Following the critique I develop in chapter 1 regarding Said's reluctance to engage with what he calls "latent Orientalism," I argue in this chapter that this is precisely the site where the *unconscious* desires and fantasies of the "other" and "otherness" appear as powerful constituents of the so-called autonomous and rational Western subject and expose this position as structurally male. By using the Lacanian notion of fantasy, I demonstrate that the Orient as it figures in several eighteenth- and nineteenth-century European texts is a *fantasy* built upon sexual difference. My analysis reveals how the figure of "veiled Oriental woman" has a particular place in these texts, not only as signifying Oriental woman as mysterious and exotic but also as signifying the Orient as feminine, always veiled, seductive, and dangerous. Powerful "scientific," literary, humanistic or administrative discourses of colonialism and imperialism have thus constructed the world as a natural territory ready for the conquest of the "rational" and "civilized" European man as the subject of the modern world. My exploration of the articulation of cultural and sexual representation is also an attempt to bridge the gap between the historical and the psychoanalytic analyses of Orientalism. And this involves an examination of the unique ways in which the unconscious fantasies, dreams, and desires of the Western subject structures his relation to the Oriental other. I incorporate Homi Bhabha's concepts of ambivalence and mimicry to explore the ways in which the structures of desire and fantasy operate in the contradictory economy of colonial domination. Moreover, it is by way of acknowledging such an economy that I address the question of displacement and subversion of Orientalist discourse and the role the veil plays in this. By taking the representations of the veil as a test case I suggest that the presumption of a hidden essence and truth behind the veil is the means by which both the Western/colonial and the masculine subject constitute their own identity. Moreover, by demonstrating the structural homology between the representations of the Orient, veil, and feminine, I suggest that the discourse of Orientalism is mapped powerfully onto the language of phallocentricism and thereby point to the inextricable link between representations of cultural and sexual difference.

Throughout the text I use the category subject not only to refer to its sovereign status, but also to allude to the unavoidably masculine position it occupies *vis-à-vis* its cultural others. To suggest that the Western subject (irrespective of the gender identity of the person who represents the Orient) occupies not only the position of a colonial, but also a masculine subject position was not an easy task in the context of a hegemonic US feminism. My argument that Western feminism is inevitably caught and empowered by masculinism and imperialism has been met with unease by my American feminist colleagues. In chapter 3, I explore the ways in which the Orient is represented not only in the texts of women, but more specifically in those ones that have a more "feminine" rhetoric. The epistemic violence in Western women travellers' discourse, as I trace it in Lady Mary Montagu's *Turkish Embassy Letters,* has helped me to sketch out the peculiar nature of the relation between Western women and men as they proceeded in their journey into the Orient. It is the Derridean notion of supplement which helps me to examine this relation and suggest that Western women, as the excluded other of Western men, nevertheless occupy a masculine position in relation to Oriental women.

Chapter 4 addresses the complicitous relationship between Western/ imperialist interests and the emancipatory project of Enlightenment and how this configuration has affected and shaped the emergence and consolidation of an imperial Western feminist gesture. It is again the question of the veil which becomes my test case. I demonstrate the ramifications of this articulation through a reading of ethnographic texts by Western women who have a more visible "feminist" rhetoric. In reading these texts, my concern is to highlight the point that the Western feminist desire to lift the veil of the Oriental woman in the name of "liberating" her reflects the historical, cultural, psychical, and political obsessions of the culture that produced Western women. I thus examine the emergence of a colonial feminist position which is both a product of and at the same time constitutive of the modernist/Enlightenment project in the early-twentieth-century ethnographic texts. I also suggest that the colonial feminist discourse to unveil Muslim women in the name of liberation was linked not only to the discourse of Enlightenment but also to the scopic regime of modernity which is characterized by a desire to master, control, and reshape the body of the subjects by making them visible. Since the veil prevents the colonial gaze from attaining such a visibility and hence mastery, its lifting becomes essential. I argue that the desire to unveil women should not be seen simply as an uncovering of their bodies, but as a re-inscription, for the discourse of unveiling is no less incorporated in the existential or embodied being of Oriental women than the discourse of veiling.

Chapter 5 examines Third World nationalisms as a Western/Orientalist construct and hence traces the project of Enlightenment in the discourse of nationalism. I therefore propose to see the discourse of nationalism as the inscription of Western hegemony in the Third World as part of the many-leveled and complex Orientalist discourse. By offering a different reading of nationalism I contest nationalism's own narrative which offers itself as the means of emancipation from colonialism. Contrary to such claims of emancipation, I propose to trace it as one among several effects of colonial inventory. However, what is at stake in my refusal is not an attempt to substitute nationalist discourse with a "politically correct alternative" discourse, but to underscore the fact that the colonial and post-colonial subjects of the Third World are constituted by the experience of colonialism and nationalism. I examine the contours of the nationalist discourse in Turkey and Algeria and explore the ways in which the question of woman in general and the veil in particular have been articulated with their discourse. By examining this articulation, I suggest that although women and the veil occupy a particular place in the nationalist project of the Turkish elite and in the Algerian anti-colonial struggle, they occupy such a position in so far as they become the ground of the struggle between the patriarchal power and Orientalist hegemony: it is the effacement of sexual difference which keeps both the male and the colonist dominant.

1

Mapping the field of colonial discourse

The Orient: a suppressed authenticity or an idea without a referent?

Edward Said's *Orientalism*[1] offers a powerful analysis of the structure of those varied Western discourses which represent the Orient and Islam as an object for investigation and control. By covering a historical corpus of literary, scientific, and diplomatic discourses, Said brings to our attention a textual universe which draws an imaginative geographical distinction between the peoples and cultures of the West and East. We learn from Said that a vast array of rhetorical figures and discursive tropes were employed by the West to *represent* and *know* the Orient.

However, Said's work is not merely about how Europe represented the Orient, it also raises some significant general theoretical and political questions. By offering a rich panorama of the ways in which Orientalist texts constitute the Orient as a racial, cultural, political, and geographical unity, *Orientalism* also provides a fruitful arena where questions of a more general nature, questions that pertain to the representation of cultural and sexual difference and the nature of the discursive constitution of otherness, could be raised. Said's analysis demonstrates that what is at stake in the constitution of the Oriental other is the West's desire to set boundaries for itself as a self-sustaining, autonomous, and sovereign subject. He illustrates the dialectics of self and other that is at play in Orientalist discourse by continually alluding to the establishment of a binary opposition between the Orient and Occident as the primordial technique operating at its very core.

Said's analysis also focuses on how the Western desire to represent the Oriental other is interlocked with its will to power. Situating the emergence of Orientalism within the peak period of colonialism, Said extends Michel Foucault's concept of power/knowledge nexus to the representation of the Orient and demonstrates the close ties between Western knowledge and its will to power. The relationship between colonial expansion and Orientalism that Said's analysis demonstrates has been picked up by his critics. For example, Lata Mani and Ruth Frankenberg argue that Said's definition of Orientalism alludes to the "complicity between Orientalism and imperialism" and how "Orientalism has informed and shaped the colonial enterprise."[2] Likewise, Robert Young, by referring to Orientalism's close ties with enabling socioeconomic and political institutions of colonialism, argues that Said's analysis demonstrates how Orientalism "*justified* colonialism in advance as well as subsequently facilitating its successful operation" (emphasis added).[3] James Clifford is another critic who points to this important connection and argues that Said correctly identifies how the essentializing and dichotomizing discourse of Orientalism "functions in a complex but systematic way as an element of colonial domination."[4] However, a closer look at Said's work reveals that in referring to the power of Orientalism, he does not in any simple and limited way refer to the economic, political, and administrative institutions of colonial domination, although such institutions constitute a significant part of it. By pointing to the configurations of power, Said *also* emphasizes that Orientalism is an *apparatus of knowledge with its will-to-truth*. However, this connection is not given sufficent consideration in the analysis of the above commentators. This enhanced emphasis upon the articulation of Orientalism with forces of colonial domination implies a confinement of the efficacy of Orientalist discourse to an *ideological supplement* and thus to an effacement of the power implied in the production and dissemination of academic and other forms of knowledge. Seen from the perspective of power/knowledge nexus, Said's analysis could very well be extended to historical periods that exceed territorial colonialism. To emphasize this connection we need to pay close attention to the nature of the relation Said establishes between representation, knowledge, and power.

As a distinct style of representation, Orientalist discourse offers an interpretive strategy or a body of knowledge about the cultures and peoples of "Oriental" localities. By emphasizing the discursive mechanism of Orientalism, Said aims to go beyond Marxism's base–superstructure model in which the role of ideology is understood to be the legitimation of the material, or economic conditions.[5] His insistence on Orientalism as a discursive regime constitutes a valuable intervention against an understanding of Orientalism as an ideological instrument that is "fabricated" in the service of colonial power. As I noted above, by using Foucault's notion of discourse, Said unravels how Orientalism is intimately connected with apparently objective academic scholarship. This emphasis on the complicity between academic knowledge and the forms of subjugation and

administration of other cultures shifts the analysis towards an examinina-
tion of the discursive mechanism of Orientalism which prescribes what can
be said and recognized as the "truth" of the Orient. Thus, for Said, the
process of the production of the knowledge of the Orient and the process
of its subjugation by colonial power do not stand in an external relation to
each other. The incorporation of Foucault's insight in the analysis of
Western ethnocentricism needs to be understood as an effort to understand
the *productive* nature of the discourse of Orientalism. However, although
Said occasionally alludes to the constitutive role of Orientalist discourse,
we still need to question to what extent he successfully elaborates this
important point.

Let us first delineate briefly Foucault's notion of power. He objects to a
notion of power understood in a narrow sense; a notion according to which
the effects of power are assumed to be negative or repressive. Contrary to
the understanding of power that is presumed to be independent of knowledge or truth statements, Foucault wants to capture its productive nature –
power induces forms of knowledge and forms of discourse. Seen in this
way, power produces effects of truth, which are in themselves neither true
nor false. Following Foucault's argument, Said suggests that the effect of
Orientalist discourse is "to formulate the Orient, to give it shape, identity,
definition with full recognition of its place in memory, its importance to
imperial strategy, and its 'natural' role as an appendage to Europe."[6] The
conclusion we can derive from the above statement is that the "truth,"
"identity," or "reality" of the Orient is not something that stands in an
external relationship to the discourse of Orientalism and something against
which we can measure the "truthfulness" of representations. Indeed, to use
the formulation Judith Butler[7] develops in a different context, both the category of the Orient as well as the declaration of its exteriority to discourse
is constituted by the very discourse of Orientalism as the founding principle of its claim to legitimacy. Said suggests that the discursive strategy
deployed by Orientalism is homologous to realism. The utilization of this
realist mode of representation creates the Orient. As he puts it:

Philosophically, then, the kind of language, thought, and vision that I have been
calling Orientalism very generally is a form of radical realism; anyone employing
Orientalism which is the habit for dealing with questions, objects, qualities and
regions deemed Oriental, will designate, name, point to, fix what he is talking or
thinking about with a word or phrase, which is then considered either to have
acquired, or more simply to be, reality.[8]

They [figures of speech associated with the Orient] are all declarative and self
evident; the tense they employ is the timeless eternal . . . For all these functions it is
frequently enough to use the simple copula *is.*[9]

Therefore, the Orientalness of the Orient, for Said, is not something that is given as a fact of "nature." Rather, the essentializing discourse of Orientalism, which is achieved by the copula *is* not only construes the Orient as the place of sensuality, corrupt despotism, mystical religiosity, sexually unstable Arabs, irrationality, backwardness, and so on, but also makes the Orientalists' inquiry into the nature of "Islamic mind" and "Arab character" perfectly legitimate. It is precisely through such essentializing claims that the Orient is *Orientalized*. The repertoire of these images, figures, tropes are the very means by which the Orient is *made* Oriental. As Said puts it, "the Orient was Orientalized not only because it was discovered to be 'Oriental' in all those ways considered commonplace by an average nineteenth-century European, but also because it *could be . . . made* Oriental";[10] knowledge of the Orient, because generated out of strength, in a sense *creates* the Orient, the Oriental, and his world.[11]

By following the above line of reasoning, we can suggest that geography must not be understood simply as a knowledge about a "natural" referent, but is inextricably linked with cultural signification. The very knowledge produced in and by the Orientalist discourse "creates" the Orient:[12] Such discourses "*create* not only *knowledge* but also the very reality they appear to describe."[13] The Orient as such becomes possible only through the knowledge produced in and by these texts.

However, I should caution the reader not to be misled by my selective juxtaposition of Said's remarks regarding the constitutive character of discourse. Although it is not totally incorrect to argue that Said tends to recognize that discourse constitutes the object it speaks about, it is not possible to argue with full confidence that he is completely divorced from a conception of language as a mediation. This prevents him from radically calling into question the economy that underwrites the binary opposition between the "real" and representation.[14] The interrogation of such a dichotomy would first of all, among other things, require questioning the notion of an *extra-textual referent* which we do not attest in Said's work. Rather, the theoretical status of representation in his work can at best be characterized as fraught with dilemmas and ambivalences. James Clifford draws our attention to such a methodological ambivalence in Said's text. According to Clifford, Said's position vacillates between accepting something called "the real Orient" and regarding "the Orient" as the construct of a questionable mental operation.[15] It is to these contradictory methodological positions that I want to turn now.

It is his apparent refutation of any appeal to a notion of a "real," "authentic," or "true" Orient that sets Said's work apart from many mainstream analyses of the representation of "other" cultures. Rejecting an understanding of Orientalism as a *misrepresentation* of the truth of the Orient, Said argues that the methodological problems of Orientalism cannot be delineated by simply claiming that the "real" Orient does not correspond to the image depicted in Orientalist texts. He explicitly refutes the thesis that "there is such a thing as a real or true Orient (Islam, Arab or whatever)."[16] Instead, his analysis exposes the category of the Orient as an effect of a specific formation of power. He does not seem to look for a genuine or authentic Oriental identity/reality, but aspires to examine the processes by which institutions, practices, and discourses posit and designate an essential or original Oriental identity and the political stakes involved in such processes. Hence Said disputes the notion of an Oriental culture which can be defined on the basis of some essential quality. Contrary to such widespread assumptions, Said suggests that "the Orient itself is a constituted entity."[17] Having argued that the Orient "was reconstructed, reassembled, crafted, in short born out of the Orientalists' effort,"[18] Said then proposes "to look at styles, figures of speech, setting, narrative devices, historical and social circumstances, not the correctness of the representation nor its fidelity to some great original."[19]

However, Said's attempt to understand the constitutive power of Orientalist discourse is not very convincing at times, for his analysis poses a set of theoretical problems that he does not fully engage with. As I mentioned above, on the one hand he argues that Orientalism "creates" the Orient and on the other hand he cautions us not to conclude that *the Orient is just an idea, with no corresponding reality.*[20] This, for James Clifford, should be regarded as a manifestation of an important contradiction in Said. One of the reasons why such a contradiction exists in Said should be sought in the notion of language that Said uses. One such example can be seen in his ready acceptance of the rather simplistic account of the notion of representation offered by Barthes. This can be taken as one indication of the restricted notion of language Said deploys for understanding Orientalism: "representations are formations, or as Roland Barthes has said of all the operations of language, they are deformations."[21] The notion of language Said uses seems to be limited to linguistic activity. For example he argues in a rather unquestioning manner that "the Orient was a *word* which later accrued to it a wide field of meanings, associations, and connotations, and that these did not necessarily refer to the *real* Orient but to the field surrounding the word"[22] (emphasis added).

If Said readily accepts such a notion of language, then he must be moving further away from a notion of discourse as a process which constitutes the very object it represents, for it implies that language is merely a collection of words and associations, and is a device in the service of image making. Such a notion of discourse is clearly limited to a linguistic activity and establishes a dichotomy between the real/material (which is assumed to be extra-discursive) and the discursive. Having argued that the Orient is created, constituted, and born out of these representations, the above distinction between the discursive and extra-discursive, between words, ideas, and the "real," constitutes a major contradiction which Said leaves unresolved.

Following the concept of discourse employed by Ernesto Laclau and Chantal Mouffe, we can suggest that Said operates with an assumption of the *mental character of discourse.* According to Laclau and Mouffe, to suggest that the object of discourse is constituted does not imply a rejection of the materialist idea that there is a world external to thought. Nor does this thesis have anything to do with the opposition between realism and idealism – a trap which Said seems to fall into. What Laclau and Mouffe contest is not that there are objects existing in the world, but the assumption that "they could constitute themselves as objects outside any discursive condition of emergence."[23] Hence, with a restricted notion of language, Said's analysis is bound to consider Orientalist discourse as a collection of images and ideas about the Orient, having no real efficacy in the construction of its materiality or the Orientalness of the Orient. Such an understanding runs counter to his continual emphasis on the "creation" and "constitution" or the Orientalization of the Orient in and by the discourse of Orientalism.

Robert Young follows a different path in his critique of the same point. For Young, Said attempts to make two points at once: on the one hand, he denies any correspondence between the "real" and representation of the Orient; on the other hand, he argues that the knowledge produced in and by Orientalism was put in the service of colonial conquest. These two arguments, according to Young, contradict each other, for, if Said wants to claim that Orientalism as a body of knowledge became effective at a material level as a form of colonial power and control, this means that the representations had to encounter the "actual" Orient. According to Young, however, Said denies that there is any actual Orient which could provide a true account against Orientalist representations. And he asks: "how can then Said argue that the "Orient" is just a representation, if he also wants to claim that "Orientalism" provided the necessary knowledge for the actual colonial conquest."[24]

Young's critique does not seem to be well taken, for in attempting to overcome the dualistic account which characterizes Said's analysis, he himself develops another dualism, that of between reality and representation. The notion of the "actual" which Young too readily accepts does not seem to be sufficiently developed to enable us to engage with the "representation" versus "real" problem that Said's text poses. It is rather naive to approach Said's work as if he is claiming that there is no "actual" geographical place called the Orient, or there are no "actual" Oriental people living on these geographical spaces, or the "actual" colonial conquest did not happen. It is, after all, Said who in the first place establishes the indissociable link between the colonial conquest and Orientalist knowledge. In a way, criticisms such as Young's reiterate what Said's text has already demonstrated. The epistemological problem that needs to be mapped out in Said's text is certainly more complex than Young suggests and cannot easily be resolved by claiming that there is an "actual" Orient and that this can be proved by pointing to the "fact" of colonial conquest. In other words, Young far too easily assumes that if Said does not really elaborate the theoretical status of the complex relationship between representation and reality, then he must be naively refusing the referentiality of the Orient. While there is no doubt that the theoretical status of the notion of representation or discourse in Said's text is cryptic, the pressing theoretical question cannot easily be reduced to the question of the "actualness" of the Orient. If we want our analysis to exceed the common understanding of discourse as a kind of linguisticism, then we should entertain the possibility that the materiality of the Orient is indistinguishable from the essentializing discourse of Orientalism. The efficacy of the discourse of Orientalism should thus be sought in its power to produce the phenomena it names and speaks about. Moreover, we also need to acknowledge that the notion of the "actual Orient" as preceding language is itself posed retrospectively by the very discourse that Orientalizes the Orient. A deconstructive reading of Orientalism would reckon that the Orient is always-already articulated in a discursive field and that this articulation entails the materialization or incorporation of the Orient within such representations. The evocation of the Orient's always-already constituted character within discursivity need not imply suspending reference altogether, but should be seen as an invitation to think about the complex nature of the referentiality itself.[25]

The status of the referent and its involuted relationship with discourse or textuality has been preoccupying critics working in various different fields who aim to reformulate the referent's material and at the same time discursively constituted character. The question of discursive constitution of the object has also been on the agenda of feminist criticism. One such exemplary attempt comes from Judith Butler.[26] In interrogating the worthiness of the ostensible duality between discursive and non-discursive, Judith Butler's aim, in *Bodies that Matter*, is to rethink the complex nature of the referent called the body.[27] Her refutation of the notion of a pure body is an attempt to alter the meaning of referentiality and theorize its materiality by questioning the common assumption that accords it an extra-textual status. As she suggests, "to refer naively or directly to such an extra-discursive object will always require the prior delimitation of the extra-discursive. And in so far as the extra-discursive is delimited, it is formed by the very discourse from which it seeks to free itself."[28] Thinking that materiality is the most productive effect of power, Butler locates this materialization as a "kind of citationality, as the acquisition of being through the citing of power."[29] Thus the materiality of the referent needs to be seen as the materialization and citational accumulation of this regulatory norm. Critical of the constructivism versus essentialism opposition, Butler reminds us that the point is not simply to suggest that "everything is discursively constructed" but to understand construction as a process of materialization which is stabilized over time through a forcible reiteration of a founding interpellation that reinforces a naturalized effect.[30]

Of course, such attempts do not remain unchallenged. Critics who reduce discursive constitution to determinism claim that agency has been foreclosed in such constructivist arguments. Engaging with such an interlocutor, Butler counters the notion of a voluntarist subject whose resistance is assumed to require its existence detached from the regulatory norms. For her, the question of agency needs to be located in the appropriation or rearticulation of the regulatory norm, for the citing of the law implies that it can be produced differently. For Butler, the necessity of reiteration demonstrates that this materialization is never fully completed or the body never completely complies with norms. The need for re-materialization indicates a potential for turning the regulatory norm against itself. Reiteration must not, therefore, be understood as a final fixing or reduced to determinism, for it is through this reiteration that "gaps and fissures are opened up as the constitutive instabilities in such constructions."[31] Such instabilities, for Butler, demonstrate a deconstructive possibility as the object constituted escapes or exceeds the norms. Moreover, as Foucault's notion of subjectivation (*assujetisement*) suggests, discourses which constitute the subject are at the same time the condition of possibility of its empowerment. Therefore, the critical question does not lie merely in positing the agency of the subject, but in acknowledging the double bind logic of the process of subjectification, a bind that subjects as well as enables.

If we turn to the question of the constitutive force of Orientalism, conceptualizing the Orient's reality as a material effect of the process of signification requires redefining the Orientalist discourse as a process of materialization. The Orient "as such" needs to be comprehended as a discursive effect, as a textual referent which is always-already entangled with its representation, always articulated within a political field of signification. The point here is not to give up on the idea of the referentiality of the Orient, but to reconceptualize this referentiality as an embodiment of a certain discursive production, to understand the process of signification as an Orientalization of the Orient. Such an understanding will undercut appeals to an extra-textual referent and foster an understanding of why an outside of the text of Orientalism is unthinkable, for the Orient, in this reconceptualization, will be seen as already a manifestation of a particular discursive articulation.

The emphasis on the material constitution of the Orient by the discourse of Orientalism also implies not divorcing language from the constitution of subjectivity. To redefine the problematic of representation so as to see the Orientalist discourse not as a mediation between an extra-discursive signi-fied and a process of signification, but as a practice that *constitutes not only the object but also the subjects who are investigated* also undermines the validity of the criticisms about the repudiation of agency. The foreclosure of agency and counter-histories is one of the widespread criticisms advanced against Said's analysis. It is suggested that by portraying Orientalism in totalizing terms, *Orientalism* leaves no room for appreciat-ing the agency of the Other. When Orientalism as a cultural representation is not seen simply as a constraining or distorting process, but as a practice of active constitution of subjectivity, enabling and empowering as well as dominating, then resistance to colonial power or the restoration of the col-onized as the subject of history cannot be theorized apart from the Orientalist discourse. The discursive constitution of the subject does not connote merely a total pacification or a process of producing the being of the Oriental subjects as a stable category fixed in a position of subjugation, but an enabling process as well. When this paradox of subjectification is recognized, suggestions about theorizing agency as outside Orientalist dis-course become simply untenable. I will discuss this point further in chapter 2. But now let me turn to the discussion of binarism that seems to be one of the major weaknesses in Said's analysis.

Binarisms of Orientalism

In characterizing the discursive economy of Orientalism through a set of binary terms, Said posits a polarity or duality at its very center. The fol-lowing definition of Orientalism is an instance of such a polarity:

Orientalism is the generic term that I have been employing to describe the Western approach to the Orient; Orientalism is the discipline by which the Orient was (and is) approached systematically, as a topic of learning, discovery and practice. But in addition I have been using the word to designate the collection of *dreams, images and vocabularies* available to anyone who has tried to talk about what lies East of the dividing line. These two aspects of Orientalism are not incongruent, since by use of them both Europe could advance securely and unmetaphorically upon the Orient.[32] [emphasis added]

The two senses of Orientalism used above are further elaborated in the following pages. Here Said makes a distinction between *latent* and *manifest* Orientalism – a distinction which has profound implications for reformulating the structure of Orientalist discourse. *Manifest* Orientalism is "the various stated views about Oriental society, languages, literatures, history, sociology and so forth," whereas *latent* Orientalism refers to "an almost unconscious (and certainly an untouchable) positivity."[33] Thus *latent* Orientalism reflects the site of the unconscious, where dreams, images, desires, fantasies and fears reside. Orientalism, then, simultaneously refers to the production of a systematic knowledge and to the site of the unconscious – desires and fantasies; it signifies how the "Orient" is at once an object of *knowledge* and an object of *desire*.

Latent Orientalism seems to have a fundamental significance in Said's overall analysis, for he argues that it is through this *latent* structure that Orientalism achieves its doctrinal and doxological character, its everydayness and natural-ness, its taken-for-granted authority. It thereby provides travellers, writers, historians, and anthropologists with an "enunciative capacity"[34] which could be mobilized for handling any concrete, unique issue at hand. In other words, latent Orientalism is "transmitted from one generation to another" partly because of an "internal consistency about its constitutive will-to-power over the Orient."[35] Thus, this permanent, consistent, systematic, and articulated knowledge of Orientalism establishes a discursive field, or as Said describes it, a "textual attitude" through which any concrete Oriental detail could be made sense of.

However, in implying a kind of sub-structural, disseminating, and authorizing knowledge, the distinction between the *latent* and *manifest* Orientalism seems to have wider implications than Said himself recognizes. It is analogous to the distinction made in psychoanalysis between the *latent* and *manifest* content of the dream.[36] Although Said refers, in passing, to the concept of *latent* Orientalism as the realm where unconscious desires, fantasies, and dreams about the Orient reside, he never elaborates its nature nor the processes and mechanisms involved in its working. He does not engage in a discussion of its role in the constitution of the relationship between the Western subject and its Oriental other by subjecting this unconscious site to a more detailed psychoanalytic reading. However, I do not in any way want to imply that psychoanalysis is *the* theory that can lead us in the most correct way for understanding the workings of Orientalist discourse. Although psychoanalytic theory has been used in quite an inspiring way for developing a theory of colonial discourse, especially the account offered by Bhabha, his framework is not completely unproblematical either. The reason I dwell on Said's reluctance to further elaborate the above point in psychoanalytic terms is mainly because the distinction he introduces between the *manifest* and *latent* content is one that has its origins in psychoanalysis. In chapter 2, where I demonstrate the intermingling of representations of cultural and sexual difference by reading the unconscious structure of Orientalism, psychoanalytic theory proves to be useful. However, this should not imply that I regard psychoanalysis as *the* theory which can offer the most accurate account of Orientalism. Nor does it imply that I believe psychoanalysis can be unproblematically applied to the analysis of Orientalism. I use psychoanalysis not because I believe it offers the truth, and that truth can once more be demonstrated by applying it to the discourse of Orientalism. It is rather the other way around: my point of departure is the Orientalist discourse itself, which I believe exhibits important material that can be usefully examined in terms of ideology and subject constitution, and psychoanalysis provides convincing theoretical tools for comprehending their functioning in Orientalism.[37]

As I suggested above, Said's text is also imbued with the binary economy he criticizes. The various definitions of Orientalism he offers are trapped within this economy. As Young also mentions, even though "*Orientalism* is directed against the hierarchical dualism of the "West" and "East," other dualisms ceaselessly proliferate throughout his text."[38] Hence, the field of Orientalism is characterized in discrete terms: it is a topic of learning and a site of dreams; it has both a *manifest* (stated knowledges about the Orient) and *latent* content (an unconscious positivity); it is also characterized by synchronic essentialism (making the Orient synonymous with stability and unchanging eternality) and diachronic forms of history (recognition of the possibility of instability which suggests change, growth, decline and movement in the Orient). Rather than treating this aspect of Said's text as an indication of weakness, Homi Bhabha takes it as a starting point from which to develop a more refined analysis of colonial discourse in order to understand the articulation of cultural difference. According to Bhabha, by resolving the oppositions he set earlier, Said loses the inventive character of his diagnoses, because in unifying the two, at times contradictory, systems that characterize Orientalism, Said moves further away from engaging with the problem of ambivalence and the contradictory economy that structures and sustains it. For Bhabha, what lies behind Said's definition of a monolithic and closed system is the assumption of a unitary intention on the side of the Orientalist who is conceived of as "motivated" by a desire and will to govern the Orient. [39]

The question of sexuality

Said is certainly not unaware of the nature and extent of the sexual implications of the unconscious site of Orientalism to which I have referred above. He mentions, for instance, "how latent Orientalism also encouraged a peculiarly . . . male conception of the world" and how Orientalism "viewed itself and its subject matter with sexist blinders."[40] When he talks about Nerval's work, he points to the sexual dimensions of his representation of the Orient.[41]

On another occasion, when he discusses the ways in which the Oriental woman is represented in Flaubert's works, he alludes to the uniform association established between the Orient and sex. However, in the following few lines Said confesses the limits of his analysis:

Woven through all of Flaubert's Oriental experiences, exciting or disappointing, is an almost *uniform association between the Orient and sex*. In making this association Flaubert was neither the first nor the most exaggerated instance of a remarkably persistent motif in Western attitudes to the Orient . . . *Why the Orient seems still to suggest not only fecundity but sexual promise (and threat), untiring sensuality, unlimited desire, deep generative energies, is something on which one could speculate; it is not the province of my analysis here, alas, despite its frequently noted appearance.* Nevertheless one must acknowledge its importance as something eliciting complex responses, sometimes even a frightening self-discovery, in the Orientalists, and Flaubert was an interesting case in point.[42] (emphasis added)

If the uniform association between the Orient and sex is such a constitutive trope in Orientalist discourse, how can we regard these as issues belonging to a separate province? What are the implications, for his overall analysis, of Said's decision to leave the discussion of the the the sexual/unconscious site of Orientalism to a distinct field?

Said's reluctance to engage with Orientalism through psychoanalytic categories has an inhibiting effect on his pioneering analysis. For example, it prevents him from fully demonstrating the inextricable link between the process of understanding, of knowing the other cultures, and the unconscious and sexual dimensions involved in this process. The utilization of images of woman and images of sexuality in Orientalist discourse is treated as a trope limited to the representation of Oriental woman and of sexuality. In other words, neither the images of woman nor the images of sexuality are understood as important aspects of the way Orientalist discourse is structured. Rather, they are treated as belonging to a sub-domain of the Orientalist discourse, thus implying a risk of mirroring the divisional, disciplinary, and expertise-oriented structure of Orientalism. Consequently, we are left with, on the one hand, the representations of the Orient and Oriental cultures, and on the other, representations of Oriental women and of sexuality.[43] When the articulation between the two levels is left unexplored, *latent* Orientalism, or the unconscious site of Orientalism, remains a separate domain, clearly distinguishable from the realm of Orientalism as scholarly discipline.

To engage in an analysis of the unconscious site of Orientalism should not be seen as an alternative to its historical analysis. Indeed, if the power of Orientalism is not, as vulgar Marxism would have it, a mere reflection of an economic power, but is rather a power that is rooted in the production and dissemination of knowledge, concepts, and commonsense, then we must be able to root this knowledge itself in a certain libidinal economy that drives it. Therefore we need to subject Orientalist discourse to a more sexualized reading. By doing so we can understand how the representation of otherness is achieved simultaneously through sexual as well as cultural modes of differentiation. The Western acts of understanding the Orient and its women are not two distinct enterprises, but rather are interwoven aspects of the same gesture. Thus, in referring to the scene of the sexual and the site of the unconscious, I do not simply mean the ways in which the figure of the Oriental woman or Oriental sexuality is *represented*. I am rather referring to the ways in which representations of the Orient are interwoven by sexual imageries, unconscious fantasies, desires, fears, and dreams. In other words, the question of sexuality cannot be treated as a regional one; it governs and structures the subject's every relation with the other. Understanding this (double) articulation in Orientalist discourse therefore requires an exploration of the articulation of the historical with fantasy, the cultural with the sexual, and desire with power. It is this connection that I want to elaborate in chapter 2. By organizing my interrogation around the figure of the veil. I will try to show how the Orientalist construction of the Orient is the Western subject's means of securing an identity for itself mediated by the other. It therefore needs to be understood as being structured by the fantasy framework in the Lacanian sense, which provides the coordinates of the Subject's desire for the other. However, before engaging in such an analysis, let me turn to Homi Bhabha's psychoanalytic approach about the question of representation of cultural difference in colonial discourse. Bhabha attempts to fill in the lacuna left by Said's analysis, especially by addressing the questions regarding the effectiveness of colonialism as a subject constituting practice and by articulating the question of sexual difference to his analysis of colonial discourse.

The limits of Bhabha's analysis

The originality of Bhabha'a approach lies in the way he articulates the problematic of cultural representation with the problematic of subjectivity. This is an issue that Said drew to our attention but left unelaborated as he was not granting sufficent attention to the notion of discourse deployed in post-structuralist and psychoanalytic theories, namely the notion of discourse as a subject constituting practice.

In characterizing the mode of representation of otherness in the discourse of colonialism as polymorphous and perverse, Bhabha attempts to capture the multiple and cross-cutting determinations of the constitution of colonial subjectivity. Refusing to assume the nature of colonial discourse as unified and unidirectional (for it is not only the colonized but also the colonizer who is simultaneously constituted in it) as Said does, Bhabha discerns a *productive ambivalence* at the very center of colonial discourse. Such an understanding avoids the pitfalls of assuming both the colonizer and the colonized as fixed once and for all, and the colonial discourse as being based on a final closure and ultimate coherence. On the contrary, it designates the conflictual economy upon which colonial discourse is based.

The articulation of the Foucauldian model of subject constitution with psychoanalytic theory enables Bhabha to understand the articulation of history with fantasy, pleasure and desire with domination and power. Understanding this articulation is necessary for understanding how the subject of colonial discourse is constituted simultaneously in the field of a *disciplinary form of power* (as it functions productively as incitement and interdiction) and of *fantasy*.

Among other things, the novelty of Bhabha's analysis lies in his engagement with the question of sexual difference in developing a theory of colonial discourse. The concept of *fetishism* occupies a central place in Bhabha's analysis of the ways in which colonial discourse operates. Before I discuss Bhabha's adaptation of the formula of fetishism to colonial discourse, let me first briefly explain the concept of fetishism in psychoanalysis. Fetishism refers to a *contradictory belief* structure which enables the infant to deal with the shocking discovery of sexual difference. The male infant discovers that woman's/mother's body is different, for she does not have a penis, and substitutes this lack with what thus later becomes a "fetish-object." The fetish can be any object that can serve in place of the penis with which the shocked male infant would complete the woman/mother.

The function of the fetish is to *disavow* the perception of difference. The constitutive formula of fetishism is the statement, "I know very well, but nevertheless . . ." In other words, the notion of fetishism refers to the structure of a belief which maintains a fantasmatic unity and sameness in the face of contradiction and difference. The belief (that the woman/mother does not have a penis) is retained, but it is also denied and is substituted with a fetish object. This implies that the structure of fetishism as a contradictory belief is always characterized by an ambiguity or ambivalence, by a productive tension that results from the simultaneous recognition and refusal of difference. It is this implication of fetishism that Bhabha is concerned with.

In the construction of discriminatory knowledges, fetishism "provide[s] a process of splitting and multiple/contradictory belief at the point of enunciation and subjectification." [44] The ambivalence and splitting of colonial discourse, reflected in its fetishistic mode of representation, can be illustrated in the conflictual way pleasure and fear, strangeness and familiarity, recognition and refusal of difference are articulated. The irreconcilable logic of fetishism offers the subject of colonial discourse "a primordial either/or" structure which in turn facilitates its denial of recognition of difference.

By applying the psychoanalytic theory of fetishism to explain the mode of operation of colonial discourse, Bhabha elucidates the ways in which cultural difference is represented. Bhabha translates "penis" into skin/race/culture and formulates the following structure to explicate the constitutive ambiguity in the articulation of otherness. As he puts it, "fetishism is always a 'play' or vacillation between the archaic affirmation of wholeness/similarity – in Freud's terms 'All men have penises,' in ours 'All men have the same skin/race/culture; and the anxiety associated with lack and difference' – again, for Freud 'Some do not have penises'; for ours 'Some *do not* have have the same skin/race/culture.'"[45]

Bhabha is certainly aware of the problems of translating the theory of fetishism – which is developed primarily to understand the construction of sexual difference – into the domain of colonial discourse as part of his effort to understand the nature of the representation of cultural difference. For example, he tries to delineate the significant differences between the general (read sexual) theory of fetishism and his specific use of it for understanding the discourse of colonialism. First, he argues, that, unlike the fetish of sexual difference, the fetish of colonial discourse is not a secret. The skin, which is quite visible, is a key signifier of racial and cultural difference and thus functions at the center of the racial drama which characterizes the colonial encounter. Second, the fetish of cultural difference –

unlike the sexual fetish which is registered as a "good object" and is lovable and facilitates sexual pleasure – validates the colonial relation which is based on power. Although Bhabha acknowledges the problem such a translation poses, the solution he offers for resolving it is a rather uninspired one. For this purpose he goes back to Freud, who states that in the treatment of the fetish, affection and hostility run parallel to each other, for they both are based on disavowal and acknowledgment of castration. However, Bhabha fails to recognize that the problems involved in transferring fetishism from the domain of sexual difference to the question of cultural difference are more complex than being two sides of the same coin. The main reason why the perceived "lack" of woman/mother is disavowed and then substituted for with another object is that such a lack poses a threat of castration and hence induces fear and anxiety in men. One of the avenues available to dissipate the anxiety provoked by castration is to substitute a fetish object to disavow sexual difference. Given that "castration anxiety" and hence the threat it constitutes is key in the theory of fetishism, it is not clear how the perceived lack (all men do not have the same skin/race/culture) of the cultural other constitutes a threat for the colonizer. Moreover, it is not clear how a specific color is translated into lack.

Bhabha, in specifying the conditions and defining features of the discourse of colonialism, attempts to articulate the representation of sexual difference with cultural difference. This is certainly a remarkable endeavor, for most of the analyses of representation of difference ceaselessly reproduce the dualistic framework in which the representation of cultural difference is treated as belonging to a separate domain, clearly distinguishable from the representation of sexual difference. And we should also remember that Said's analysis was not free from this dualism. However, despite Bhabha's efforts to breach this dualism and conjure up the much more complicated nature of constitution of difference, he nevertheless leaves the question of sexuality unexamined. He recognizes this problem in a footnote, yet this does not quite help him in resolving the dualism in the analysis of cultural and sexual difference. As Young rightly observes in elaborating the structure of colonial discourse, the question of sexuality and of sexual difference is elided in Bhabha's analysis. The question of a gendered colonial subject is not worked out in detail, but simply regarded as a metaphor of colonial ambivalence in Bhabha's analysis.[46]

A new binary: theoretical unity versus historical particularity

In recent years Said's work has stimulated a wide range of discussion and hence has became an indispensable reference point for the work done in the field of post-colonial theory. Not only the conceptual pairs of the colonized and colonizer, West and East but also the term post-colonial have been met with skepticism. In this section I would like to discuss the debates and reasons surrounding this skepticism.

In a recent collection entitled *Colonial Discourse/Postcolonial Theory*,[47] critics such as Ela Shohat, Peter Hulme, and Anne McClintock point to the pitfalls of using such general categories to account for the particular texts produced in particular historical contexts. Criticisms voiced by Nicholas Thomas in his recently published book *Colonialism's Culture* [48] and to a certain extent by Robert Young in his *Colonial Desire* [49] are generally centered around the usefulness of the concept of colonial discourse as a general category. The question of the legitimacy of employing colonial discourse or the colonized as a general category in dealing with a diversified and heterogeneous phenomenon such as colonialism has been raised quite frequently in the studies of colonial discourse.

It has been suggested that the prevalent perception of colonialism and of colonial discourse is characterized in unitary and essentialized terms. By evoking colonialism as a transhistorical and global phenomenon, such terms not only imply a homogenizing vision of colonialism but also suggest that colonialism was a coherent imposition, implying that it was all pervasively efficacious in dominating and assimilating the colonized.[50] Such a unitary understanding of colonialism also implies that the discourse of colonialism operated identically across the colonized space and throughout time.[51] In this respect, it is claimed that by employing the Manichaean division between self and other, colonizer and colonized, colonial discourse theory perpetuates the terms and dominance established by colonial history that it aims to scrutinize.[52] Benita Parry criticizes colonial discourse theory for being complicit with the postulates of colonial discourse, because it retains colonialism's undifferentiated identity categories. In opposition to this, she suggests that the range of possible subject positions can never be wholly determined by any system of coercion. [53]

Belief in the geographical homogeneity and all-encompassing nature of colonialism has also been criticized on the grounds that by exaggerating colonial power, colonial discourse studies elide the subjectivity of the colonized and the various forms of indigenous resistance against colonialism. The question of agency and the concern for reinstating and recovering the subjectivity of the colonized is reflected in attempts to revise Said's work, which is believed not to foster an analysis of counter-histories, for it allegedly implies that there is no alternative to Orientalism. Moreover, Said's work is thought not to encourage inquiry into the actual and historically specific conditions of colonialism.[54] For Parry, by implying a totalizing potency for the colonial apparatus, colonial discourse theorists "misrepresent the colonized as being produced as a stable category fixed in a position of subjugation."[55] This understanding, for her, precludes the possibility of theorizing resistance and affirming the power of the reverse discourse and anti-colonialist writing that subverts the colonial ideology. Similarly, for Thomas, the prevalent understanding of colonial discourse entails a denial of the sovereignity and autonomy of the colonized and fails to show how colonial histories were shaped by indigenous resistance and contestation. Thus for Thomas, subjectivity is elided in post-structuralism in general, and in colonial discourse theory in particular. In contrast to this, he suggests that emphasis should be placed on agency.[56]

This concern about undoing colonial discourse as a homogenizing category and pointing to its historically specific articulations so as to give the local and the particular due consideration can be regarded as the most salient feature of Nicholas Thomas's work. A similar concern, though as not quite strongly expressed, also prevails in Young's study. But it is important to point out that, despite critiquing the lack of historical specificity and the tendency of anti-Eurocentric theory to homogenize the Third World and the West, Young is careful to avoid leaping into empirical and geographical particularity. For example, he reminds us that Third World theorists (such as Fanon, Said and others) felt it necessary to construct such a general category in order to be able to constitute an object of analysis and resistance. Moreover, he suggests that setting homogenization against historical specificity and geographical particularity might imply repeating colonialism's own partitioning strategies.[57] To be able to delineate the differences between the two critics it is important to discuss them separately.

Thomas's main interest is to localize and pluralize colonialism by historicizing it. By suggesting that colonial projects and relationships are inevitably fractured, he wants to point to the dispersed and conflicted character of colonial discourse and thereby challenge the common fundamental division set between the colonizer and colonized, to undo the notion of colonialism as a coherent object. In an effort to bring attention to the complex, variable, and ambivalent nature of colonial ideologies, he aims to reveal the enormous variation in different colonial contexts and different historical moments. To historicize and pluralize colonialism, Thomas suggests that we need to change our understanding of colonialism from a model of *signification* to a model of *narration* or from a model of *signs* to a model of *practices*, for there is always a gap between projection and performance of colonialism. The endurance of colonial relations and their representational codes are not due to their reproduction as a structure, but due to performance and practical mastery.[58] For Thomas, such a dynamic model of colonialism will allow us to identify not only the continuities but also the failures, displacements and ruptures of colonial projects, for such projects are continually constructed, misconstructed, adapted, and enacted. It is not simply the fundamental division between the colonized and the colonizer, but also the divison within the strategic colonizing projects and visions of the civilizing mission (for example, assimilationist versus segregationist) which inevitably fractures colonial projects and colonialists. Nor should we assume that there is one overriding discourse at a particular time. Thus, historicization of colonialism necessitates that we localize colonialism in encounters so as not to see it as an inescapable system. By referring to the inevitable fissure at the heart of colonialism, Thomas does not refer simply to its degree of success or failure, but to the ways in which colonial projects are altered, contested, adapted, and redefined by indigenous societies, as well as to the internal debates and contradictions within colonial projects.

Thomas is not unaware of the risk that such pluralization carries: the danger of restricting analysis to mere empirical particularity. While he is concerned with identifying the epistemological breaks and ruptures, and hence with establishing the distinctiveness of different historical periods, he is also careful to recognize continuity across periods and the ways in which perception of otherness remains salient and available in varying degrees over time.[59] Thomas suggests that by describing the distinctive character-istics of colonialist imagination of each period, we will avoid setting up a binary opposition between empirical particularity and an essentialist idea of Orientalism.[60] But then one wonders whether this periodization is any different from empirical particularity or from a designation of the peculiar characteristics of *different national styles* (say British versus French coloni-alism) that Thomas himself does not necessarily endorse as a way of getting out of the totalizing notion of colonialism. He suggests that although it might be useful to identify the contrasts between French and British models of colonialism, this can only be done at the expense of ignoring the diver-sity within French and British practices. But we should ask to what extent this emphasis on epochal frame or historical typification (or the designa-tion of historical peculiarity) is useful in overcoming the problem of empir-ical particularity. One is also tempted to ask, after this emphasis on internal contradictions and debates within colonial ideologies, whether this histor-ical typification does not also imply another unified or homogeneous notion of colonialism. In other words, by doing this, does not one simply displace the criterion for the unity of colonialism from space to time? Although Thomas seems to promise a theory of colonialism that can acco-modate multiple histories, cultures, and geographies, what we are offered eventually is a historicist periodization which is no less unifying than the predominant conceptions of colonialism. Therefore, we can bring the same objection to Thomas that he himself develops against the idea of contrasting different national styles. The identification of the salient features of a historical period can be made only at the expense of masking the diversity and multiplicity within that specific period. Anticipating such a possible objection Thomas develops his defense as follows: "At this heuristic level, an analytical fiction that postulates distinctions between colonial epochs is more valuable than a history of colonialism, though it needs to be understood that such a fiction is a rhetorical device: it is constructed in order to subvert easy totalities or progressive histories."[61]

If the designation of defining characteristics of an epoch can be treated as a rhetorical device, why can one not also accept the general category of colonialism as a rhetorical device? In other words, if the issue here is simply a matter of constructing a rhetorical device, one wonders why totalizing implications of one device but not the other is preferable and acceptable. Does not this epochal rhetorical device disguise diversity? Although I am not particularly concerned with the diversities existing within a historical period, what I want to point out here is the sterility of the framework that posits multiplicity as a solution to homogenization, essentialism or unity. What I want to underline here is the impasse we hit when we imagine that we can challenge essentialism when we simply reverse it and privilege multiplicity and plurality instead. I will try to elaborate this point further in the following pages, but let me turn now to a discussion of Robert Young's study.

In *Colonial Desire* Robert Young expresses his dissatisfaction with how post-colonial criticism has constructed the colonizer and the colonized or self and the other as two antithetical groups. For him, post-colonial criticism tends to reproduce the static and essentialist categories that it aims to dismantle by constructing such Manichean divisions. Questioning the legitimacy of colonial discourse as a general category, Young points to the difficulty of avoiding the accusation of idealism involved in the use of such a general category as a way of dealing with the "totality of discourses of and about colonialism."[62] Although he is prepared to accept that colonialism was to a noticeable degree geographically and historically homogenous, nonetheless he is not fully convinced that the category of colonial discourse warrants its general use so as to imply that colonialism has operated everywhere in a similar enough way. The differences between French and British colonialism, for example, as well as the varieties within racism, constitute the basis of Young's reluctance to claim that theoretical paradigms of colonial discourse analysis work equally well for all the different versions of colonialism. For example, French colonialism, which was designed to assimilate, was based on egalitarian Enlightenment assumptions of the sameness of all human beings, and British colonialism, which was designed for indirect rule, was based on the assumptions of difference and of inequality. By pointing to this and other historical differences, Young aims to point to the heterogeneity within colonial domination as well as the different outcomes colonialism has given rise to. Young's study implies that if we cannot confidently assume that colonial discourse operated identically across space and time then it becomes quite legitimate to question the validity of a "general theoretical matrix that is able to provide an all-encompassing framework for the analysis of each singular colonial instance."[63] However, Young is careful not to simply set homogenization against the varieties of historical and geographical instances and thus drift into empirical particularism as he acknowledges the necessity of constructing a general category such as colonialism to counter-attack the colonial power. As Young acknowledges, the attempt to further develop the theoretical parameters set by Said and others cannot be achieved simply by producing new archival material.[64] Indeed, especially in his chapter entitled "Colonialism and Desiring Machine," where he applies Deleuze and Guattari's framework and particularly the concepts of desire, machine, territorialization, and reterritorialization, the necessity of using a general and unified notion of colonialism becomes more visible.[65] Here Young, following Deleuze and Guattari, characterizes colonialism as a machine, as a determining and law-governing process. His endorsement of David Trotter's understanding of "colonialism as a text without an author" should be seen as part of the same attempt to emphasize the importance of retaining the notion of colonialism as a general category.[66] By designating the role of capitalism as the determining motor of colonialism, Young conceives the procedures of global capitalism as a form of cartography/inscription or as a territorial writing machine in which the physical appropriation of land and the seizure of cultural space are fundamental. But Young warns us that such processes of appropriation and seizure should not be understood as a simple destruction of native cultures or a simplistic grafting of one culture onto the other. In an effort to point to the complexities involved in such processes he proposes to see the decoding and recoding processes (processes through which colonial practices are inscribed on the territories and peoples subjected to colonial power) as a layering of cultures on top of each other. Such imbrication of cultures with each other shows that colonial culture never simply repeats itself. In other words, colonialism is not a simple process of production of a new mimesis. When colonial cultures are inscribed to colonized contexts, they are always translated and become hybridized and thus give rise to an "uncertain patchwork of identities" and produce "polymorphously perverse peoples who are white but not quite." The term Young proposes to capture this complexity is "palimpsestual inscription."[67]

This characterization of colonialism is in accordance with Young's approval of Homi Bhabha's concept of hybridity which he rightfully thinks allows an understanding of colonial discourse as open to the trace of the language of the other. Since the command of colonial authority does not have a univocal grip on native cultures, it is important that we have concepts to enable us to formulate how structures of domination are reversed, and get translated and displaced. As Young correctly points out, the concept of hybridity at the same time refers to a moment of challenge and resistance and thus questions the validity of the essentializing logic of the opposition set between colonizer and colonized. Hence Young recognizes that Bhabha's characterization of colonial discourse as a production of hybridity grasps the double logic upon which colonial discourse is based: on the one hand, it hegemonizes and creates new structures, spaces, and scenes and, on the other hand, it diasporizes, enables intervention, subversion, translation, and transformation. In fact, Young tries to further elaborate the double logic of colonialism by introducing Jacques Derrida's notion of "brisure" which refers to the moment of breaking and joining simultaneously. Thus, for Young, hybridity is the concept that enables us to understand how difference and sameness exist in an apparently impossible simultaneity. As he suggests, "hybridity thus makes difference into sameness, and sameness into difference, but in a way that makes the same no longer the same, the different no longer simply different."[68] It is this "binate operation," for Young, which comprehends the simultaneous repetition and subversion of colonialism.

Young's above formulation implies that he recognizes that Bhabha does not simply suggest the pluralization of the concept of colonial discourse in an effort to understand its potential subversion, for he formulates it in such a way that it enables us to see the fracture, splitting, and multiplicity within its consistency. Moreover, Young also acknowledges the usefulness of the concept of ambivalance which Bhabha proposes as it "shows the different kinds of framing that Western culture receives when translated into different contexts."[69] But let it suffice to mention here that despite Young's acknowledgment of the use of the concept of hybridity and ambivalance, he still insists on the necessity of understanding the historical specificity of the discourse of colonialism. The problem is not simply Young's insistence on specificity, but the formulation he proposes to achieve it. As if Young himself has not already endorsed hybridity and ambivalance as enabling the recognition of the differential articulations of colonialism (which in fact should be taken as the recognition of its inescapably historically specific nature), towards the end of the book he suggests that we should acknowledge the simultaneous working of *other forms* of racial distinction alongside the model of the *self–other*. Being critical of the Hegelian dialectic, Young suggests that racism or colonialism has not simply operated according to the same–other or black and white model but was also based on the "computation of normalities and degrees of deviance from the white norm."[70] After recognizing the merits of the concepts of hybridity and ambivalance, one is struck by the threadbareness of such a formulation which claims to recognize the historically specific varieties of colonialism and thus to avoid the problem of binarism and the totalizing gesture of the theoretical paradigms of colonial discourse. What Young suggests implies no more than a simple pluralization of the allegedly unified and totalizing notion of colonial discourse. Any attempt to avoid the self/other, colonized/colonizer, West/East opposition should not feel satisfied simply by such pluralism. What we need instead is a theoretical framework, one that is no less generalized than those already in existence, that will enable us to show how colonial discourse can never be identical with itself, how it is inevitably fractured within itself and never repeats itself identically as it constitutes its unity; how it changes while it retains its hegemony and adapts to different circumstances. In other words, the point is to show the sameness within the difference of colonial discourse. Young himself also tends to make a similar suggestion when he tries to understand the changes that occurred in racist discourse. As he observes, the scientific theories measuring cultural difference have always used earlier ideas whereby the multiple meanings of race were grafted onto each other. This, he characterizes as the *oneiric logic* of race theory which "allows it to survive despite its contradictions, to reverse itself at every refutation, to adapt and transform itself at every denial."[71]

The "computation of normalities and degrees of deviance from the white norm" that Young suggests as a way of overcoming the binarism implied in the Hegelian dialectical model of the same and the other is also quite problematical. Such a model can be interpreted not simply as referring to two antithetical groups, but more productively to understand a model where the other represents the excluded site against which the subject constitutes its identity. While being expelled from the privileged domain of subjectivity, the other is nevertheless an integral part of the subject as its effaced foundation. The force of this effacement ensures the subject's illusory claims for self-sufficiency and self-certainty.[72]

The same–other dialectic should be taken as the prototype of an exclusionary scheme by which the subject is constituted as sovereign and autonomous. Thus the very process of the computation of normalities and degrees of deviance from a norm does not refer to a different mechanism, but can be seen as one variant of the exclusionary scheme that the same–other model designates. In other words, the so-called computation of normalities and degrees of deviance do not refer to *other forms* of racial distinction alongside the model of the *self–other*. Rather than multiplying the variants of this model with an additive logic, we should emphasize that the important point is to understand what is relegated to the status of "outside the norm" is also produced in a mode of exclusion by the subject who claims to be self-constituting.[73] Such exclusions, be they in the form of black and white, or computations of normalities, are all attempts at securing the seeming self-sufficiency of the subject.

If we return to the issue of the historical specificity and the recognition of varieties of colonialism, the question that needs to be asked should be about the gains we can achieve by an uncritical celebrating of colonialism*s* instead of colonialism. Similarly, we should also ask about the dangers and risks such a pluralization implies. As Barker, Hulme, and Iversen warn us, commitment to particularity does not imply rejection of the possibility of generalization. In trying to avoid unity and homogeneity we should not fall back into "obsession with specificities which can become another empiricist fallacy in which all attempts to theorise are answered by the supposedly irrefutable case of a counter-example."[74] We should also remember that in trying to bring into the picture the historically specific articulations which colonial discourse supposedly homogenizes we are introducing a new binarism, this time between the homogeneity and the specificity of colonial discourse in the name of avoiding the Hegelian model of the same and the other, the colonizer and the colonized. Thus the supposed triumph of the totalizing notion of colonialism cannot be remedied by a straight reversal which celebrates historical particularity and specificity. Such criticisms are made in the name of avoiding the essentializing and totalizing gesture of colonial discourse theory. But what such critiques ignore is that essentialism inheres precisely in binary opposition. In this sense, a forthright reversal of the binary is far from interrupting the economy that underpins it. As Vicki Kirby notes, "essentialism is not an entity that can be identified and dissolved by saying yes or no to it."[75] Rather, the question, as she suggests, should pertain to "the how" of essentialism, to the ways in which "essence" is "made proper and naturalized within our thought or being."[76]

There are other good reasons also why we have to retain the general and generalizing term colonialism. In talking about the term neocolonialism

Spivak notes that "historically these terms are always heterogeneous and so is neocolonialism. You have to posit a great narrative in order to be able to critique it."[77] Similarly, Bruce Robbins suggests that we must avoid the "easy generalization" and retain the right to formulate "difficult generalizations."[78] Thus the first and foremost reason for posing such a generalized category as colonialism is that it enables us to critique it.

In insisting on retaining the general category of colonial discourse or colonialism, I am in no way suggesting we see its unity as a simple harmonious totality. Rather, what I am suggesting is that we see the *complexity within such a unity*. As I try to show in chapter 3 it is the citationary nature of orientalism that maintains its constancy, unity, and hegemony. Thus to understand the complexity of the unity of colonialism and colonial discourse we need to conceive of it as a network of codes, imageries, signs, and representations which serve as a reference system and function as a regulatory principle of a discursive regime that we can label as colonial. It is this reference system or regulatory principle that facilitates the recognition of a discourse as colonial. Thus colonial discourse should be seen as an episteme in the Foucauldian sense. The colonial episteme is maintained by a reiteration or citation of certain statements and representations. It is this citational nature of colonial discourse that guarantees its "factual" status, its "naturalness," while simultaneously concealing the conventions upon which it is based. Paraphrasing Derrida in this context, white mythology or colonial discourse is a process of erasure of the fabulous scene that has produced it. However, it is a "scene that nevertheless remains alive and stirring."[79] But if it is citationality that is essential in the sustenance of colonial discourse, it at the same time constitutes the possibility of its subversion and displacement. The repetition of the colonial dictum by the colonized, taken outside its original context where it has been deployed as an instrument of oppressive power, can pave the way for its differential articulation. It is this potential subversive reiteration that Bhabha's formulation of colonial discourse recognizes.[80]

2

Veiled fantasies: cultural and sexual difference in the discourse of Orientalism

If one wants to understand the racial situation psychoanalytically . . . considerable importance must be given to sexual phenomena.
Frantz Fanon, *Black Skin, White Masks*

The phantasy is the support of desire; it is not the object that is the support of desire. The subject sustains himself as desiring in relation to an ever more complex signifying ensemble.
Jacques Lacan, *The Four Fundamental Concepts of Psycho-Analysis*

Unveiling as political doctrine

Erecting a barrier between the body of the Oriental woman and the Western gaze, the opaque, all-encompassing veil seems to place her body out of the reach of the Western gaze and desire. Frustrated with the invisibility and inaccessibility of this mysterious, fantasmatic figure, disappointed with the veiled figure's refusal to be gazed at, Western desire subjects this enigmatic, in Copjec's terms, "sartorial matter," to a relentless investigation. The practice of veiling and the veiled woman thus go beyond their simple reference and become tropes of the European text in Hayden White's sense: "the data resisting the coherency of the image which we are trying to fashion of them."[1] It is no surprise that there are countless accounts and representations of the veil and veiled women in Western discourses, all made in an effort to reveal the hidden secrets of the Orient. The very depiction of the Orient and its women, "like the unveiling of an enigma, makes visible what is hidden."[2] The veil is one of those tropes through which Western fantasies of penetration into the mysteries of the Orient and access to the interiority of the other are fantasmatically achieved. The most blatant example of the fear of the other and the associated fantasy of penetration is French colonialism's obsession with the woman's veil in Algeria. As we learn from Fanon, "the Algerian woman, in the eyes of the observer, is unmistakeably 'she who hides behind a veil'."[3] Fanon continues: "this enabled the colonial administration to define a precise political doctrine: 'If we want to destroy the structure of Algerian society, its capacity for resistance, we must first of all conquer the women: we must go and find them behind the veil where they hide themselves and in the houses where the men keep them out of sight.'"[4]

I propose to take this "precise political doctrine" seriously, because it provides us with several possibilities at once: first, a critique of the critiques of the ethico-political program of European Enlightenment from the point of view of the double articulation of global-cultural and sexual differences, hence a new way of dealing with the entanglement of questions of imperialism and gender; second, a critique of the critiques of colonial discourse from a feminist point of view, hence the development of a new feminist perspective in the analysis of colonial discourse. I must warn my reader that I claim no privilege for the veil as an object of study. The grand narrative of the imperial, sovereign subject is complex and constantly changing, and the veil is privileged only to the extent that it enables us to see some of the complexity of this narrative.

The question of why the veiled woman has such a high profile in the French colonization of Algeria seems obvious at a first glance: in the colonizer's eye Algerian resistance is condensed in the veil which is seen as an obstacle to his visual control. Conquering the Algerian women is thus equal to conquering Algeria, the land, and people themselves. This is surely not a simple military question in a narrow sense, but it is rooted in a problematic of power, which not only takes Algeria as a land to be conquered, but which establishes such conquest in terms of an epistemological superiority.[5] One of the axioms of the European Enlightenment is "the disenchantment of the world" in which "knowledge, which is power, knows no obstacles."[6] In his study on modern forms of discipline, Michel Foucault demonstrated that this problematic of knowledge as power is tied to a social program and strategy according to which space is organized in a particular way which makes its individual occupants and their behavior visible and transparent. With modernity comes a new form of institutional power which is based on visibility and transparency and which refuses to tolerate areas of darkness. The epitome of this modern form of power, Bentham's model prison, the panopticon, embodies the concept of an eye which can see without being seen.[7] For Foucault, the social practice of transparency completes the philosophical ideas of the Enlightenment, for instance Rousseau's well-known dream of a perfectly transparent society (we might also say that it reveals the other side of these ideas).[8] Foucault's view is supported by Jean Starobinski's interesting study on the theme of transparency and obstacle in Rousseau. Starobinski shows that Rousseau attached a negative value to anything hidden or mysterious and elaborated a whole theory of unveiling the truth.[9] Indeed, in the political doctrine of French colonialism, the veiled woman is made "a case which at one and the same time, constitutes an object for a branch of knowledge and a hold for a branch of power," and Muslim women are classified as a group of people "who have to be trained or corrected, classified, normalized, excluded, etc."[10] As Foucault has succinctly argued, these objects of discourse are not a pure creation of discourse, they are rather objects (and subjects) identified by discourse as problems to be dealt with, and objects to be known and controlled (only once they are identified, they enter into a process of construction in and by discourse). Surely, the veiled woman is already other-ed in her own culture, gender-ed in and by a particular form of dressing, but she is other to the Western subject in a way that differs from her position relative to the dominant male subjects of her culture. I would like to argue here that the case or tropology of the "veil" is not simply a signifier of a cultural habit or identity that can be liked or disliked, be good or bad, but "in a world bewitched by the invisible powers of the other" for a subject, i.e., for the European subject in our case, it signifies the production of an "exteriority," a "target or threat," which makes possible for that subject to "postulate a place that can be delimited as its own and serve as the base."[11] This enables him to produce himself *vis-à-vis* an other while simultaneously erasing the very process of this production.

The veil can be seen as the resisting data or tropology of this modern power whose program aims to construct the world in terms of a transparency provided by knowledge as power. However, limiting itself to Europe as the sovereign subject of history, Foucault's analysis of such power has remained blind to the role played by these technologies and their epistemological and subjective import in the European colonization of the world. Gayatri Spivak suggests that we write against the "possibility that the intellectual is complicit in the persistent constitution of other as the self's shadow." I take her words as a warning:

The clearest available example of such epistemic violence is the remotely orchestrated, far-flung and heterogenous project to constitute the colonial subject as Other. This project is also the symmetrical obliteration of the trace of that Other in its precarious Subject-ivity. It is well known that Foucault locates epistemic violence, a complete overhaul of the episteme, in the redefiniton of sanity at the end of the European eighteenth century. But what if that particular definition was only a part of the narrative of history in Europe as well as in the colonies? What if the two projects of epistemic overhaul worked as dislocated and unacknowledged parts of a vast two-handed engine? Perhaps it is no more than to ask that the subtext of the palimpsestic narrative of imperialism be recognized as 'subjugated knowledge'...[12]

The sub-text of the palimpsestic narrative of imperialism is demonstrated in the fact that, whether he likes it or not, for the European subject, there is always more to the veil than the veil. A very interesting example is Gaëtan Gatian de Clerambault, the nineteenth-century French psychiatrist who was fascinated with the foldings of North African dressing and took hundreds of photographs of veiled people. Clerambault seems to constitute the unique instance of a subjective approach to North African Islamic culture which needs to be explored further. According to Gilles Deleuze, if Clerambault's interest in Islamic folds "manifests a delirium, it is because he discovers the tiny hallucinatory perceptions of ether addicts in the folds of clothing."[13] The Islamic veil is considered by Clerambault and Deleuze as providing a unique form of perception of a world of "figures without objects."[14] I see this as a legitimate area of research into the Islamic veil/fold, but I am interested here in a dialectics of seeing and gazing. Although Deleuze considers this a more restricted area of the "optical fold,"[15] I argue that its ethico-political implications exceed its epistemological limits. A general study of the fold and of its varieties remains limited in a different way, if we remember that, writing against the always-already existing possibility of the constitution of the other as the self's shadow, Spivak's "two-handed engine" would ask for a re-inscription of the Islamic fold/veil as *subjugated knowledge* of the Western imperial palimpsest in Clerambault's psychological "discoveries." And Malek Alloula's well-known *Colonial Harem* undeniably demonstrates the place of sexual difference in the signification of the Islamic fold/veil. Alloula's semiological classification and reading of erotic postcard pictures of half-veiled Algerian women opens up the problematic of cultural difference into a problematic of sexual difference. Although his approach is a semiological/Barthesian one which does not employ a thematics of fold, I suggest that we take this work as a warning for the Deleuzian overlooking of sexual (and cultural) difference in the fold/veil.[16]

The rhetoric of the veil: Orientalist travel writing in the nineteenth century

In a sentence which predicts Alloula's work, "in the Arab world" writes Fanon, "the veil worn by women is at once noticed by the tourist ... (it) generally suffices to characterize Arab society."[17] Can this immediate attention be considered as an instance of the celebrated Lacanian "triumph of the gaze over the eye"?[18] If I am wary of Foucault's complicity with the very form of power he analyzes because he overlooks its working outside Europe, or of Deleuzian analysis of the fold, I am also wary of a kind of psychoanalysis which is blind to the historical inscription of its conceptual apparatus. The question posed by François Wahl to Jacques Lacan in his seminar on the gaze is instructive in this sense. Against Lacan's insistence that all eye is evil eye, Wahl brings up the example of the "prophylactic eye" (an eye that protects one from disease) in the Mediterranean cultures. Lacan's answer is that the prophylactic eye is allopathic, i.e. it cures the disease by exciting a dissimilar affection, and that the prophylactic objects are clearly symbols of the phallus. In the same place, he refers to the North African–Islamic "baraka" and, despite a few places where he admits that he hesitated, concludes that the eye is always maleficent rather than benef-icent.[19] I take the hesitation rather than the conclusion as my guide, but I am interested in a deconstruction of the sovereign subject rather than an ethnography of Islamic culture. In other words, I am more interested here in demonstrating the *historical determination* of the Lacanian gaze, of "the form of a strange contingency, symbolic of what we (they) find on the horizon, as the thrust of our (their) experience, namely the lack that con-stitutes castration anxiety."[20] Within such an approach, I consider the European's immediate object of attention in the horizon of Muslim culture as *his* construct: the veiled woman is not simply an obstacle in the field of visibility and control, but her veiled presence also seems to provide the Western subject with a condition which is the inverse of Bentham's omnipotent gaze. The loss of control does not imply a mere loss of sight, but a complete reversal of positions: her body completely invisible to the European observer except for her eyes, *the veiled woman can see without being seen*. The apparently calm rationalist discipline of the European subject goes awry in the fantasies of penetration as well as in the tropolog-ical excess of the veil. This is why the precise political doctrine is not simply a military matter, but, as I will demonstrate below, the strategic desire which defines it is structured through fantasy. Drawing upon his experience as a psychiatrist, Fanon emphasizes the violent play of this reversal:

Thus the rape of the Algerian woman in the dream of a European is always pre-ceded by a rending of the veil . . . Whenever, in dreams having an erotic content, a European meets an Algerian woman, the specific features of his relations with the colonized society manifest themselves . . . With an Algerian woman, there is no pro-gressive conquest, no mutual revelation. Straight off, with the maximum of violence there is possession, rape, near-murder . . . This brutality and this sadism are in fact emphasized by the frightened attitude of the Algerian woman. In the dream, the woman-victim screams, struggles like a doe, and as she weakens and faints, is pen-etrated, martyrized, ripped apart.[21]

The veil is then part of or an element of a highly charged fantasmatic scene. Nevertheless, the fantasy of penetration is only one aspect of a more complex ideological-subjective formation which oscillates between fascination and anger and frustration. In the nineteenth-century European travellers' obsession with the veil, the "precise political doctrine" dissolves into a textual inscription which is witness to an underlying enunciative (and subjective) formation traversing different fields of writing. These texts clearly display the veil's specific polysemy. As is well known, in Lacan's approach the gaze is not seen, but is imagined by the subject in the field of the other.[22] Orientalist writing is the European imagination at work in the field of the other. The veil attracts the eye, and forces one to think, to speculate about what is behind it. It is often represented as some kind of a mask, hiding the woman. With the help of this opaque veil, the Oriental woman is considered as not yielding herself to the Western gaze and therefore imagined as hiding something behind the veil. It is through the inscription of the veil as a mask that the Oriental woman is turned into an enigma. Such a discursive construction incites the presumption that the real nature of these women is concealed, their truth is disguised and they appear in a false, deceptive manner. They are therefore other than what they appear to be. Edmondo de Amicis' statements reveal this figure of deception: "it is impossible to say what they contrive to do with those two veils . . . making them serve at once to *display*, to *conceal*, to *promise*, to *propose* a problem, or to betray some little marvel unexpectedly"[24] (emphasis added).

The figure of the masquerade is frequently employed. Theophile Gautier, in his description of the women of Istanbul, expresses both his denunciation of the veil and his identification of the true nature of the city through this same figure: "an immense female population – anonymous and unknown – circulates through this mysterious city, which is thus transformed into a sort of vast masquerade – with the peculiarity, that the dominoes are never permitted to unmask."[24] Edmondo de Amicis describes the women on the streets of Istanbul in a similar manner:

The first impression is most curious. The stranger wonders whether all those white veiled figures in bright colored wrappers are masquerades, or nuns, or mad women; and as not one is ever seen accompanied by a man, they seem to belong to no one, and to be all girls and widows, or members of some great association of the "ill-married" . . . One is constrained to stop and mediate upon these strange figures and stranger customs.[25]

The veil gives rise to a meditation: if they wear a mask, or masquerade or conceal themselves, then there must be a behind-the-mask, a knowledge that is kept secret from us. The *mystery* that is assumed to be concealed by the veil is *unconcealed* by giving a figural representation to this mask and to the act of masquerading as an enigmatic figure. However, what is thus unconcealed, i.e. the "masquerade," the "veil," is the *act of concealment itself*. The veiled existence is the very truth of Oriental women; they seem to exist always in this deceptive manner.

This metaphysical speculation or mediation, this desire to reveal and unveil is at the same time the *scene of seduction*. The metaphysical will to know gains a sexual overtone. Troubled with this mask, the Western subject is threatened and seduced at the same time:

These then, you think, these are really those "conquerors of the heart," those "founts of pleasure," those "little rose leaves," those "early ripening grapes," those "dews of the morning," "auroras," "vivifiers," and "full moons." These are the *hanums* and the mysterious odalisques that we dreamed of when we were twenty years old . . . It is a costume at once austere and sweet, that has something virginal and holy about it; under which none but gentle thoughts and innocent fancies should have birth.[26]

Since he is devoid of any true perspective on the Oriental woman, Amicis can never be sure. The Oriental woman/Orient is so deceptive and theatrical. With her, everything is an enigma. Amicis continues: "that jealous veil that, according to the Koran, was to be 'a sign of her virtue and a guard against the talk of the world' is now only a semblance."[27]

This fear of being deceived by the masquerading Oriental woman is also what characterizes Loti's representation of the Oriental woman in *Disenchanted*. In this novel, two Turkish women and a French writer, Marc Helys, write a letter to Loti, simply because they want some divergence from their monotonous life and would like to teach him a lesson by making him an object of ridicule. The women approach Loti under their veils, thus remaining completely incognito.[28] Uncomfortable with their invisible presence, Loti asks them to remove their veils, but they refuse to do so. During their conversations, when the women speak a few Turkish words with each other, Loti immediately warns them that he knows the language sufficiently well and would be aware if any "uncivil remark" was being uttered about himself.

This short scene sums up the whole theme of the novel: it is about how Loti is seduced but at the same time mocked by these veiled women. As they themselves express through their attitude, it is precisely with their veils that Oriental women can seduce, mock, and threaten him. The veil places them at a distance Loti can not reach. In warning them that he knows Turkish, that he can understand them, he in fact expresses his own anxiety. This anxiety is caused by his lack of a true, fixed perspective; he can not position himself *vis-à-vis* them. He reminds them of his knowledge of their language precisely because this knowledge does not seem sufficient to him to gain control over their veiled presence, for they masquerade and their dress is deceptive. It is this incapacity to fix and control that is unsettling and terrifying and yet so seducing.

A variety of reasons are offered by the European subject to explain this obsession with the Oriental veil: "civilizing," "modernizing," and thereby "liberating" the "backward" Orient and its women, making them speaking subjects. These are the manifest terms of the political doctrine. But then what do we make of the above texts obsessed with the veil? Joan Copjec suggests that no rational explanation can account for the West's preoccupation with lifting the veil, for this is a preoccupation sustained by fantasy and hence belongs to the realm of desire. According to Copjec:

What was capital in this fantasy was the surplus pleasure, the useless *jouissance* which the voluminous cloth was supposed to veil and the colonial subject, thus hidden, was supposed to enjoy. Every effort to strip away the veil was clearly an aggression against the bloated presence of this pleasure that would not release itself into the universal pool.[29]

Simultaneously attracting and repelling the subject, the veil occupies the place of the *object petit a*, the object causing desire in Lacanian psychoanalysis. Lacan writes that "the object a in the field of the visible is the gaze."[30] However, such an object does not exist objectively, in itself, but is constructed retroactively by the subject. Although any object might potentially be an object of desire, what transforms an object into *object petit a* is, in Slavoj Zizek's words, "an interested look, a look supported, permeated and distorted by desire."[31] Such a look is possible within fantasy. Fantasy is basically a scenario filling out the fundamental lack in the subject caused by a splitting in the language. In Heath's words, "no object can satisfy desire – what is wanting is always wanting, division is the condition of subjectivity."[32] The concept of fantasy is crucial in Lacan's account of sexual relationship: Jacqueline Rose shows that it is at the level of fantasy that man achieves his identity and wholeness: "the idea of a complete and assured sexual identity belongs in the realm of fantasy," and "the man places the woman at the basis of his fantasy, or constitutes fantasy through woman" by transposing *object a* onto the image of woman who then acts as its guarantee. "The absolute Otherness of the woman, therefore, serves to secure for the man his own self-knowledge and truth."[33] We have seen above how the veiled Oriental woman is given precisely such a status in Orientalist discourse. In Orientalist writing, *discourses of cultural and sexual difference are powerfully mapped onto each other*. What is crucial in this process is that the very act of representing the veil is never represented; the desire that represents the veil can not be represented. The subject can not represent (see) himself representing (seeing) himself.[34] The metaphorical excess of the veil is thus an effacement of the *process of production* of the subject. Placing desire on the side of the being rather than on that of the thing, Jacques Lacan writes: "This lack is beyond anything which can represent it. It is only ever represented as a reflection on a veil."[35]

Orientalist travel writing of the nineteenth century reveals that the ethico-political program of the Enlightenment in the East can not be dissociated from a patriarchal subjectivity disturbed by the presence of the veiled woman, fading under her sign. As we learn from these writers, this is a disturbance and obsession which they also strangely enjoy, leading to a textual dialectic which, with its rhetorical excess, gives rise to the tropology of the veil. Such a rhetoric should be considered as an act of subjective *incorporation*, a transformation of difference into a manipulable and enjoyable object of discourse, hence providing the European with a sense of the fictive unity and command of his experience.

This fictional unity of command and experience, however shaky, is produced by a plurality of narrative themes and elements, both subjective and epistemological and metaphysical, evoked by the figure of the veiled Muslim woman. *The Oxford English Dictionary* registers this metaphorical dimension of the veil: it is "an article of attire, especially worn by women to conceal or protect the face"; but also it is "something which conceals, covers or hides," it is a "disguising medium, a cloak or mask"; it refers to "the act of hiding or concealing the true nature of something," it is "that which refrains from discussing, keeping from public knowledge"; it refers to a "membrane, membranous appendage, serving as a cover or screen"; and it is that which "conceals from apprehension, knowledge or perception."[36] Whenever the signifier "veil" is used in the Orientalist context, all these different, yet interrelated meanings work as tropes of representing the Orient, its women, and their dressing. Veil is thus a multilayered signifier which refers at once to an attire which covers the Muslim woman's face, and to that which hides and conceals the Orient and Oriental woman from apprehension; it hides the real Orient and keeps its truth from Western knowledge/apprehension. It is also a metaphor of membrane, serving as a screen around which Western fantasies of penetration revolve. It is this polysemous character of the veil which seems to play such a crucial role in the unique articulation of the sexual with cultural difference in Orientalist discourse.

The reference of the veil thus exceeds its sartorial matter, it is in everything that is Oriental or Muslim. The Western eye sees it everywhere, in all aspects of the other's life. It covers and hides every single Oriental thing that the Western subject wants to gaze at and possess; it stands in the way of his desire for transparency and penetration. Writing on Cairo, Nerval observes that "the town itself, like those who dwell in it, unveils its most shady retreats, its most delightful interiors, only by degrees."[37] In the Orientalist chain of signification, the veil signifies not only (Oriental) woman, but also the Orient itself. And it is precisely through this excess that the veil and woman come to represent, in Mary Harper's words, "the most characteristic aspect of the 'mysterious East' – the quintessential Orient."[38] The metonymic association of the figure of the veiled woman and the Orient constitutes an overdetermined totality whose residue persists in the unconscious of the subject.

The veil is thus turned into a privileged concept-metaphor in the construction of the reality of Orient; its very ontology. We can not over-look the important role it plays in the production of an *essential* "Oriental-ness." The veil is central to the discursive constitution of the referent, namely what the Orient is; it constitutes the condition of possibility of the copula "is." But this is a unique strategic-rhetorical move, precisely because it is assumed to conceal not only Oriental woman but also, through her, the very being of the Orient. It incites an inquiry into an ontology or presence which does not just remain beyond knowledge but is closed to it as a requirement of its essential being. In Western eyes, the Orient is always *more and other* than what it appears to be, for it always and everywhere appears in a veiled, disguised, and deceptive manner. It is by way of its veiled appearance, by the very act of its concealment, that the Orient reveals itself, reveals that there is Orient, a place, a culture, an essence that needs to be grasped, known, and apprehended. But precisely because this essence is grasped "in" and "as" concealment, the essence *as essence* is never grasped. One always misses it – the veil is that curtain which simultaneously conceals and reveals; it conceals the Orient's truth and at the same time reveals its mode of existence, its very being – a being which always exists in a disguised and deceptive manner, a being which exists only behind its veil. Therefore, the veil represents simultaneously the truth and the concealment of truth. The truth of the Orient is thus an effect of the veil; it emerges in the traumatic encounter with its untruth, i.e. veil.[39] As Oliver Richon suggests, these Orientalist motifs of uncovering and unveiling a hidden essence imply a metaphysical fantasy.[40]

Hegel's theory of subject provides Orientalist rhetoric with a metaphys-ical framework. As Slavoj Zizek explains, in his dialetic of the production of meaning and of subject, Hegel does not simply oppose appearance to essence, but shows their unity: "if there is deception we cannot subtract it from the Thing; it constitutes its very heart. If, behind the phenomenal veil, there is nothing it is through the mediation of this 'nothing' that the subject constitutes himself in the very act of misrecognition."[41] The doctrine of unveiling is more interested in the constitution of veil as object and target than in unveiling Muslim women. The veil is necessary to the European, and it is irrelevant in this sense whether there is "nothing" or "something" behind it. What is important is the fact that the European subject is able to secure his identity through this supposition or through, to use Teresa Brennan's phrase, this *imaginary anchor*.[42] The veil and the reality that is presumed to be hidden by it serves the subject's need for an imaginary component, the Lacanian *object petit a*, in the act of constituting himself. It is not that the question of "what is behind the veil that is more than the veil" does not bother him. It is precisely this kind of vexation which constitutes his subjectivity. In other words, the answer is the question by which the European traveller or colonizer establishes the required imaginary anchor for himself to securely assert his subjectivity as sovereign. In imagining this hidden Oriental/feminine essence behind the veil as the repository of truth, the subject turns the Orient into an object that confirms his identity and thereby satisfies his need to represent himself to himself as a subject of knowledge and reason. It is not for nothing that I have not said a word on the veiled woman herself so far, as my analysis here concerns man's question, his subjectivity and not hers. The attempt to represent what is concealed behind the veil and what the veiled being of the Orient/feminine is, is one that starts and ends with the subject of representation.

Hence the Orientalist's production of his identity through difference. The method of this constitution is to make the veiled Muslim woman other, that is to say, to turn her into an object of curiosity or marvel, and "an exterior target or threat."[43] In his excellent book *Colonising Egypt*, Timothy Mitchell argues that Orientalism does not simply provide knowledge about Oriental societies, but is itself constitutive of "absolute differences" which enable the European to code the Oriental as his reverse image or as the "exterior of the West." However, as Mitchell points out, "what is outside is paradoxically what makes the West what it is, the excluded yet integral part of its identity and power."[44]

Once constructed as signifying the truth of the Orient, and particularly of the Islamic Orient, the veiled woman is not necessary for the employment of the veil as a rhetorical figure. Edmondo de Amicis' description of Turks as an Oriental people reveals the presence of an enigmatic gaze, frozen, mute and deadening, imagined by the subject in the field of the other:

the Turks have the aspect of people who are thinking about some remote and inde-
terminate thing. They look like philosophers all bent upon one thesis, or somnan-
bulists, walking about unconscious of the place they are in, or the objects about
them. They have *a look in their eyes as if they were contemplating a distant horizon*;
and the vague sadness hovers around the mouth, like people accustomed to live
much alone, and *shut up within themselves.* All have the same gravity, the same com-
posed manner, the same reserve of language, the same look and gesture . . . Their
faces are cold, revealing nothing of their mind or thought . . . *Every face is an
enigma; their glance questions but makes no response; their lips betray no movement
of the heart.* It is impossible to express the *deadening weight* upon the stranger's soul
produced by those *mute, cold masks,* those *statuesque attitudes,* those *fixed eyes* that
say nothing. Sometimes you feel an almost irresistible impulse to shout out in the
midst of them: – "Come, more like other men for once! tell us who you are, what
you are thinking of, and what you see in the air before you, with those *glassy eyes!*"
It is all so strange, that you doubt its being natural, and imagine for a moment that
it is the *result of some agreement among themselves*, or the passing effect of some
malady common to the Mussulmans of Stamboul.[45] (emphasis added)

The impenetrability of Orientals evokes uncovering, unconcealing,
knowledge. However, since they are always other than what they appear
to be, it is difficult to study these people. There is no possibility of mixing
with them because they are reserved; moreover, even when one observes
them or communicates with them, one can never be sure, for dissimulation is their essential characteristic. With such people one should always
go beyond appearances, one should always be on guard against the
possibility of deception. Edmondo de Amicis argues that apparently
there is

reciprocal manifestation of respect among all classes. But this is only on the surface.
The rottenness is concealed. The corruption is dissimulated by the separation of the
two sexes, idleness is hidden under tranquility, dignity is the mask of pride, the com-
posed gravity of countenance, which resembles thoughtfulness, conceals the mortal
inertia of the intellect, and that which seems temperance of life is nothing but an
absence of life in its true sense.[46]

Therefore, the Orient is nothing but an endless dissemblance and dissimulation; the Orientals are people who are characterized by dissimulation
and dissemblance, which is why it is so hard to understand them, to penetrate their minds. The Orientals are hidden not only behind their words but
also behind their silence, for even their lips are a veil; true life is missing, its
absence is dissimulated by appearances and masks. But it is paradoxically
this doubt which makes the observing subject certain that there is something hidden in this infinite play of dissimulation, dissemblance, and
concealment. The veil *must* be hiding some essential truth, some mystery
or secret. By hindering a true perspective on the Orient, the veil gives birth

to an irresistible urge for knowledge and control, and at the same time, an irresistible urge for travel, for being there.

We have thus seen the cultural inscription of the "precise political doctrine" of conquering the women of the colonized country. Veiled women are not simply an exterior target or threat, but a target, object or subject who are engaged epistemologically, literally, and metaphysically. It is this textual engagement which turns the veiled woman into a metaphor for the Oriental culture. We have also seen that this engagement reveals another figure, that of the author: the European patriarchal subjectivity which is obsessed with the veiled woman.

Woman as veil: Nietzsche and Derrida, or limits of the deconstruction of metaphysics

We have then a very precise relationship established between the veil, masquerading, truth, and woman. These themes are familiar in post-structuralist, psychoanalytic and feminist theories. By a detour through these theories, I am going to argue that, since the veil is a figure essential in the construction of femininity in a patriarchal order, the European's strange obsession with the veiled woman also has implications for a more general analysis of patriarchy.

The representation of "womanliness as masquerade" finds one of its most powerful expressions in Nietzsche's work, where he associates femininity with the tropes of truth and veil.[47] For him, woman, like the truth, is enigmatic and has a deceptive appearance. She adorns herself and by adorning herself she seduces and fascinates man: "woman, conscious of man's feelings concerning herself, walking beautifully, dancing, expressing delicate thoughts: in the same way, she practices modesty, reserve, distance – realizing instinctively that in this way the idealizing capacity of man will grow."[48] She has no truth nor she does or can want enlightenment about herself;[49] Her truth is her adornment and her style is appearence and disguise. She is nothing but a pure spectacle.[50] Here is Nietzsche's description of the feminine:

Unless a woman seeks a new adornment for herself that way – I do think adorning herself is part of the Eternal-Feminine? – surely she wants to inspire fear of herself – perhaps she seeks mastery. But she does not *want* truth: what is truth to woman? From the beginning nothing has been more alien, repugnant and hostile to woman than truth – her great art is the lie, her highest concern is mere appearance and beauty.[51]

Faced with this destabilizing, fearful and enigmatic figure, we find a perplexed man who tries to grasp the essential femininity that lies behind her mask. Nietzsche's "nothing but pure spectacle" is only apparently opposite to the veil as a dark figure or as an obstacle to vision. The underlying question is the same as de Amicis' or Loti's: how can he attain the knowledge of this enigma, how can he reveal what lies behind her veiled appearance (i.e. the lie as her great art)? These are the questions de Amicis, Gautier, and Loti ask in their search for the truth of the Oriental woman as an appearance of femininity. In their rhetorical and epistemological move which I describe as the double articulation of cultural and sexual diference, culture and gender are other-ed through each other. These European men bring their insight and knowledge, their intuition and contemplation to the task of uncovering her hidden truth, yet they are not successful. Their solution is to posit the truth of a particular culture from within a certain patriarchal metaphorics: deception and dissimulation are essential characteristics of Oriental cultures. According to Nietzsche, however, woman's deceptive style does not mean that she conceals an essence behind her appearance and adornment. She is deceptive *because* she has no essence to conceal. It is her masquerading style which makes one think that she hides an essential truth.

Nietzsche's aim in establishing an association between the tropes of woman, truth, and veil is to develop a critique of the philosophy of truth, which is the problematic commanding European Orientalist writing. An analysis of the veil occupies an important role in his attack on metaphysical discourse and the various set of oppositions established within it. The parallelism he establishes between the movement of truth and the deceptive feminine gesture enables Nietzsche to criticize, but at the same time to reinscribe the tropological system of metaphysics. The veil functions to make "truth profound, to ensure that there is a depth that lurks behind the surface of things."[52] It is precisely by attacking this figuring of the veil that Nietzsche is able to take a critical distance from the metaphysics of truth and the essentialism immanent in such discourses as Loti's or de Amicis'. He refutes the idea that there is an essence or "real" behind the veil and increases the value attached to appearance over truth or real: "we no longer believe that truth remains truth when the veils are withdrawn; we have lived too much to believe this. Today we consider it a matter of decency not to wish to see everything naked, or to be present at everything, or to understand and 'know everything.'"[53]

Metaphysical discourse is able to secure the various sets of oppositions it constructs between appearance and reality, surface and depth, precisely through the figuring of the veil as that opaque curtain which conceals, covers, hides or disguises an essential nature. Nietzsche, by distancing himself from the idea of a "real" residing beneath appearance and by valorizing the appearance over this 'real,' attempts to undermine the oppositional structure that characterizes metaphysical discourse. However, as

Doane rightly points out, while taking up a critical distance from the metaphysics of truth, Nietzsche reinforces the association between woman and dissimulation or deception, for "the pronoun *she* plays a major role in delineating the operation of this mode of deception."[54]

Despite his attempt to devalorize the association of truth with what is behind the veil, Nietzsche's work still retains the categories of deception and femininity as deception. Although in Nietzsche's philosophy, there are no negative connotations attached to deception and appearance (on the contrary he values them), Doane argues that these categories nevertheless "place the woman as the privileged exemplar of instability."[55] In other words, despite his attempt to dissociate the value attached to truth, Nietzsche still remains locked within the binary logic which construes truth and appearance as opposites. What Nietzsche fails to address is posed by Irigaray, as her criticism targets the very opposition between real and appearance itself and the *interest* that resides underneath such an opposition: "*what* that we should question has been *forgotten*, not about a truer truth, a realer real, but *about the profit that under-lies the truth/fantasy pair?*"[56]

The profit that underlies the truth/fantasy pair is what I have described as the European's fictional unity and command of experience, i.e. the production of their subjectivity, which de Amicis, Gautier, and Loti had managed by a textual proliferation of discourses through the tropology of the veil.

Joan Riviere's important work "Womanliness as masquarade" also brings out an implicit criticism of the Nietzschean critique of metaphysics by providing us with a powerful discussion of how the figures of woman or feminity and veil/mask are closely associated in a masculine order.[57] Unlike Nietzsche's approach, Riviere's exposes man as the one who formulates the question: for Riviere, the term "masquerade" refers to the *male's representation* of woman on the one hand and how this representation constitutes her identity on the other. These two aspects are closely related, for the question of representation is at the same time a question of constitution.

The concept of "womanliness as masquerade" refers to a male's representation, to masculine construction: "The masquerade is a representation of femininity, but then femininity is representation, the representation of woman."[58] This trouble with masquerade is man's trouble: "the conception of womanliness as a mask, behind which man suspects some hidden danger, throws a little light on the enigma."[59] It is man's assumption of femininity which turns it into an enigma. As Stephen Heath observes: "Man's suspicion is the old question, *Was will das Weib?, das ewig Weibliche* (what does woman want? Eternal feminine) all the others, always the same . . . the masquerade is the woman's thing, hers, but it is also exactly *for* the man, a male representation."[60] The question "what does she want?" is paradigmatic here: de Amicis articulates this question when he "wonders whether all those white veiled figures in bright colored wrappers are masquerades, or nuns, or mad women" or when he cries, in fervor, before the cold mute masks: "come, more like other men for once! tell us who you are."[61] We learn from Riviere's psychoanalytic-feminist criticism that the question of what woman wants is the man's question. According to her, it is precisely this characterization of femininity that incites contradictory desires; the desire to know and uncover her truth on the one hand, and the desire to distance her and thus avoid the threat her unpredictability and inaccessibility pose, on the other. Consequently, the man is seduced and mocked and threatened all at the same time. Such a contradictory and ambivalent desire, caused by *the continual displacement of his perspective on or lack of knowledge of the woman*, lends itself to an overrepresentation (the excess of the veil) and to an endless investigation of the feminine in an effort to evade such a lack and constitute his subjectivity. As such, the instability he experiences is dissipated by projecting it onto the feminine and characterizing her as the sex which is unpredictable and deceptive. At this point we also need to remember Freud's endless attempts to evade his inability to know and conquer the "darkness" that hovers around the feminine sexuality – *at the same time a darkness he himself construes through his own representation*. For example, he is as confident to study and know men's sexuality as he is totally puzzled by the other sex: "That of women – partly owing to the stunning effect of civilized conditions and partly owing to their conventional secretiveness and insincerity – is still *veiled* in an impenetrable obscurity" (emphasis added).[62] As Doane suggests, "the horror or threat of that precariousness (of both sexuality and the visible) is attenuated by attributing it to the woman, over and against the purported stability and identity of the male. The veil is the mark of that precariousness."[63]

Derrida is another critic of Nietzsche and the last figure in our detour through post-structuralist theory. Although affirming Nietzsche's attack on the metaphysics of truth through the metaphor of woman as the name of untruth, Derrida nevertheless gives it another twist in his *Spurs*. His concern is, like Nietzsche, to undo the metaphysical discourse that sets truth and untruth as opposites. While Nietzsche compares woman's deceptive veiled gesture to the movement of untruth, Derrida compares the feminine gesture to *writing* or *style*. The concept *writing* is one of the central instruments in Derrida's deconstruction of metaphysical binaries. Refuting the idea that woman has an essence, Derrida argues that "there is no such thing as the truth of woman, but it is because of the abyssal divergence of the truth, because that untruth is 'truth.' Woman is but one name for that untruth of truth."[64] The metaphors Nietzsche uses for femininity such as instability and dissimulation are also deployed by Derrida. In his case, she appears as the figure for undecidability (associated with but repressed by metaphysics), but as a figure nevertheless:

It is impossible to dissociate the questions of art, style and truth from the question of woman. Nevertheless, the question "what is woman?" is itself suspended by the simple formulation of their common problematic. One can no longer seek her, no more than one could search for woman's femininity or female sexuality. And she is certainly not to be found in any of the familiar modes of concepts or knowledge. Yet it is impossible to resist looking for her.[65]

Derrida represents a step further than Nietzsche in deconstructing the metaphysics of truth. But his deconstruction of metaphysics by way of associating woman with undecidability and unpredictability implies turning woman into a ground or instrument of deconstruction. However radical this aim is, she becomes a vehicle of deconstruction rather than a subject of it. In Spivak's words, "as the radically other she does not *really exist*, yet her name remains one of the important names for displacement, the special mark of deconstruction."[66] As Spivak rightly suggests, to avoid this "double displacement of woman," what is needed is the deconstruction of the "opposition between displacement and logocentricism itself." Spivak further argues that the task of deconstructing the sovereign subject cannot be accomplished if we limit our investigation to the question of what woman is, for this is only another way of asking the question "what does woman want?" With this question, woman is still posed as the *object* of investigation. Rather, the feminist gesture requires asking the question that will allow the woman the *subject* status and the positioning of a questioning subject: what is man? what does he want? It will then be possible to "bring back the absolutely convincing deconstructive critiques of the sovereign subject."[67]

I take Spivak's suggestion that a deconstruction of the opposition between displacement and logocentrism is necessary in order to pose the question of the itinerary of man's desire in an attempt to deconstruct the imperial European subjectivity.[68] The question of what man wants, of "the itinerary of his desire," does not only make women subjects of inquiry but it also opens the inquiry to a *global socio-economic and cultural inscription*, for which nineteenth-century Orientalist writing is but one remarkable instance. We are now in a better position to ask what "interest" is involved here and what is "the profit that underlies the truth/fantasy pair."

The constitution of the European subject as sovereign

Two modes of differentiation, the sexual and the cultural, are thus not simply two distinct, singular moments in the representation of *difference*, but rather, as Homi Bhabha phrases it: "within the apparatus of colonial power, the discourses of sexuality and race relate in a process of *functional overdetermination.*"[69] The structural affinity between the two with respect to the display of difference establishes a chain of equivalence in which woman is the Orient, the Orient is woman; woman like the Orient, the Orient like the woman, exists veiled; she is nothing but the name of untruth and deception. If the Oriental is feminine and if the feminine is Oriental, we can claim that the nature of femininity and the nature of the Orient are figured as one and the same thing in these representations. This equivalence positions the Orientalist/Western colonial subject as masculine: the other culture is always like the other sex.[70] This is why the Western subject, *whether male or female*, is always fascinated by the veil or harem, the truth of culture in the space of woman, in the body of woman. But then what does he see when the mask is lifted? Is it ever lifted? How can the subject of knowledge know and be certain about what lies behind the mask? Nietzsche refutes the view there is an essence behind the veil. Riviere reinscribes the question as man's, but then reads it also as constitution of femininity (which is representation of woman).[71] Irigaray also resists differentiating between the veil and what exists underneath it, by writing that "beneath the veil subsists only veil."[72] But for her – and especially we might say, if representation is constitution – there is an interest in the question and a profit in the discourse which it produces.

What do we make of these Orientalist and masculine representations which presuppose and pose a place and a cultural/sexual secret behind the Oriental feminine veil? We have seen that European writers first posit the Oriental veil as an object of investigation and presuppose that there is something behind it, but then this very presupposition is both denied and accepted by the conclusion that the very nature or being of the Orient is veiled. On the surface, this is a process in which the veil is incorporated as an object of discursive and textual play. These two processes however, political and cultural, as separate they are, are not simply chronologically ordered. While the political project has been a precise strategy of unveiling, i.e. an implementation of the European principle of government based on an ideal of transparency and visibility, the textual and conceptual dimension, the inscription of the veil in the European text is witness to a constitution of subjectivity, an imaginary unity and command of experience in the encounter with the other. A careful reading of this constitution might enable us to see that the profit that underlies the truth/fantasy pair is not a simple plus on the side of European subjectivity. Since such profit, such surplus of subjectivity is in the *excess* of the tropology of the veil, it is subjected to a mechanism which remains *beyond its control*. What the Orientalist texts manifest in their paradoxical attempt to other the veil is that the reference is always veiled and remains other to what it signifies. This is the point where "real" politics (the world of conflict) and textual "sublation" (*belles lettres*) are necessarily conflated with each other. What appears through this conflation might be called an *ethos*. The ethos in question, that of the sovereign subject of Europe, is described by Marx in his critical reading of Hegel. Gayatri Spivak observes that, according to Marx, "Hegel's picture of the subject appropriating the object" was really charged by "a deep hostility." In Marx's own words, "the appropriation . . . must proceed from indifferent alienness to real hostile engagement."[73]

If Europe's outside is made an integral part of its identity and power in discourses such as Orientalism, this is, paradoxically, only by the creation of such outside in terms of an absolute and essential difference. If the veiled woman/culture remains always different or infinitely dissimulating in Orientalist logic, this is *not* because of the complexity of her/their being-in-the-world, in which one might find continuities as well as discontinuities with one's own culture/subjectivity, but because they are always and absolutely different. They *should* remain different, because I should remain the *same*: they are not/should not be a possibility within my own world, which will thus be different. This is the "deep hostility" which is pointed out by Spivak and Marx, in resonance with essentialism conceived as a philosophy of the "proper." That is to say, such hostility does not refer to a mere prejudice or uncultivated aggressive behavior which can be corrected or repaired by simply taking a more peaceful, good-natured, tolerant or sympathetic attitude. Deep hostility is not merely a subjective or personal characteristic, changing from one person or group to another, and thus adaptable or normalizable. While personal or even group characteristics might well be affected by education, to think that such an education will thus erase the *subject position* is rather disingenuous. It is not a question of liking or disliking the Orientals, their women, and their culture. The hostility expressed here is the force of negation which constitutes the subject *as* sovereign, that stern force which drives the machine of his self-production in the dialectical, restricted economy of the production of the self as same. It is therefore a necessary moment in his encounter with the culturally/sexually different.

The hostility in question must perhaps be associated with fear and anxiety. "What is in the other other than the other" is a persistent inquiry that we come across in representations of cultural, racial, and sexual difference. By posing and presupposing that the veil is hiding something, concealing some ungraspable essence, the subject turns the veil into a mask – a mask behind which the other is suspected of hiding some dangerous secret threatening his unity and stability. If they are wearing those masks, then there must be a behind-the-mask that needs to be penetrated: "What does (veiled) woman want?" "What does Jesse Jackson want?" "What is in Saddam's mind?"[74] The question has something to do with the subject's inability or incapacity to engage the other's desire in a positive way, to *respond to* her. The French colonial doctrine of unveiling, the fantasy of penetration, the metaphysics of the veil can all be seen as the avoidance of such *responsibility vis-à-vis* the other, denied by the very structure of sovereign subjectivity. The grand narrative of colonial gaze is a deaf tropology of the veil, made up of tales of unveiling, fantasies of penetrating the inaccessible world of the other, the metaphysics of discovering her truth, fantasies of domesticating and reforming and thus controlling her. In other words, the subject effaces his own constitution by representing the veil over and over again. And this process of effacement ensures that the desire which represents the veil itself is never represented.

Mimicry and the question of the veil

I have argued above that if the concept-figure of veil provides the Orientalist with an imaginary control of his colonial displacement, its textual inscription nevertheless remains beyond his control. I have thus located an incessant movement of desire at the center of orientalist discourse. This is part of an attempt to transform and reformulate the very means by which we identify the nature of colonial oppression and hence rethink the problematic dichotomies between self and other, structure and agency, domination and resistance.[75] To re-think Orientalism's discursive field through the psychoanalytic concept of desire enables us to conceive colonial domination as being based on an ambivalent and conflictual economy. To give an account of otherness through the concept of desire implies a formulation of the process of colonial identification not as an affirmation of a pregiven identity, but as a *process* in which both the "Western subject" and the "Oriental other" are mutually implicated in each other and thus neither exists as a fully constituted entity. As Bhabha suggests, "the desire for the Other is doubled by the desire in language, which *splits the difference* between Self and Other so that both positions are partial; neither is sufficient unto itself."[76] My purpose, in pointing to the complexity and contradiction of desire in the representations of cultural and sexual difference, is twofold: to understand the process of exclusion and differentiation through which the Western self is constituted and achieves the appearance of an autonomous identity precisely by veiling its dependency and indebtedness from its excluded and marginalized other; second, to capture the unavoidable trace of the other in the subject and the consequent resistance it exerts upon him.

At this point it might be useful to briefly recapitulate Said's depiction of the relationship between the colonized and the colonizer and Bhabha's useful intervention. As I emphasized earlier, by introducing a polarity between the manifest and latent content of Orientalism Said introduces a crucial split between the historical and fantasy; between Orientalism as a topic of learning and as a fantasy of the other. However, as Bhabha's reading of Said points out, he contains and resolves the ambivalence between these two economies by *assuming* a unified system of representation. As I noted in chapter 1, Bhabha suggests that Said's analysis loses its inventive character because of his reluctance to engage with the conflictual economy that splits the Orientalist discourse, for he unifies and contains the oppositional structure as a congruent system of representation.

Contrary to Said's containment of this ambivalence, Bhabha's insistence on the concept of ambivalence as constituting the ground of the conflictual economy of colonial discourse allows us to go beyond the rather simplistic and oppositional politics of the marginalized, where a mere reversing of the oppositional structure was suggested as a viable strategy of subversion of the hegemonic operations of colonial power. It is by inquiring into the "mechanism" of desire that, I believe, we can begin to understand the ambivalent and contradictory nature of the economy of colonial domination.[77] And it is precisely by acknowledging the impossibility of the final closure of this economy in and upon itself that "we can avoid the increasingly facile adoption of the notion of a homogenized Other, for a celebratory, oppositional politics of the margins or minorities."[78] The corollary of such an oppositional logic, which today structures and frames many analyses in the field of "cultural studies," is the assumption of two full identities confronting each other. Unfortunately Said's analysis is not free from this simplification, for, as Bhabha observes, he does not pay sufficient attention to the concept of representation "that articulates the *historical and fantasy (as the scene of desire)* in the production of the 'political' effects of discourse."[79]

Positioning the colonizer and the colonized other in a relation of dialectical opposition as in the Hegelian model of master/slave, self/other opposition suggests that the politics of subversion resides in the act of inversion of such opposites. Such a strategy of reversal, which forgets that the reversal itself remains locked within the same logic, should be seen as an inevitable extension of the adoption of a totalizing dialectics of self and other.[80] The current forms of "identity politics" that surface in various struggles today and more importantly the simplistic praising of the authentic/native voice expressed in the "native informant" or "let the native speak" syndrome[81] both by the Western and post-colonial intellectuals in the name of subversive politics, carry the trace of such a unified notion of subject. Contrary to this, Bhabha's concept of ambivalence implies a refusal of a total and unidirectional theory of colonial power and thereby works as a fundamental conceptual tool for us to transform the theoretical frame by which we recognize and identify the problematic of human agency.

If we do not want to contain this ambivalence in a simple oppositional structure, and if we want to be able to offer an analysis of the other's unsettling and disturbing presence for the subject (and not just assume it as given), it is necessary that we recognize the inability of colonial power to fix difference in a once-and-for-all manner. If the menace of the other is always inscribed within the economy of colonial domination and never comes simply from outside, then what are the conceptual tools through which we can formulate the nature of this menace? Are there specific conceptual tools we need to develop to understand the resistance the veil *might* imply?[82] Where does such a quality of the veil, which might function to unsettle the colonial desire for its other, stem from?

The notion of ambivalence and the contradictory economy as developed by Bhabha enables us to understand the excesses or slippages within colonial discourse.[83] Such excesses or slippages imply the impossibility of formulating the relationship between the Western subject and its colonial other in dualistic terms which implies setting up oppression and agency as two different poles of a binary opposition. My reiteration of the concept of desire should thus be conceived of as an effort to displace the notion of colonial discourse as an affirmation of a pregiven Western identity. The crux of my argument is that *not only the very identity of the Western subject is constituted in the movement of desire, but also the potential resistance to this constitution is also inscribed in this very process.* Fanon's observation is pertinent for understanding this dynamic: "when it encounters resistance from the other, self-consciousness undergoes the experience of *desire* . . . As soon as I *desire* I am asking to be considered."[84]

As Fanon's statement (above) implies, the desire for recognition is precisely what makes possible the precariousness and uncertainty of the colonial relation. It implies that we recognize that wherever there is resistance, there is desire; resistance is the condition of possibility of desire. Although Fanon's statement is written in the context of his debate with Hegel, it actually bears a certain similarity to Foucault's view of power and resistance. If I may briefly remind the reader, Foucalt notes that power and resistance are not external to each other, for "wherever there is power, there is resistance"; since there is no final or absolute beyond of power, one is said to be always "inside power" for there is always a law that one is subject to and subjected by. The points of resistance have to be and are diffused, multiple, and plural and "by definition, they can only exist in the strategic field of power relations."[85]

Without imagining desire, one cannot imagine the resistance the otherness might generate against the subject. If the Western subject's relation with its Oriental other is not given and determined once and for all, it is precisely because, desire, as the moving motor of the subject, posits its own object in an effort to constitute its own identity. As Metz suggests: "It is true of all desire that it depends on the infinite pursuit of its absent object."[86] Being an endless pursuit it implies that "the subject of desire is never simply a Myself . . . the Other is never simply an *It-self*, a front of identity, truth or misrecognition."[87] It is this endless movement, which, by inaugurating the contradictory and ambivalent economy that structures the relation between the subject and its other, simultaneously constructs and destabilizes the colonial domination. Bhabha suggests that it is in this ambivalent space between desire and fulfilment that we locate the strategy of colonial resistance.[88]

Before I proceed to the discussion of the ways in which the veil *might* acquire a subversive quality, I would like to recapitulate what I have been suggesting regarding the moment of colonial resistance. To inquire into the "mechanism" of the Western subject's constitution through the psycho-analytic concept of desire is not to suggest that its identity is fully determined.[89] On the contrary, it should be seen as an attempt to explain the constituted character of the subject and thereby to argue that both the closure of the subject's identity and the resistance of the other is never final, but always partial and relative. As Judith Butler warns us, it is erroneous to assume the subject in advance so as to protect its agency, because to argue the constituted character of the subject is not to suggest that it is determined. In other words, the power that constitutes the subject does not cease to exist "after" constituting its subject, for the subject "is never fully constituted, but is subjected and produced time and again."[90] Therefore, if we are not in search of an *a priori* guarantee for the agency of the subject, then we cannot afford not to scrutinize the process of the constitution of the subject. The inquiry into the agency of the subject can be made only when it is not presumed and such an inquiry is contingent upon understanding its constituted character.

How does the desiring subject's ceaseless pursuit of its absent object and
the disruption of the stability of this desire refigure itself in the context of
colonial discourse? If we claim that the subject can never achieve a full
closure in constituting his identity, what role does the unique text-ile of the
veil, a text-ile which "conceals" and "hides" the other from the colonial
gaze, play in this process? How can we seek out the residues, the remains or
traces of the veiled other which exceed the phallocentric and Orientalist
representations? Where can we locate the moments of recalcitrance? What,
if any, role do the unique characteristics of the veil play in this?

We have seen above that the colonial subject's desire to control and dominate the foreign land is not independent from his scopic desire, from his
desire to penetrate, through his surveillant eye, what is behind the veil. *The
invisibility the veil secures for the colonial other is simultaneously the point
at which desire is articulated and the ground upon which the scopic drive of
the subject is displaced*, for there is always the threat of the return of the
look of the other. In Fanon's words, "it was the colonialist's frenzy to
unveil the Algerian woman, it was his gamble on winning the battle of the
veil."[91] In this battle "the occupier was *bent on unveiling Algeria*," [92]
because "there is in it the will to bring this woman within his reach, to
make her a possible object of possession."[93] But what explains the obsession with lifting the veil is something that is always-already inscribed in this
unique sartorial matter. The veil is seen as a border which distinguishes
inside from outside, as a screen or cover, and women are associated with
the inside, home and territory in the native Algerian culture. [94] Of course
at the same time the veil demarcates a boundary and delimits the colonial
power. As Malek Alloula's analysis of the French colonial picture-post-
cards demonstrates, the veil that covers the Algerian woman indicates a
refusal to the French soldier. The photographer, whose scopic desire is discouraged, experiences disappointment and rejection.[95] Similarly for
Fanon, since the veil allows women to see without being seen, it disallows
reciprocity, and implies that the woman is not yielding herself, making
herself available for vision.[96]

It is this disappointment and frustration which disturbs the voyeuristic
look of the subject. Unlike looking at a photograph or a screen, by looking
at a veiled other, the subject cannot have the security of "I look at it, but it
does not look at me looking at it,"[97] because there is always the threat of
the return of the look of the other. This implies that the pleasure of seeing
is not entirely on the side of the subject, but he himself is subject to a look
and hence is not inscribed, to borrow from Metz again, as an "invisible"
subject.[98] The structure of voyeuristic pleasure which is based upon the
"invisibility of the subject" and the "visibility of the object" is being

reversed here into its opposite. Instead of being looked at, the object now looks at.[99]

The subject cannot ignore that he is being looked at as he tries to unveil the other in order to satisfy his voyeuristic pleasure and thus fails to fantasize himself as a full subject.[100] The look that filters through the tiny orifice of the veil is the statement of the absent and invisible other and this statement can be translated, to borrow a formulation from Bhabha, into: "as even now you look/but never see me."[101] In other words, the invisible other speaks from its absent location. The countergaze of the other should be located in this absent-presence, in this space of the in-between. It is the veil which enables the Oriental other to look without being seen. This not only disturbs the desire of the Western/colonial subject to fix cultural and sexual difference, but also enables the colonial other to turn itself into a surveillant gaze. It is in this space of absent-presence that there emerges the challenge of the "invisible," "hidden" other. To recapitulate, *it is through the veil that the colonial/Western desire to see emerges and is erased simultaneously*, and this is what enables the veiled other to destabilize the identificatory process of the subject. It is this moment of seeing or these eyes that filter through the veil which frustrate the voyeuristic desire of the colonialist and displaces his surveillant eye.

If it is through this uncanny look, which her absence/invisibility provides to her, that the other constitutes its "I" and thereby unsettles the colonial gaze, then one might ask what the difference is between my account of the other's resistance through its enigmatic absence and the representation of the veil in Orientalist discourse? Are these two discursive systems not based on the recognition of the other as absent, invisible, hidden, and do not both register this absence as enigmatic?

In his discussion of the Algerian liberation struggle, Fanon claims that during the anti-colonial resistance movement, the veil "has been manipulated, transformed into a technique of camouflage, into a means of struggle."[102] What transformed the veil from being an element of tradition into an element of strategy of subversion? Fanon at times claims that the veil was used by women as a protective mask in order to carry bombs and weapons for the revolutionary movement – "every veiled woman, every Algerian woman, became suspect."[103] But this is not a sufficient explanation because many women during the revolutionary process reveiled themselves in order to affirm "that it was not true that woman liberated herself at the invitation of France and of General de Gaulle."[104] Apparently what used to be an "oppressive" item which confined women to the private domain of the home now enabled them to assert their subjectivity and agency.[105] The affirmation of the veil in the anti-colonial struggle was a direct response to the colonial desire to unveil, reveal, and control the colonized country. It is not surprising after all that women's agency emerged out of the *texture* of their own culture. Or, given the immense significance of the veil for both sides, should we not say that the anti-colonial resistance emerged under the banner of a metaphor – veil – that belongs to, that is woman? However, this culture was no longer the same. In taking up the veil as a constituent symbolic element of their subjectivity, the Algerian women did not simply continue their traditional roles, because the veil had now become the *embodiment of their will to act, their agency*. It was thus re-inscribed and re-charged in the colonial situation and acquired a symbolic significance that directly *affected* the struggle. I will talk about the consequences of this situation for the relationship between nationalism and women in "decolonized" societies – the question of the manipulation or control of women by "post-colonial" nation-states – in chapter 5. Now I should like to explain how the veil turned out to be a subversive element. In order to do this, I want to use the concept of mimicry as explained by Luce Irigaray.

In her critique of phallocentrism, Irigaray insists that a mere reversal of this system cannot constitute a subversive politics, for it remains locked within the same economy that it aims to shatter. What could displace and hence shake the ground of the phallocentric representations is a purposeful but distorted imitation of the characteristics attributed to the feminine:

There is, in an initial phase, perhaps only one "path," the one historically assigned to the feminine: that of *mimicry*. One must assume the feminine role deliberately. Which means already to convert a form of subordination into an affirmation, and thus to begin to thwart it . . . To play with mimesis is thus, for a woman, to try to recover the place of her exploitation by discourse, without allowing herself to be simply reduced to it. It means to resubmit herself – inasmuch as she is on the side of the "perceptible," of "matter – to "ideas," in particular to ideas about herself, that are elaborated in/by masculine logic, but so as to make "visible," by an effect of playful repetition, what was supposed to remain invisible: the cover-up of a possible operation of the feminine in language. It also means "to unveil" the fact that, if women are such good mimics, it is because they are not simply resorbed in this function. *They also remain elsewhere.*[106]

Following Irigaray's formulation, I suggest that by claiming and playfully repeating the very attributes of concealment and dissimulation, the Algerian women managed to stay elsewhere, indeed to create an "elsewhere," an "outside" that displaced the French colonial power. But how does one distinguish between a subversive repetition and a loyal one? For Irigaray, parodic repetition differs from mere loyal repetition, for it consists of simultaneous recognition and denial of the dominant codes of femininity. However, repetition of the dominant norms in and of itself may not be enough to displace them, for there is a risk involved in it. The trap here is becoming complicit by receding back into the old definitions that one seeks to combat. Hence mimicry does not automatically produce a subversive outcome; it can achieve such an effect to the extent that it is, as Braidotti notes, "being sustained by a critical consciousness."[107] That is, it can be subversive on the condition that the naturalized gender codes are critically reflected upon. The re-articulation, re-working and re-signification of the discursive characteristics of phallocentrism can open the possibility of an in-between ambivalent zone where the agency of the female subject can be construed. In our case, the colonization of land and culture in Algeria was strategically entangled on the body of women – such is the articulation of the historical and fantasy. This created a unique situation for native women and produced a historically specific kind of critical consciousness. Always-already articulated as the most inner core of culture, of the very nativity and territoriality of culture, Algerian women had become able to embody their difference *vis-à-vis* the hostile foreign power. It is in this very particular kind of historical conjuncture that the veil shifted from a traditional to a subversive role. This is no doubt a historically specific situation or conjuncture of our modern times, that is repeated in so many anti-colonial and national resistance struggles, a strange and unique historical moment or process in which tradition does not simply disappear in loyalty to the forward march of progress but instead ceases to be traditional and loyal and becomes the signifier of an active, resistant, and transformative subjectivity, a moment of empowerment and agency. Surely this is not an unproblematical moment, given the nationalist elite's patriarchal framework. But blindness to women's irreducible power and seeing their difference as simply contained within nationalist leadership is indeed to re-inscribe the power of female agency into the grand illusion of the forward march of history. I will turn to this question in chapter 5.

The Algerian women thus turned the Orientalist representation into an affirmation and thereby instilled a new definition of the act of concealment by, in Mary Ann Doane's words, "enacting a defamiliarized version" of the Orientalist representations of the veil. What the colonial gaze saw in the Algerian women's disturbing mimicry was a displacement of its own representation of the veil. Hence what was once familiar and recognizable *as* concealment, mask, masquerading, has now become unfamiliar, disturbing, and uncanny. Therefore, what was implied in this manipulative use of the veil was *not* a strategy of reversal of the Orientalist discourse, for such a strategy would have implied an effort to demonstrate that they were hiding *nothing* behind colonialism's so-long-held object of suspicion.

Mimicry revealed that there was nothing but the veil behind the veil. In resuming and reclaiming the veil, Algerian women parodied the Orientalist discourse which construed the veil as a mask. Their strategic use of the veil thus *doubled* the Orientalist representation of cultural and sexual difference and this doubling brought a new mode of representation of the veil as a positive, self-affirming political force. The calling into question of Orientalism's claim on the naturalness of the veil through a mimetic repetition enabled women to constitute a space where they engendered their own subjectivity. The subversive quality the veil achieved in this decolonizing gesture was enabled by the very conditions that construed it. There is an affinity between Algerian's women's struggle and deconstruction which, in Derrida's words, "operate(s) necessarily from the inside, borrowing all the strategic and economic resources of subversion from the old structure, borrowing them structurally."[108]

Naomi Schor, in reading the meaning(s) of the concept of mimicry in Irigaray, suggests that, in mimicry, difference is signified as a positivity; it refers to the reclaiming of the characteristics attributed to the feminine. The difference that is brought about in this joyful reappropriation is not only beyond masquerade and mimicry, but signifies "an emergence of the feminine and the feminine can only emerge from within or beneath . . . femininity within which it lies buried. The difference within mimesis *is* the difference within difference."[109] Following Schor, I would suggest that we see the difference within the Algerian women's mimicry as the difference within difference – a difference that came out of their doubling of the Orientalist/masculinist representations of difference. In other words, what is revealed in this doubling is the sub-sistence of the "quite Other" behind its mere difference. The difference represented in the subversive mimicry of the Algerian women is the *unrecuperable* or *undomesticated* difference that the colonial Subject has ferociously tried to deny. In Irigaray's words:

Beneath all those/her appearances, beneath all those/her borrowed finery, that female other still sub-sists. Beyond all those/her forms of life and death, still she is living. And as she is dis-tant – and in "herself" – she threatens the stability of all values. In her there is always the possibility that truth, appearances, will, power, eternal recurrence . . . will collapse. By mimicking them all more or less adequately, that female other never holds firm to any of them univocally . . . Truth and appearances, and reality, power . . . she is – through her inexhaustible aptitude for mimicry – the living foundation for the whole staging of the world. Wearing different veils according to the historic periods.[110]

In exploring the articulation of sexual and cultural difference in the discourse of Orientalism, I have pointed to the inextricable link between the masculinist and colonialist position the Western subject occupies in relation to its Oriental others. A Western reader, more specifically a feminist reader, might feel uneasy about this suggestion, wondering whether the representations of the Orient, veil, and woman might be different if the gender identity of the representing agency were woman. I now want to turn to a discussion of the role Western women have played in the construction of the Orientalist imagery and the nature of the relation that has been established between the texts of male and female Orientalists.

3

Supplementing the Orientalist lack: European ladies in the harem

The citationary nature of Orientalism

Since its publication Said's *Orientalism* has been subjected to critical evaluation, at times appreciative and at other times quite disingenuous. Strikingly, attention to Orientalism's entanglement with issues of gender has been missing in such critical assessments. In recent years we have witnessed the publication of numerous books that attempt to fill this lacuna by examining the missing link between Orientalism and Western women's discourse.[1] In addition, studies that highlight the masculine nature of categories of Orientalist discourse have also proliferated.[2] As Said himself also recognizes in *Culture and Imperialism*, studies about the Middle East have been dominated by masculism, and he acknowledges the important role feminist works play in undermining this hegemonic attitude by demonstrating the "diversity and complexity of experience that works beneath the totalizing discourses of Orientalism and of Middle East (overwhelmingly male) nationalism."[3]

It is hard to disagree with Said's recognition of the importance of such feminist works. However, it is also interesting to observe that Said does not engage these feminist arguments in his own work. Can we regard these works as unequivocally "corrective" of the problems of *Orientalism,* just for the sake of conceding feminism? What would the implications of such an easy embracing for feminist politics? I think, accepting the importance of such feminist works should not leave us blind to the controversial propositions advanced in some of these projects simply because they interrogate *Orientalism*'s totalizing gesture by demonstrating the (feminine) diversity beneath the discourse of Orientalism. Despite the problems in *Orientalism*, it still remains an important piece of work that needs to be revisited precisely for such a "rectifying" task. However, my argument is not a recommendation for complementing Said's work with a gender-conscious analysis, but of developing a critical engagement with it so as to generate useful clues for feminist purposes.

Before I discuss what might be useful in Said's text for such a purpose, I would like to outline briefly the principal points of contention that are advanced in Sara Mills's *Discourses of Difference*, and Reina Lewis's *Gendering Orientalism*. I will discuss Lisa Lowe's *Critical Terrains* separately in the following pages in a more detailed fashion.

Both Mills and Lewis are concerned with undoing Said's allegedly monolithic account by emphasizing the multiple and diverse positions within Orientalist discourse. For Lewis, Said presents us with a discourse that is homogeneous, presumed to be enunciated by a unified colonialist subject. Hence *Orientalism* is criticized for its inability to address the conflicts inherent in colonialism and for lacking a sense of either the Orient's resistance or the internal splits within Orientalism. Mills suggests that colonialism should not be seen as a unified phenomenon, for there are diverse elements within Orientalism that both contest and affirm the dominant discourses. Therefore, differences of discursive frameworks need to be recognized, for attention to diversities within the Orientalist text is assumed to allow us to grasp the differential negotiations with the rules of discourse. Gender appears to be one of the factors that produce such differences. One major reason why women's discourse is advocated as the site where such differences could be discerned is the unique position it occupies in relation to the discourse of colonialism and the discourse of femininity. Women's texts on the Orient are imbued with contradictions, sometimes straightforwardly Orientalist and other times undermining the dominant discourse, and for Mills, such contradictions can function as a critique of other colonial texts. Another characterizing feature of women's texts is that they are informed by the discourse of feminism, since in the nineteenth-century feminist debates were influencing a wide range of issues. Although Mills does not deny that women's discourse was inscribed in an imperialist ideology, she nevertheless argues that women's discourse was more heterogeneous and such heterogeneous or contradictory elements acted as a critique of the colonial gesture. Similarly, for Lewis, although women did produce imperialist images of the Orient, their differential and gendered access to the dominant imperial position constructed images that were less pejorative of the Oriental other and of difference. Therefore, women's discourse functioned to cultivate a critique of the unified and male colonial subject.

Could a revisit to *Orientalism* help us to develop a different perspective about the issue of unity? I suggest that the so-called unified nature of Orientalism such critiques discern in Said's analysis is not something that we should simply throw away, but is an issue that requires to be thought over in order to develop a more complex understanding of the nature of Orientalist discourse. In this text Said makes a very important suggestion that we can utilize for such a purpose. He suggests that it is the *latent* structure of Orientalism which provides individual travellers with an enunciative capacity; it is by way of its "unanimity, stability, and durability" that the Orientalist hegemony maintains its constancy.[4] However, Said's emphasis on the unity of the Orientalist structure does not preclude the recognition of individual or authorial differences in style and form of presentation. Rather, he encourages us to view such differences in a different register. As his close reading of various Orientalist texts reveals, it is through such differences that the *manifest* content of Orientalism is constituted. But Said's concern is less with these idiosyncrasies and styles of presentation than with what enables individual writers to keep "intact the separateness of the Orient, its eccentricity, its backwardness, its silent indifference, its feminine penetrability, its supine malleability."[5] The *manifest* content is therefore a function of the West's "repetitious consistency about its will-to-power over the Orient."[6] Thus we can find variations, differences, deviations, multivalences, and paradoxes (even writings that challenge other Orientalist representations) in various individual accounts of the Orient. Moreover, we can delineate certain features that differentiate British and French Orientalism, differences between the eighteenth, nineteenth, and twentieth-century Orientalisms, and the disparate ways in which the Orient is represented in the texts of male and female Orientalists. But the question that needs to be kept alive is, "what is it that compels us to name these representations Orientalist, despite their differences?" What enables Orientalism, as Said puts it, to "survive revolutions, world wars and the literal dismemberment of empires?"[7]

One of the principal mechanisms that sustains this *latent* structure is what Said calls the "citationary nature of Orientalism." Orientalism, for Said, is constructed as a systematic symbolic universe not simply because various representations constitute a unity through their reference to a common geographical place called the Orient. Although the large number of writings on the Orient give the appearance of a multifarious body of work, they are in fact "a reworking or direct repetition of earlier descriptions."[8] In this sense, each individual representation functions as a referent for another text. Various writings, by referring back and forth to one another and by borrowing elements from predecessors, constitute a systematic body of knowledge about the Orient. In this systematic body, the Orient for Said, is:

less a place than a *topos*, a set of references, a congeries of characteristics, that seems to have its origin in a quotation, or a fragment of a text, or a citation from someone's work on the Orient, or some bit of previous imagining, or an amalgam of all these. Direct observation or circumstantial description of the Orient are the fictions presented by writing on the Orient, yet invariably *these are totally secondary to systematic tasks of another sort.*[9] (emphasis added)

To suggest that Orientalism establishes its systematic character through its citationary nature does not mean that every single text is nothing but a simple repetition of another. These series of representations are not constituted merely through an additive or cumulative process. For, as Said observes:

the growth of knowledge is a process of selective accumulation, displacement, deletion, rearrangement, and insistence within what has been called a research consensus. The legitimacy of such knowledge as Orientalism was during the nineteenth century stemmed not from religious authority, as had been the case before the Enlightenment, but from what we can call the restorative citation of antecedent authority.[10]

Following Said (and perhaps even taking his suggestion further than he does), I suggest that it is misleading to assume that the contradictions and splits within Orientalist discourse as expressed by different authors, or sometimes even in the same text by an author, constitute a challenge to its unity and hegemony. When we come across texts that question another text's loyalty to the truth of the Orient, it is quite problematical to claim that they constitute an intervention against the symbolic universe of Orientalism. In other words, we should not simply look for the re-statement of the Orientalist topos in the act of simple repetition of earlier ideas and images, but also in displacements, divergences, and even in the dissemination of dissenting ideas. Thus the heterogeneous and multivariant character of the texts on the Orient cannot simply be regarded as a refutation of either the hegemonic power or the unity of the Orientalist tradition. In fact, it is not difficult to notice that each Orientalist text opens up its own space within the wider Orientalist hegemony by re-announcing its own truth value, and this announcement is often predicated upon its renunciation of the truth claims of previous texts. This, then, is to claim that the apparent contradiction and heterogeneity that characterize the cluster of texts we call Orientalist belong to the *manifest* content of Orientalism. Indeed, the *manifest* content cannot come into existence without the multiplicity, heterogeneity and contradictions that characterize the relation between these texts. Orientalist hegemony could not possibly sustain itself without its unique articulation in various forms and in different historical periods. To insist on the unity of Orientalist discourse is not to claim that it is a monolithic block. But, if the legacy of Orientalism is with us today, and if it has been able to survive despite the collapse of empires, it is

because it has articulated itself differently in each instance. As an unconscious memory it reappears through displacement, association, disruption;
it intersects with newly emerging discourses. Each intersection, each interruption and displacement does in fact multiply and complicate as much as
it fixes the discursive unity of Orientalism.

In the light of these concerns, I would like to inquire into the role and
status of representations of the Orient and its women by Western women
in the formation (and perhaps contestation) of Orientalist imagery. My
concern in focusing on Western women's representations is neither simply
to discern the "feminine idiosyncrasies" assumed to be expressed in their
texts, nor to see their accounts as a reflection of their gender. Rather, my
concern in examining such texts as a separate cluster is, first, to point to the
necessity of recognizing the complicity between Orientalism's imperialist
operations and a certain type of Western "feminist" gesture. For, as Spivak
suggests, feminism "must recognize that it is complicitous with the institu-
tion within which it seeks its space"; and "varieties of feminist theory and
practice must reckon with the possibility that, like any other discursive
practice, they are marked and constituted by, even as they constitute, the
field of their production."[11] Second, my aim is to discern how Western
women's representations are positioned in relation to texts by men. And
third, I wish to delineate the specific features that characterize women's
texts and how they differ, if at all, from their male predecessors.
Understanding these characteristics might be helpful in revealing the specific nature of Western women's relationship to the Orient and Oriental
women and how these features have been influenced by already existing
tropes of the Orientalist discourse. If, as Timothy Mitchell suggests, "the
East itself is not a place . . . but a further series of representations, each one
reannouncing the reality of the Orient but doing no more than referring
backwards and forwards to all the others,"[12] then we need to understand
the nature of this backward and forward movement between men's and
women's narratives. Are there specific means by which Western women
writers authorize their representation of the Oriental other? If Orientalist
imagery is not a simple reproduction of existing tropes and ideas, in what
ways do Western women's writings diverge from and converge with men's
writings?

Western woman as supplement

I have suggested in chapter 2 that whether male or female, the Western
subject's desire for its Oriental other is always mediated by a desire to have
access to the space of its women, to the body of its women and to the truth

of its women. What explains such an obsession with the Oriental woman is the metonymic association established between the Orient and its women. The Orient, seen as the embodiment of sensuality, is always understood in feminine terms and accordingly its place in Western imagery has been constructed through the simultaneous gesture of racialization and feminization. As Mary Harper notes, "the Orient is its women for many of these travellers."[13] In this imagery, the inquiry into the Orient always implies a need to investigate its women. It is through the simultaneous mobilization of these two lines of inquiry, which are brought together and bear and reflect upon each other, that the Orient is comprehended in feminine terms. The process of Orientalization of the Orient is one that intermingles with its feminization. The interlocking of the representation of cultural and sexual difference is secured through mapping the discourse of Orientalism onto the phallocentric discourse of femininity. Consequently, one can not only find sections consistently devoted to women, the harem, and the veil in most texts on the Orient, but also on various spheres of Oriental life that are comprehended through feminine iconographies. Thus one can easily see that within the symbolic economy of Orientalism, the typography of femininity as enigmatic, mysterious, concealing a secret behind its veil is projected onto the iconography of the Orient. The horror and threat of what is assumed to be hidden behind the Oriental/feminine veil is revealed in and by these representations.

The desire to penetrate the mysteries of the Orient and thereby to uncover hidden secrets (usually expressed in the desire to lift the veil and enter into the forbidden space of the harem) is one of the constitutive tropes of Orientalist discourse. An obsession with a "hidden" and "concealed" Oriental life and with the woman behind the veil and in the harem has led to an overrepresentation of Oriental women in an effort to evade the lack posed by a closed "inner" space. It is this trope of concealment which has led many male travellers to denounce the hateful mystery of the harem and the veil. However, despite this overrepresentation, the Orientalist's desire is always left unsatisfied. The more the Orientalist subject has tried to know and conquer the zone of darkness and mystery, the more he has realized his distance from "authentic," "real" knowledge of the Orient and its women. It is the nostalgia for the "real" Orient that motivates the Western subject's irresistible urge to enter this forbidden space. The following lines from Jean Jacques Ampere illustrates this: "Oriental life is only found today in all its splendour within the house, where travellers cannot enter."[14]

Ampere repeats most of the common tropes one can find in Orientalist imagery. The "real" characteristics of the Orient are assumed to be found in the space of its women. It is in this closed domestic space that the Western subject seeks the most "glorious" and "delightful" aspects of the Orient. In order to fully grasp the Orient, in order to reveal the truth of it, he has to see this domain; hence not only the primacy of vision as the ultimate guarantor of truth and knowledge, but also the necessity of the gaze in the voyeuristic economy of colonial desire. Moreover, it is no accident that the space where Ampere locates the "essence" of the Orient is the space of the woman. Hence the Orient is identical to its women; they are its essence. He states this rather explicitly: "the Orient is for me, today, like a masked woman who has revealed only her face."[15] He cannot regard himself as having acquired the full knowledge of the Orient without knowing and understanding its essence, i.e. its women. He knows that no matter how hard he tries to rip off the veil of the harem that conceals the Oriental other from the Western subject, his effort is destined to fail. Moreover, not only is the space of the Oriental woman "hermetically sealed" from men, thus incapacitating their voyeuristic pleasure, but also the native resists giving any information regarding this "inner" space. Here is Théophile Gautier expressing this battle to gain access to the knowledge of the interiority of the other: "It is, therefore, easy to understand, that it would be singularly unbecoming to ask from a Turk any details as to the habits or customs of the harem, or the character and manners of the women . . . Civilization in this particular, has not advanced a single step."[16]

Since the masculine gaze is determined to have access to this "hidden" space, it uses every single means that is available. Accounts and descriptions of Western women are utilized as a means of evading the lack that lies at the very heart of the Orientalist/masculine desire. Despite his ability to freely enter the Orient and move in and out as much as he wishes, the Western subject is frustrated by the closure of the space of the Oriental woman; he had no option but to speculate on the details of harem life, its mysteries, and the lascivious sexuality the other-sex enjoys behind that closed curtain. Moreover, the veil and its mystery, which most Western travellers denounce, is dropped in this "inner space." When the "inner" space is closed in this way, the only available means for the Western man is to rely on the Western woman's accounts of the harem's forbidden space, her description of the unveiled women, the details of their everyday life, etc. It is thus only through the assistance of the Western woman (for she is the only "foreigner" allowed to enter into the "forbidden zone") that the mysteries of this inaccessible "inner space" and the "essence" of the Orient secluded in it could be unconcealed; it is she who can remedy the long-lasting lack of the Western subject. The inability to see and have access to the interiority of the other and to the space of woman reminds men of their limit, their *lack*. It is at this point that they resort to the accounts and descriptions of the Western woman who can "remedy this gap." Gautier expresses this as follows: "the only method to employ, in order to really obtain any authentic information, is to request some European lady, who is well introduced and has access to harems, to recount to you faithfully that which she has seen."[17]

Men's frustration about the inability to see the "interiors" is so strong as to compel Gautier to suggest that only "women should go to Turkey," for what men are able to see is very much "marginal" when compared to what women can see, which is the "real" Turkey:

> In Constantinople, when our curiosity is allowed to run the streets, enter the houses, it irritates us to be unable to go past the selamlik with our cups of coffee and chobouks, we often say to ourselves "Only women should go to Turkey – what can a men see in this jealous country? White minarets, guilloche fountains, red houses, black cypresses, many dogs, hammals with loaded camels . . . or photographs and optical views." Nothing more. For a woman, on the contrary, the odalisque opens itself, the harem has no more mysteries; those faces, doubtless charming, for which the bearded tourist searches in vain . . . she contemplates stripped of their veil, in all the brilliance of their beauty; the fredge [cloak], a domino from Islam's permament carnival, could not conceal more gracious bodies and splendid costumes.[18]

Jean Jacques Ampere's praising of Lady Mary Montagu and Sophia Poole as competent agents for filling men's lack with their accounts and observations is also noticeable:

> Fortunately the female tourists, whose numbers are increasing daily, are in a position to *remedy this gap* and have already done so with success, Lady Montagu set the example for Constantinople. Mistress Poole followed this for Cairo: the sister of M. Lane, to whom we owe the most reliable book on *The Modern Egyptians*, she has *completed* the valuable work of her brother with much felicity. In her pleasant little book entitled *The Englishwoman in Egypt,* we find the splendid costumes, mounds of jewels, fairytale meals, beautiful slaves, in short, the whole harem; it is in the harem that the most exquisite and brilliant aspects of Oriental life have taken refuge and still remain hidden.[19] (emphasis added)

This appeal to the accounts and observations of Western women recalls the citationary nature of Orientalism. However, the nature of the backward and forward movement of the citation among Western male and female Orientalists is not independent from the inscription of relations of sexuality, from the staging of masculine and feminine relations.

Being called upon to supplement the masculine subject's lack, Western woman is happy to report "faithfully" what she witnesses in this hermetically sealed world. In fact, as many of them say, they see themselves as fulfilling an important function for their male counterparts: completing their deficiencies. For example Edward Lane's sister, Sophia Poole's identity is constructed in relation to her brother. She does not have an independent identity, but is known in the field as 'Edward Lane's sister'. Not only others, but also she herself, identifies herself in relation to her brother, as she does not hesitate to regard her own writings on the Orient as mere additions to her brother's accounts. She states this in the following manner:

My brother's account of the harem, and all that he has written respecting the manners and customs of the women of this country, I have found to be not only minutely accurate, but of the utmost value to me in preparing me for the life which I am now leading. His information, however, on these subjects, being derived only from other men, is of course imperfect; and he has anxiously desired that I should *supply its deficiencies*, both by my own personal observation, and by learning as much as possible of the state, and morals of the women, and of the manner in which they are treated, from their own mouths.[20] (emphasis added)

Hence Western woman, as the one who completes through her addition, functions to constitute the fullness and coherence of the narratives of man. She supplies him with what he lacks, i.e. the knowledge of the inside. But, on the other hand, precisely because her function is seen to complete the picture, implying that the "essential" picture of the Orient is already there, but needs few other additions, her account is not regarded as an essential part of the Orientalist plenitude. This longing for Western women's accounts as a necessary supplement in fact operates to distinguish essential from inessential, original from additional/optional extra, center from margin, interior from exterior. This gesture which dissociates the texts by women from the "primary" text is the very gesture by which the masculine subject distinguishes his text as the "originary" one. What Sophia Poole's writing does, which the other Western men's accounts cannot do (her brother has already derived his knowledge of the harem from other men and this is precisely the reason why it is imperfect), is to *add* in order to complete the "fullness" of her brother's writing.

At this point it is important to briefly explicate the concept of supplement developed by Derrida, for it can enable us to understand the economy that structures the relationship between male and female travellers' texts and the specific features of the dynamic between the backward and forward citation between them.

Derrida distinguishes two meanings of the supplement. The first meaning implies that, "the supplement adds itself, it is surplus, a plenitude enriching another plenitude, the *fullest measure of presence.*"[21] Within this logic, writing is seen as an addition to speech and as such functions to secure the presence of speech. The logic that accords writing the status of an addition at the same time privileges speech as being a natural expression of thought, for it sees language as primarily made to be spoken. If this is so, then writing must be serving to supplement it. Or take the example of masturbation. Its function is to supplement the "natural sex." It is nothing but an addition, a surplus which enriches the self-sufficient plenitude. It is this logic of supplementarity which determines the set of oppositions which constitute the core of the metaphysics; nature versus culture, man versus woman, speech versus writing, origin versus history are all functions of this economy of supplementarity. According to the second meaning, the supplement "adds only to replace. It intervenes or insinuates itself *in-the-place-of* ; if it fills, it is as if one fills a void . . . Compensatory [*suppéant*] and vicarious, the supplement is an adjunct, a subaltern instance which *takes-(the)-place* [*tient-lieu*]."[22]

The example Derrida gives for this second meaning of the supplement is the sign. It is conceived as a supplement to the thing itself. What is important is that, whether seen as an addition or a substitution, within this economy, the supplement is always "*exterior*, outside of the positivity to which it is super-added, alien to that which, in order to be replaced by it, must be other than it."[23] What is common to both meanings of the term is that the logic of supplementarity assumes and also undermines a self-sufficient originary presence. By the fact of being pushed into the margin, the function of the supplement is to restore the fullness of the one. But the necessity of the supplement implies that there is a lack in this plenitude, despite its fullness. This longing, this necessity for the supplement, the very fact of necessity for something to be added indicates that it fulfills the function of filling a void, of remedying an imperfection in the origin. The very movement of the supplement which restores presence at the same time effaces it and insinuates it as the non-presence. It thus appears as nothing more than an optional extra, an appendix to the original, to what was complete in itself; but it adds in order to compensate for the lack in this presence that is "supposed to be complete." In other words, "that supplementation is possible only because of an originary lack."[24] As a non-presence, the supplement, then, is the condition of possibility of the interior and thus cures the deficiencies in the origin or compensates for its lack. This implies that what lies at the core of the logic of supplementarity is the process of exclusion which constitutes exteriority and interiority simultaneously.[25]

Investigating the status of Western women's writings within the Orientalist tradition reveals the logic of supplementarity at work in the process of citation between male and female Orientalists and the process of internal exclusion through which Orientalism constitutes its unity and fullness.

In their call to Western women to provide them with the knowledge of the sealed interior space of the Orient and its women "hidden" behind the veil and the harem, the Western/masculine subject simultaneously constitutes his own text as the primary one and thereby positions the texts by women as mere additions. The fact that such accounts are positioned as simple additions implies that they are in fact "no-thing" because they are added to a full and completed account of the Orient. But, on the other hand, there is a sense in which the masculine subject's comprehension of the Orient is not complete unless he incorporates this supplementary information. Each additional piece of information that comes from Western women is conceived as an integral part of the knowledge of the Orient, but at the same time it is seen as standing on the outskirts of the primary texts, thus implying the fullness and completeness of the masculine subject's representations. This move, by designating the status of the information dug out from Western women as additional information construes what counts as *the* knowledge of the Orient. But what is added, despite residing outside, takes the place of the default or fills in a fundamental lack in the Orientalist plenitude. The lack that characterizes the Western subject here is precisely the lack of access to the interior space of the Orient and as such the Orientalist plenitude is far from being self-sufficient. The Western woman's descriptions of the harem and of Oriental women, this supplement, this plus, by the very fact that it substitutes the lack of the Western subject, is also less than the originary text. It does not have an independent definition of itself. It *is what it is* only in relation to men's writing. It is through this double operation – residing only in the exterior and serving as an appendix to the originary set on the one hand, and fulfilling the function of an extra which cures the lack in the masculine subject on the other – that the Western woman's text is recognized and disavowed at the same time. This explains why the masculine subject needs to have women's accounts as a supplement, and call upon them and repel them at once. But this double movement in no way situates the Western woman's writing outside Orientalism's grasp. On the contrary, what the logic of supplementarity reveals is "this strange reversal of values whereby an apparently derivative or secondary term takes on the crucial role of determining an entire structure of assumptions."[26]

In the pages that follow, I will offer a reading of Lady Mary Montagu's *Turkish Embassy Letters*.[27] My focus on Montagu's *Letters* is not because they occupy a very special place in Orientalist discourse, but rather that her writing is a symptom of the issues I have addressed above. Montagu is by no mean the only Western woman who functions as a supplement for the masculine Orientalist texts, nor are her representations more "Orientalist" than those of other Western women who travelled to the Orient either as wives of Western officials, businessmen, as missionary workers, travellers or anthropologists. Her text is simply a convenient example through which one can discern how the tropes used by Western women converge with and diverge from the ones used by men and the specific position women's texts occupy *vis-à-vis* men's in the wider universe of Orientalism.

Lady Mary Montagu: Orientalist or feminist?

In discerning the characterizing features of Montagu's *Letters* I engage in the discussion of the main arguments developed by Lisa Lowe in her analysis of the same text in her *Critical Terrains: French and British Orientalisms.* For this reason, I first offer a brief exegesis of her argument and then discuss at which points and why my reading of Montagu's *Letters* diverges from Lowe's. In doing so, I do not claim to offer a detailed and exhaustive review of her stimulating and dynamic book in its totality, in which she offers a reading of a wide selection of Orientalist texts, ranging from Montagu, Flaubert, Forster to Kristeva, Barthes, and the group *Tel quel.* Rather, I will draw on only one strand of her diverse web of arguments, specifically, the one that pertains to Lady Mary Montagu's *Turkish Embassy Letters.*

One of the reasons why Lowe is motivated to make a reading of Montagu's *Letters* is that she wants to scrutinize and thereby resist a totalizing and monolithic conception of Orientalism. In fact, she offers this as one of the main concerns of her book. For instance, she detects in Said's *Orientalism* a tendency to generalize Orientalist discourse as a constant and monolithic entity.[28] In an effort to elucidate the "heterogeneous and contradictory sites of Orientalism," Lowe focuses her readings on the junctures at which gendered, racial, national, and class differences may complicate, and even interrupt and displace Orientalism. In locating the moments of what she calls the "destabilization of Orientalism" in such discursive intersections, Lowe aims to situate the sites of resistance to Orientalism within the very apparatus of Orientalist discourse. Following Foucault she employs the notion of heterotopicality to refer to such moments of resistance as are articulated against Orientalism from within. Lowe's search for internal sites and rearticulations as a way of understanding the moments of intervention against Orientalism is certainly a very promising project. Indeed, it is precisely by resorting to such notions of textuality and intertextuality and "internal" sites of resistance that we need to contest the simplistic praising of the authentic voice or the desire to have the other display its cultural difference in a confessional and testimonial mode – a trend which has become widespread among the "new ethnographers" as a means of "overcoming" the Orientalizing move of classical anthropology. However, despite such a promising concern, Lowe, at times, is too quick to spot sites of resistance to Orientalism. If one instance of such a quick solution lies in her multiplying Orientalism (in contrast to a binary structure, she discerns heterogeneity and multiplicity), the other becomes visible in her, at times not very elaborated, celebration of moments of resistance and intervention in Montagu's *Letters*.[29] I will limit my critical dialogue to this aspect of Lowe's text in an effort to situate Montagu's *Letters* in a different relationship to Orientalism.

Like Sophia Poole, Lady Mary Montagu emphasizes the privilege she has over Western men in terms of having greater access to the space of Turkish women and hence to their knowledge. She does not forget to remind her readers that this is mainly due to her being a woman: she has what men do not have and thus can supplement their lack. She thus authorizes her own accounts by resorting to the notion of truth – a widespread trope which not only characterizes the series of representations we call Orientalist, but also masculinist representations. Being aware of the marginal/supplementary position her text occupies *vis-à-vis* men's, she feels the need to discard their truth claims in order to open up a space for her text in the Orientalist textual universe. She emphasizes over and over again how her accounts are faithful to the truth of the Orient and its women and tries to dismiss the texts written by men as being merely a distorted and an inaccurate representation of the "reality" of the Orient. Hence the citationary nature of Orientalism which operates not simply through a process of accumulation, but also through displacement, deletion, rearrangement, and even contestation, intervention, and contradiction. For example, in her letter "To Lady —" on 17 June 1717, Lady Montagu challenges the accuracy of the French historian Jean Dumont's descriptions of Turkey:

Your whole Letter is full of mistakes from one end to 'other. I see you have taken your Ideas of Turkey from that worthy author Dumont, who has writ with equal ignorance and confidence. Tis a particular pleasure to me here to read the voyages to the Levant, which are generally so far remov'd from Truth and so full of Absurditys I am very well diverted with 'em. They never fail giving you an Account of the Women, which 'tis certain they never saw.[30]

Or in her letter "To the Countesse of —" in May 1718 she says, "I am more enclin'd, out of a true female spirit of Contradiction, to tell you the falsehood of a great part of what you find in authors; as, for example, the admirable Mr. Hill.[31] . . . But I depend upon your knowing me enough to believe whatever I seriously assert for truth".[32] And in her letter to Lady Bristol, she emphasizes her concern with truth:

Since my last I have stay'd quietly at Constantinople, a City that I ought in Conscience to give Your Ladyship a right Notion of, Since I know You can have none but what is partial and mistaken from the writings of Travellers. 'Tis certain there are many people that pass years here in Pera without having ever seen it, and yet they all pretend to describe it.[33]

This attempt to authenticate her accounts through resorting to the trope of truth while at the same time renouncing her male predecessors' Oriental pictures is quite widespread not only in Montagu's *Letters*, but also in other Western women's writings.[34] As I suggested above, the citationary nature of Orientalism functions to anchor its power. The systematic character of Orientalism is established not only through restoration and confirmation of previous representations, but also by deletion, displacement, and even contradiction.

Lowe argues that Montagu's text, unlike those of her male predecessors, occupies a paradoxical and multivalent position within Orientalist tradition, for she detects, on the one hand, elements in her texts which resonate with traditional Orientalist tropes, such as the figuring of the Orient as exotic, ornate, and mysterious. On the other hand, she claims that Montagu's *Letters* "explicitly challenge the received representations of Turkish society by the seventeenth-century travel writers who preceded her."[35] Thus, for Lowe, Montagu "distinctly sets herself apart from that tradition by criticizing the representations of women, marriage, sexuality, and custom in the travel accounts of Robert Withers, George Sandy, John Covel, Jean Dumon, and Aaron Hill."[36] Seen from the perspective of the citationary process of Orientalism, it becomes quite problematical to claim that Lady Mary Montagu's critical stance against the truth claims of her male counterparts situates her texts apart from the Orientalist tradition of travel writing, for as I have suggested above, the symbolic universe of Orientalism is *not* without any contradictions, displacements, or contestations. Orientalism establishes its *unity* despite the polymorphous nature of the texts that constitute it. The Orientalist universe, in its unity, is a multifarious or voluminous textuality, but these characteristics do not make it more vulnerable, or these characteristics do not in any simple way constitute a subversive challenge to its power and unity. On the contrary, they enrich the Orientalist discourse. Thus, I would prefer to be more cautious about locating the challenge of Orientalism either in the multivalent position of texts, or in attempts which offer a more "positive" and "good" picture of the Orient and Oriental women as opposed to "negative" and "bad" images.[37] If we translate Orientalism into a constellation of "prejudices" or "negative" images, then it is unlikely that our research can go further than evaluating those images according to a certain moral criterion. As Homi Bhabha suggests, rather than identifying those images as positive or negative, which implies assessing them on the basis of some political normativity, our analysis should focus "on the process of subjectification achieved through the production of stereotypes."[38] It is only then, for Bhabha, that we can reveal the productive nature of colonial discourse, i.e. the ways in which it constructs a certain regime of truth by transforming other cultures into objects of analysis. Seen from this perspective, Lady Mary Montagu's narrative partakes in the Orientalist construction but through a different gesture. To understand this we need to look more closely at her *Letters* and show how, despite their apparent divergence from male travellers' texts, they are inevitably implicated and caught within the *masculinist and imperialist act of subject constitution*. In doing so I will maintain my critical dialogue with Lowe's text.

Lowe's concern with the intersection of discourses of gender, class, race, and nation with Orientalism in order to illustrate the heterogeneous nature of Orientalism and with moments of intersection which may destabilize the power of Orientalism gains more concrete voice in her reading of Montagu's *Letters*. While finding resonances of Orientalist imageries in her text, and thereby characterizing Montagu's *Letters* as a work in which Orientalist representations overlap with rhetorics of gender and class, Lowe detects the emergence of a feminist discourse which "speaks of common experiences among women of different societies."[39] In the pages that follow, I will focus more extensively on Lowe's characterization of certain discursive elements in Montagu's writing as "feminist" and discuss in more detail how, despite its manifest contestatory and contradictory (multivalent) nature, Montagu's accounts of the Orient, Oriental women, and their customs cannot be disentangled from the masculinist and imperialist accounts of the Orient offered by male travellers.

According to Lowe, Montagu's discourse is characterized by a combination of two different rhetorics: the rhetoric of identification (or similitude/similarity) and the rhetoric of differentiation (difference). Lowe argues that one of the points which differentiates Montagu's text from those of her male predecessors is the rhetoric of comparison with which she likens the conditions, opportunities, and character of Turkish women to those of her Western counterparts. Montagu, for Lowe, articulates her identification with Turkish women by means of an analogy of gender and class (her comparisons are limited to women of the highest social class and she herself is an ambassador's wife). The fact that she identifies with Turkish women and their society indicates to Lowe the emergence of a feminist discourse in Montagu's text. At the same time, Lowe claims that as well as using a rhetoric of similarity, Montagu also employs a rhetoric of difference. It is this latter feature, for Lowe, which makes Montagu's text similar to the mainstream Orientalist attitude which differentiates and constructs Orient and Occident as opposites. Thus, the rhetorical strategies Montagu employs are simultaneously "antagonistic to and supportive of, the differentiating rhetorics of culture that characterize orientalism."[40] Montagu's detailed description of herself in Turkish dress is one of the moments, for Lowe, where she establishes a synonymity or identity between herself and Turkish women.[41] Lowe also notes how these two rhetorics are intertwined in Montagu's attempt to assert her identification with Turkish women. For example, she notes that "the rhetoric of similitude through which Montagu displays her intimate identification with Turkish women's culture relies simultaneously on stated and implied differentiations; the rhetorical act of likening herself to Turkish women ironically recalls an established separation of Occident and Orient."[42] The above statement is crucial in that it illustrates how Montagu's representation is not in any simple sense outside the traditional discursive strategies of Orientalism, for, according to Lowe, Montagu uses the rhetoric of differentiation for the purpose of establishing an equality between Turkish and English women. Even though she demonstrates how these two strategies can co-exist, Lowe's position becomes quite problematical when she identifies only the rhetoric of difference as a strategy that belongs to the traditional Orientalist act of separation of Orient and Occident, whereas, the rhetoric of similitude is implicitly regarded as distinct from an Orientalist strategy of knowing and representing cultural difference. The following lines from Lowe not only summarize the interplay of rhetoric of similitude and the logic of difference, but also show how she conceptualizes them:

when Montagu repeatedly likens English and Turkish women, her rhetoric of similitude directly contradicts the logic of difference that characterizes the observations of the male travel writers. At the same time, to a certain degree the rhetoric of identification through which Montagu displays her knowledge of Turkish women's culture inevitably restates an *orientalist topos of differentiation* in order to target it, ironically recalling the established separation of Occident and Orient.[43] (emphasis added)

Lowe's equation of the rhetoric of difference with Orientalism and the rhetoric of identification as external to it becomes clearer in the following

few lines: "the use of rhetoric of difference places Montagu's text in relation to a discourse of orientalism, whereas the rhetoric of identification
expresses the *critical distance* of the text from orientalism, marking it as
heterogeneous, divergent, and dissenting."[44]

What is confusing here is precisely what Lowe means by the "rhetoric of
difference," or rather the implicit assumption which seems to underscore
her entire reading of Montagu's text: the implication that the rhetoric of
similarity or identification does not belong to the Orientalist/colonial strategy of knowing the Orient, for whenever she alludes to the rhetoric of
difference she refers to it as an Orientalist one, whereas in her characterization of the rhetoric of similitude she does not invoke it as part of an
Orientalist discursive strategy. She does mention that Montagu employs the
rhetoric of difference in her identification with Turkish women, but she
never refers to the rhetoric of similitude as part of an Orientalist scheme of
knowing and representing the other. Thus, what is implied in the distinction Lowe makes between the "rhetoric of difference" and the "rhetoric of
similarity" is that they are two different modes of knowing and representing
the other; it is only the former which can be regarded as a discursive strategy of Orientalism whereas the latter enables one to intervene against it.

In order to avoid such confusions, I would like to reiterate one of the
important lessons taught by post-structuralist theory: the phallogocentric
and Eurocentric economy of signification is governed only by *one
term*. Difference, within a signifying economy such as Orientalism, is
nothing but the self's/same's own excluded but necessary negative other. It
is therefore always understood, to borrow a phrase from Spivak, "*as* unlike
(non-identical with) it yet *with* reference to it."[45] It is precisely to avoid such
confusions that we need to be vigilant about the epistemic violence of
imperialism. We need to keep in mind that the imperialist gesture of subject
constitution is always predicated upon the recognition of the other through
assimilation, through the logic of the same.[46] Such a process of assimilation
necessarily entails a translation and we should not forget that every act of
translation is an act of transformation of the radical alterity into the self's
own terms. This is precisely the site where we need to locate what Spivak
calls, the structure of "translation-as-violation."[47] Said's following short
statement is a cogent description of the violence embedded in the translation of the cultural other: "to convert them into topics of discussion or
fields of research is necessarily to change them into something fundamentally and constitutively different."[48] Seen from this perspective, the distinction Lowe makes between the rhetoric of identification and the rhetoric
of difference is unfounded, for within the apparatus of colonial power,
difference is always understood through the logic of the same, through the self,

and as such is nothing but an inverted mirror-image of the same. In the very act of identification she establishes with Turkish women, Montagu does perform the violent transformation implied in the act of translation of cultural difference into the self/same. As Irigaray suggests, one of the defining features of phallocentrism is the logic of sameness which operates precisely through what Lowe calls the rhetoric of similarity; the self always knows and represents the other through himself. Like the representation of sexual difference in a phallocentric order, the representation of cultural difference in the symbolic universe of Orientalist/colonial discourse is predicated upon the logic of the same. We can, in other words, translate what Irigaray says about the representation of sexual difference in the discourse of phallocentrism to the representation of cultural difference in the discourse of Orientalism. For Irigaray, the realm of the same is the hom(m)osexual economy of man and the other of this same is woman.[49] She suggests:

the desire for the same, for the self-identical, the self(as) same, and again of the similar, the alter ego and, to put it in a nutshell, the desire for the auto . . . the homo . . . the male, dominates the representational economy. "Sexual difference" is a derivation of the problematics of sameness, it is now and forever, determined within the project, the projection, the sphere of representation, of the same.[50]

Following Said's, Irigaray's, and Spivak's arguments (developed in quite different contexts) regarding the imperialist and masculinist subject's rendering and transforming cultural and sexual difference into a recognizable, commensurable sameness, I would argue that Montagu's apparently dissenting and critical distance from Orientalism, which she achieves through the rhetoric of identification, does not prevent her from exercising the imperialist and masculinist act of cultural translation and subject constitution. Her understanding of "difference" within an economy of sameness ensures that the other becomes comprehensible by being rendered as an object of knowledge.

It might be true that it is the rhetoric of similarity – through which Montagu understands and identifies herself with Turkish women and alludes to the common experiences she shares with them – that sets her text apart from her male counterparts. This is her difference and perhaps even her "advantage" (for it is only she, as a woman, who can enter the space of the Oriental woman) as a female writer within the Orientalist tradition over her male predecessors. But to reach a too quick conclusion that there is a feminist discourse which enables Montagu to intervene against Orientalist tradition would prevent us from conceiving the complicity between Western imperialism and feminism. What we need to demonstrate and specify, as feminist critics working in the field of colonial discourse analysis, is the nature of the feminist position Montagu occupies. In doing so, we need to demonstrate how (Western) feminism has been complicit in the project of imperialism. Given that a pure and uncontaminated position is impossible, can we then comfortably assume feminism and Orientalism as necessarily contradictory modalities? Rather than positing (Western) women's discourse in an external relation to Orientalism, we need to demonstrate how it can and has become imperialist – a "feminist" discourse which both benefits from and critizes discourses such as Orientalism. Rather than speaking as if feminism and Orientalism are clearly distinct and separable political articulations, I would suggest that we demonstrate how Western feminism, as it attempts to represent cultural difference by reiterating the economy of sameness, is inextricably complicitous with masculinism, Orientalism, and imperialism. But ironically, for Lowe, it is precisely this "feminist" discourse which allows Montagu a language, a rhetoric, and a set of arguments through which she can interrogate and intervene against traditional Orientalist writings about the Orient. As she claims, it is precisely by employing the discourse of "identification between women of the Turkish and English courts" that Montagu intervenes "in the differentiating rhetoric of orientalism."[51] For Lowe: "Montagu's interventions in the orientalist tradition are primarily articulated in a feminist rhetoric and take place in the moments when her text refutes the constructed topos of the enslavement of Turkish women."[52]

There is no question that Montagu uses her access to the interior space of the Orient as a powerful tool to claim that she is the one who possesses *the authentic* information of Turkish women. This, no doubt, by constituting a challenge to the authority and truth claims of her male "masters," helps her to proclaim truth for her representations. But to argue that this indicates a refutation of the established topos of Orientalism is to reduce the power of Orientalism to a mere constellation of "distorted" representations, and thus prevents us from grasping the more subtle Orientalizing operations of Orientalism which construe difference in a particular way. When Orientalism is conceived of as no more than a "distorted image" of the "reality" of the Orient, as opposed to its "true" and "accurate" representation, the Orientalizing economy which constructs the Orient cannot be radically called into question. Orientalism is an economy of signification in which the difference that inscribes the unequal relation between the subject and the object is constituted. In this regard, Montagu's strategy of representation can at best be considered as a simple reversal of Orientalist discourse, in that, as opposed to her male counterparts' depiction of Turkish women and their treatment within Turkish culture as enslaved in the harem, she might have portrayed them as even more liberated than

Western women. But if we accept the premise that Orientalism is not simply a question of the dissemination of negative images, as Bhabha's argument implies, then we cannot merely posit the depiction of positive images of the Orient and its women as a means of shattering the power of Orientalism. Nor we can ignore the fact that to invert the opposites and thereby install the excluded term at the center cannot constitute a subversive politics, for such a simple reversal would retain the very structure and the force and violence through which opposites are construed as opposites. However, it is precisely such a theoretical/political position which leads Lowe to detect a "feminist" discourse in Montagu's *Letters*. For example, she suggests that one of the discursive strategies Montagu employs in understanding Turkish women is comparison. In this comparative grid Turkish women are not understood through the theme of enslavement – a theme which is widespread in the texts written by men. For Lowe, in men's writings, what is targeted with the theme of "enslavement of Turkish women" is not a critique of the social and cultural practices that contribute to the subordination of women. Rather, by representing Islamic practices as "uncivilized" and "barbaric," male travellers in fact construe European women as a sign of civilized culture. Lowe claims that this is where Montagu's discourse diverges from Orientalist tradition and even contests it. Montagu, for Lowe, does evaluate the status of women through the lenses of a comparative grid, but in her accounts, Turkish women are represented as more advantaged or superior in comparison to English women. Thus according to Lowe, Montagu not only explicitly refutes the earlier travel writers' representation of Turkish women as enslaved, but also *intervenes against* the traditional tropes of Orientalism. Here, Lowe equates Orientalism with "negative" images and consequently identifies the intervention against Orientalism with the depiction of more positive images (i.e. as opposed to being represented as enslaved they are represented as free). Since her theoretical frame is predicated upon evaluating Orientalism in terms of positive versus negative images, she misses the Orientalizing move within these so-called "positive" attributions. However, if the power of Orientalism exceeds the negativity of images then we must be able to locate this power within the wider weave of discursive strategies.

Are there other tropes we can discern in Montagu's *Letters* which situate them within the tradition of Orientalism? Rather than offering merely a long list of these themes, I would like to dwell on the trope of "masquerading Oriental woman behind her veil." Closely related to this is the voyeuristic desire of the Western subject.

The widespread trope of "masquerading Oriental woman" does also refigure in Montagu's *Letters*. Criticizing the accounts of earlier travellers,

Montagu claims that the Turkish woman has more liberty than the English woman and the veil is that device which, by concealing her, gives her the liberty to wonder around without being recognized. For Montagu, the veil is such an effective disguising instrument that it does not allow you to differentiate the great lady from her slave; it basically renders unknowable what is behind it; like a mask it conceals and thereby enables these Turkish women, like masquerades, to follow their inclinations without the danger of being discovered. As such, the veil, for Montagu, is far from being an "oppressive" element; it gives Turkish women "liberty."

Tis very easy to see they have more Liberty than we have, no Woman of what rank so ever being permitted to go in the streets without 2 muslins, one that covers her face all but her Eyes and another that hides the whole dress of her head and hangs halfe way down her back; and their Shapes are wholly conceal'd by a thing they call a Ferigée, which no Woman of any sort appears without . . . You may guess how effectively this disguises them, that there is no distinguishing the great Lady from her Slave, and 'tis impossible for the most jealus Husband to know his Wife when he meets her, and no Man dare either touch or follow a Woman in Street.

This perpetual Masquerade gives them entire Liberty of following their inclinations without danger of Discovery . . . The Great Ladys seldom let their Gallants know who they are, and 'tis so difficult to find it out that they can very seldom guess at her name they have corresponded with above halfe a year together . . . Upon the Whole, I look upon the Turkish women as the only free people in the Empire.[53] (emphasis added)

As Robert Halsband, the editor of *The Complete Letters,* observes in a footnote, other travellers, such as Du Loir in *Voyages* and Robert Withers in *A Description of the Grand Signor's Seraglio,* whom Montagu criticizes for being unfaithful to the "truth" of Turkish women, also represent the veil as a "dress that assisted them in conducting their love affairs."[54] The representation of the veil as a mask which is assumed to hinder a true perspective on the Orient and the feminine is a powerful figure through which the Orientalist and phallocentric discourses are mapped onto each other. In this regard, Montagu's discourse is far from contesting the existing tropes of Orientalist discourse. On the contrary, her discourse not only repeats the already established representations, but also sutures them with a discourse that speaks from a feminine position (since I hesitate to call it feminist). According to Lowe's reading, although Montagu's characterization of Turkish women as masquerading assimilates Turkish culture to English terms and modes of cultural expression,[55] it nevertheless

involves some appropriation of their position for the purpose of intervening in the male tradition of travel writing about the Orient. Implying that Turkish women are the site of a variety of subversive actions, that veiled they are protected by an anonymity that allows them sexual and social license, Montagu makes of Turkish women a sign of liberty and freedom.[56]

Moreover, Montagu's reference to the veil is such that it contests the predominant idea, expressed in men's writing, that the Oriental women are enslaved. For Lowe, contrary to this anti-female discourse (the term belongs to her) Montagu represents the veil as a tool which enables Turkish women to

enjoy even more liberties than English women. Montagu's statement that "Upon the Whole, I look upon Turkish women as the only free people in the Empire" is significant because of the ways in which it challenges several discourses that inform seventeenth-century male travel writing. In one respect, her statement forcefully intervenes in the orientalist discourse that proposes the enslavement of Turkish women as a *sign* for Oriental barbarism. Her claim further implies that Turkish women are freer than English women, a statement that directly contradicts the anti-female discourse that is equally present in the travel writing.[57]

The assumption that the representation of Oriental women enjoying greater freedom than Western women due to their veils situates that discourse in a contestatory position *vis-à-vis* Orientalism once more recalls the opposition between "negative" and "positive" images. In order to understand how such a discursive articulation of the veil is what characterizes not only Montagu's text but Orientalist texts in general, one needs to take a short glance at the texts by men to see how Montagu's discourse is a replica of theirs. For example, Gerard de Nerval, who has travelled to Egypt and contributed largely to the formation of the symbolic universe of Orientalism, identifies the "freedom" of Oriental women with their veil and masquerading activities: "in reality, the mask and uniformity of dress would give them much greater freedom than Europeans, if they were inclined to go in for intrigues . . . There is, then, nothing in the Mussulman law which, as people have chose to believe, reduces women to a condition of slavery and abjection."[58]

Given that Lowe seems to take the writer's gender as the guarantee of meaning, Nerval's representation must pose a paradox for her. But I am confident that she will not disagree with me about situating Nerval's text as one of the constitutive texts of Orientalism. If this is so, then what compels Lowe to claim that there is a contestation of Orientalist hegemony in Montagu's letters? The only reason one can discern is the "positive" images (Turkish women are free, they are not enslaved, Turkish culture is not barbaric, etc.) through which Montagu represents the Oriental woman. However, if we admit that the power of Orientalism does not stem from the "distortion" of the "reality" of the Orient, nor from the dissemination of "prejudiced" or "negative" images about other cultures and peoples, but from its power to construct the very object it speaks about and from its power to produce a regime of truth about the other and thereby establish the identity and the power of the subject that speaks about it, then it becomes a peripheral concern whether the images deployed to this end are "positive" or "negative."

Western woman as sovereign subject

The representation of the Orient, Oriental woman, and femininity as concealed by the veil is also the point around which the desire to see and conquer this zone of ambiguity is articulated. The desire to see and the desire to penetrate this "unknown" and "unknowable" domain also positions the subject of representation as masculine. Montagu's descriptions of the harem reveal the voyeuristic desire she experiences there – a perpetual motif we come across in the discourse of Orientalism. By using the privilege her gender accords to her, Montagu is more than happy to offer detailed descriptions of the concealed space of the harem, of the beauty of Turkish women, of the pleasures they enjoy in the absence of men, etc. By rendering visible the invisible space of the harem, Montagu not only serves the purpose of fulfilling the Western voyeuristic pleasure, but also constitutes herself as the gazing Eye/I. Once again, the visibility of the other is the point at which the subject anchors his identity. Montagu, thus, not only reveals the inner space of the forbidden realm of Oriental woman, but, at the same time, lifts the veil that covers her – which men desired so strongly but were never fully successful in despite their attempt to rip it off by giving it a figural representation. For none of the women Montagu describes in the harem are veiled; they are in their "state of nature." Hence Montagu not only sees and has more access to the nature/essence of the Orient, i.e. to its women, but also she sees them in their "state of nature." Thus Montagu is *the* one who succeeds in penetrating deep into the heart of the other, its mysteries, its true nature, its essence: "without any distinction of rank by their dress, all being in the state of nature, that is, in plain English, stark naked, without any Beauty or defect conceal'd, yet there was not the least wanton smile or immodest Gesture amongst 'em."[59]

Following her successful penetration into the closed space and revelation of the other in its most "essential" aspects, Montagu experiences a somewhat bizarre voyeuristic pleasure. Her look is not entirely consumed and satisfied at this point of transparency, the scene of "stark naked" truth/essence of the other/woman. There starts another activity that transforms her objective factual look into a fictitious, dreaming, fantasmatic look. When she looks at the woman as other, that is to say, as belonging to the other culture, Montagu's look then turns into a masculine gaze. She takes up the masculine, phallic position and employs his *frame* in enjoyment, "wickedly." By imagining the presence of a male traveller such as Gervase, Montagu becomes what he is. The following lines reveal the phallic/voyeuristic enjoyment she experiences in the Oriental harem:

> To tell you the truth, I had wickedness enough to wish secretly that Mr. Gervase could have been there invisible. I fancy it would have very much improv'd his art to see so many fine Women naked in different postures, some in conversation, some working, others drinking Coffee or sherbet, and many negligently lying on their Cushions while their slaves (generally pritty Girls of 17 or 18) were employ'd in braiding their hair in several pritty manners.[60]

The above quote is important in that it not only reveals the unavoidable masculinity of the subject position the female travellers occupy *vis-à-vis* the Orient and its women, but also points to the power of the citationary process through which Orientalism anchors its hegemony. Halsband, the editor of Montagu's *Letters*, brings to our attention an important piece of information. We learn from Halsband that Ingres's painting *Le Bain Turc* (1862) shows the influence of Montagu's descriptions. He observes that "Ingres copied several passages into a notebook from this letter, beginning here, using his copy of French translation of the 1805 edition."[61]

Hence the citationary nature of Orientalism and the irreducible place of Western woman in it as a necessary supplement. As Said's argument makes clear, Orientalism's textual universe is constituted by an endless series of representations, each text taking the other as its referent. Needless to say, in this backward and forward movement, each individual Orientalist as much as strengthening the power of the discursive universe of Orientalism also secures his/her space within this broad structure. In other words, Montagu's *Letters* do in fact function as the "reality" of the Orient for Ingres. Indeed, when we consider all those paintings which provide scenes from the harem, we witness the fact that Orientalism is an endless copying; a series of representations in which each text works as a referent for another. It is this chain of references which produces what Said calls, the "textual attitude" or the unity of Orientalism in its diversity. The paradox here is that these texts construe themselves as representing the "original" and "real" Orient. As these examples illustrate, the "reality" of the Orient is a product of this citationary process; it is something that is grasped in and by these representations, i.e. the "reality" of the harem represented in Ingres's painting rests upon and thus is dependent on Montagu's representation of the harem and Turkish women.[62] This citationary process at the same time implies a process whereby the "real" versus "representation" opposition is construed and maintained. As Timothy Mitchell suggests:

We need to understand how the West had come to live as though the world were divided in this way into two: into a realm of mere representations and a realm of the 'real' . . . We need to understand, in other words, how these notions of a realm of the 'real,' 'the outside,' 'the original,' were in this sense effects of the world's seeming division into two. We need to understand, moreover, how this distinction corresponded to another division of the world, into the West and the non-West; and thus how Orientalism was not just a particular instance of the general historical problem of how one culture portrays another, but something essential to the peculiar nature of the modern world.[63]

As much as being predicated upon the "real" versus "representation" opposition, Montagu's penetration into the Turkish harem recalls the intimate connection established between the Orient, nature, and femininity. As Mary Harper rightly observes, "the Orient . . . is synonymous with the principle of life itself, symbolized in images of women both sacred and erotic."[64] Talking about Michelet's work, she argues that much of his work can be regarded "as an attempt to come to terms with the disturbing powers of this maternal and sensual figure."[65] The synonym established between the Orient and nature is achieved through the figuring of the Orient as a maternal figure, i.e. as the origin (for example, for Michelet, the Orient is "the womb of the world"). If this is so, that is, if it is by figuring it as the "womb of the world" the Orient is understood and represented, then what does it mean for Montagu, as a woman, to enter into this essence, into the heart of this maternal figure, this womb/Orient/harem? What makes one desire to go back into the womb, into the harem, into the heart of the Orient? What kind of a relationship does the desire to enter into the womb imply with respect to the sexual dynamics between the Orient and the West? How does this relation of penetration position Montagu *vis-à-vis* the Orient and its women? Irigaray's reading of the relation of the two sexes' differential relationship to the maternal figure and what this has to do with the phallocentric system is an insightful suggestion to think more thoroughly about these questions. Talking about the boy's relation with his mother, Irigaray argues that the boy can return to the origin by getting inside the mother. Such a return enables him to reestablish continuity with the origin and thus reproduce himself there. However, for the girl, the return to the place of origin is cut off; it cannot be repeated and reproduced. Since her turning back inside the mother is denied, she will never be able to reproduce herself inside her mother. Thus she is left with a void and is forced to pass through the law of man's desire.[66]

If returning to and entering into the origin is essential in the reproduction of one's own self, then what does Montagu's penetration, as a woman, into the space of the Oriental woman tell us with respect to her position *vis-à-vis* the Orient and more importantly the Oriental woman? Clearly, *as a woman*, Montagu (in the West), has been denied access to return to, to go back to her origin/mother/womb so as to be able to produce and re-produce herself. Her relation to her origin and to the womb as the space of self-reproduction has been inscribed and cut through phallocentrism's insurmountable barrier; she cannot have access to the life-giving origin. Even though she herself is the life-giving agent, she cannot establish any continuity with it. But she can, by being the ground/womb upon which man erects himself, feed the self of the masculine. She has no-thing, no sex organ through which she can penetrate and reproduce her identity. She is not capable of founding her own truth, identity/self *in the West* when she is inscribed as having no-thing, no-penis in her relationship with the masculine one. She is not capable of founding her ground upon which she can erect her self, for she herself is a ground; she is thus nothing but a void, a lack (in the West) in relation to her masculine one; she does not have a phallus, the "emblem of man's appropriative relation to the origin."[67] Therefore, to have the kind of appropriative and intrusive relation she has with the Orient and Oriental women, Montagu needs a phallic substitute. Or rather, in her relation with the Orient, she attaches a phallus to herself so that she can enter into the domain of the other, to the origin of all civilizations, to the "mother-nature-Orient," and thereby *be.* Thus she finds the life-enhancing origin, which has been denied to her (in the West) within the phallocentric economy, in the Orient, in the space of its women. It is by entering into the harem/Orient/womb that she can reproduce herself and constitute her identity. She thus becomes the One/Self in relation to the Orient and Oriental woman.

If this is so, then it is no big puzzle why Montagu, like her male counterparts, was interested in the "inner" space of the Orient, in its women, in its harem, for this is the very ground upon which her identity is anchored and founded. *Like many of her male predecessors, Montagu's desire to see the veiled and concealed Oriental woman and the consequent attempt to rip off the veil is one that starts and ends with the question of herself and her identity.* As a Western woman, her relationship with the Oriental woman is not different from the self/other relationship she experiences in the West with Western man. Thus, Montagu's discourse repeats and reproduces all the existing tropes and concerns that characterize the Orientalist/phallocentric discourses. However, unlike her male counterparts, and like her Oriental female counterparts, she herself is the ground of phallocentrism – she is both a supplement and an origin, an extra that fills out the void and a plenitude simultaneously. But this does not prevent her performing Orientalism's epistemic violence. The acknowledgment of her complicity with this violent gesture is absolutely pivotal for a feminist criticism which seeks to develop what Spivak calls an alternative historical narrative of the "worlding of the world" which has been denied in the imperialist narrativization. Such an alternative political/theoretical project is neither about "letting the Other speak" nor about trying to recover the lost authenticity of the Third World woman. But, as Spivak suggests, it is about "documenting and theorizing the itinerary of the consolidation of Europe as a sovereign subject, indeed sovereign and subject."[68]

The nature of the complicity between imperialist subject constitution and feminist representation is conditioned and constitutive of the historical period in which it is located. In chapter 4 I want to explore a contemporary version of this liaison by examining the ways in which the project of Enlightenment is articulated to feminist individualism in the discourse of Orientalism.

4

Sartorial fabric-ations: The Enlightenment and Western feminism

> The final emancipatory gesture of Enlightenment thought would thus be
> its own liberation from itself, so that it is no longer recognizable as reason.
>
> Robert Young, *White Mythologies*

Enlightenment's other

The interlocking relation between the political rationality of colonial
power and modernity has been demonstrated in many studies.[1]
Enlightenment reason, resting on the belief of the irreconcilability of non-
modern ways of life with Western models of progress, serves as the con-
necting tissue between colonial and modernist discourses. The signifiers of
the project of Enlightenment and humanism such as progress, modernization, and universalism have also functioned as legitimizing categories in the
civilizing mission of colonial power. As Sartre notes, this relationship was
more than a mere historical or conjunctural coincidence: the formation of
universal humanism's ideal is predicated upon a racist gesture, for, in order
to be able to proclaim its humanity, the West needed to create its others as
slaves and monsters.[2] In a different register, Gayatri Spivak commented on
the affinity between the imperialist subject and the subject of humanism, as
both share the sovereign subject status of authorship, authority, and legitimacy.[3] Thus, to set up its boundaries as human, civilized, and universal,
the Western subject inscribed the history of its others as backward and
traditional, and thereby placed cultures of different kinds in a teleological
and chronological ordering of history. It is this ordering which enabled the
West to construe and affirm its difference from its others as temporal distance.[4] This temporalizing gesture, therefore, has enabled the West not only
to invent itself as the universal subject of history, but also to assert its cultural domination and superiority by assuming one true story of human

history. What lies at the core of this "worlding of the world" is the West's stabilization of its project of global domination by defining a universally applicable norm of development and progress. The economic, political, and cultural dominance of the West is thus inextricably linked to its discovery of, in Castoriadis' words, "*the* way of life appropriate to all human society."[5] In this regard, the ideology of Enlightenment functioned, in Radhakrishnan's words, "as a free-floating signifier seeking universal confirmation."[6] However, the very production of this modernity and universality is based on a fundamental contradiction, for the imposition of modernity in colonial conditions was predicated on the denial of freedom and autonomy to native cultures.[7] The construction of a normative temporality stipulated the ground for the dissimulation of the violence exercised in the occupation of native lands as the dissemination of the benefits of modernity to uncivilized cultures. Therefore, the project of Enlightenment needs to be understood not only as a by-product of, as David Lloyd puts it, "the intersection of liberal humanism with the necessities of imperial polity,"[8] but also as a process of temporalization which fostered a certain narrative of the world within which the West is anchored as the center.

In order to be able to construe the West and the Orient in different and distant temporalities, the machinery of colonial discourse does not need terms, as Fabian suggests, that are manifestly temporal. It can very well achieve its distancing and temporalizing function by using terms such as "primitive," "backward," "traditional" and so on. The use of such temporalizing devices as a means of distancing or pushing the cultural other back in time[9] implies a specific inscription of the relation between the West and the East. More specifically, it involves a specific articulation and ordering of cultural difference, for, as Homi Bhabha notes, "to represent the colonial subject is to conceive of the subject of difference, of an-other history and an-other culture."[10] However, the representation of cultural difference through such temporal categorizations was not simply due to prejudice or overt racism, but, as Mohanty puts it, was "primarily because of uncritical application and extension of the very categories with which the West has defined its Enlightenment and its modernity – Reason, Progress, Civilization."[11]

The colonial task of mastering the other was backed up by anthropological representations.[12] The unequal relation between the West and the Third World was articulated in anthropology's will to know and make the other epistemologically available to the observing Western gaze, most notably by construing a linear time through which the relation between the West and the rest was inscribed as a temporal distance. Fabian's observation regarding the role of anthropology in the colonial enterprise is in order here:

Among the historical conditions under which our discipline emerged and which affected its growth and differentiation were the rise of capitalism and its colonial-ist-imperialist expansion into the very societies which became the target of our inquiries. For this to occur, the expansive, aggressive, and oppressive societies which we collectively and inaccurately call the West needed space to occupy. More profoundly and problematically, they required Time to accommodate the schemes of a one-way history: progress, development, modernity (and their negative mirror images: stagnation, underdevelopment, tradition). In short, *geopolitics* has its ideo-logical foundations in *chronopolitics*. [13]

In so far as the Orient was concerned, the anthropologist's concern in knowing and representing it has become one of demonstrating what it *lacks*. Talal Asad suggests that the Orientalist's concern in comparing and contrasting the Orient with his/her own civilization is to show the absence of "liberty," "progress," and humanism in Islamic societies, and that the reason for this absence is located in the religious essence of Islam.[14] The lack of freedom is traced in the Asiatic despotic mode of production, irra-tionality is discovered in tradition, barbarism is evidenced in various cul-tural and religious practices. In short, all these "discoveries" implied that the barbaric Orient had to be tamed and civilized. Such a taming required the dissemination of rational procedures of Western institutions of law and order and the reorganization of the capillaries of Oriental cultures along the principles of "modern," "progressive," and "civilized" West.

The question of woman gained a particular significance in the articula-tion of colonial and anthropological discourses. The anthropological dis-course on the Muslim or Middle Eastern woman is characterized with an articulation of colonial and liberal feminist rhetoric in which woman's status is used as the proof of the backwardness of Eastern cultures. While pro-viding the necessary legitimizing force for colonialism, Enlightenment thought has also supplied Western liberal feminism with a whole battery of discursive strategies to know and understand its ethnographic other, and thus to secure the integrity of its own identity *vis-à-vis* its dark and uncanny double. Such a discursive lineament was crucial in the emergence and consolidation of what we might call, "an imperial Western feminist gesture."

Lifting the veil, modernizing the woman

Within the grim picture of the Orient, the situation of its woman, who is secluded behind her veil, looked even more gruesome to the Western colo-nial gaze. Her situation thus required a much more serious working, for the most essential features of the culture are assumed to be inscribed onto her; she is taken as the concrete embodiment of oppressive Islamic traditions which the Orient desperately needed to break up in order to reach the level of development the West achieved a long time ago. In fact, one of the central elements in the ideological justification of colonial culture is the criticism of the cultural practices and religious customs of Oriental societies which are shown to be monstrously oppressing women. Hence, the barbarity of the Orient is evidenced in the way cultural traditions shape the life of its women.

This Enlightenment rhetoric (in its feminist career) took "backward" and "barbaric" Islamic customs, which are assumed to be central in the enslavement and imprisonment of Muslim women, as the target upon which to work. It was believed that the conditions that perpetuate the non-modern social structures and values of Oriental cultures needed to be uprooted for new and modern conditions to be put in place to produce the desired effects in women's status in the Middle East. Therefore, the systematic breakdown of the "backward" cultural, economic, and political conditions was essential if these cultures were to be improved in the direction of modern Western ideals. For example, Woodsmall, in *Woman in the Changing Islamic System*, first published in 1936, is confident that it is the West which can provide the desired model in this process: "change behind the veil is being made along lines of Western imitation in clothes with a steady improvement in taste and more discrimination as to suitability in dress . . . Social life within the harem now definitely follows the European model."[15]

As in all other Orientalist texts, the temporal problematic, which Fabian calls "pushing the Other back in time" is one of the defining characteristics of anthropological texts on Middle East women. As I mentioned above, it is also the founding principle in the construction of the universality of Western time and progress. The essential difference between the East and the West is premised on this temporal lag. Such societies are by definition deemed "stagnant"; their temporality and dynamism are not understood to be simply different. This difference is negated, denied, pushed back in a temporality which is construed in linear and progressive terms. As Said exemplifies in the case of Massignon, within the Orientalist imagery, "the essence of the difference between East and West is between modernity and ancient tradition."[16] The time lag that characterizes the religious/traditional Orient is its despotic time which remains practically stagnant. Woodsmall expresses this widespread tendency in the following way:

In the East the social system has until the last decade remained practically unchanged throughout the centuries. The Islamic world, with its integrated system of religion and society, has preserved with little if any variation, the social customs of the seventh century. Between the social practices of the East and of the West, there has always been until recently the cleavage of centuries.[17]

Even when Eastern societies undergo social transformation, the situation of women is assumed to remain the same. As Leila Ahmed notes, Western civilization has produced volume after volume regarding the supposed backward and oppressive conditions under which Muslim women live. The unchanging condition of women in these societies is expressed by Juliet Minces, writing in the 1980s, in the following way:

What is particular and problematic is that while women elsewhere gradually liberated themselves – to some extent – from the total supremacy of men, *most women in the Muslim world continued to be totally subordinate. They live under a system which has barely changed despite the undeniable evolution of their societies* and of certain would-be "revolutionary" governments to grant women greater equality and rights, in keeping what we would call desire for "Modernization".[18] (emphasis added)

It is striking that although there is a forty-year time span, there is no difference between the observations of Minces and Woodsmall. It seems that both observations were made within the same representational framework. In the identification of the locus of change, the question of woman gained particular importance. The ability of the Orient to modernize itself is assumed to be possible only by its radical break from tradition. The oppressive and unfree condition of the Oriental woman is not only morally condemned, but also she is transformed into, as Chatterjee notes in the context of India, "a sign of the inherently oppressive and unfree nature of the entire cultural tradition of a country."[19] The metonymic association between the Orient and its women, or more specifically the representation of woman as tradition and as the essence of the Orient, made it all the more important to lift the veil, for *unveiling and thereby modernizing the woman of the Orient signified the transformation of the Orient itself*. It is this metonymic association between tradition and woman that can explain the continual obsession and the fundamental weight given to women's unveiling as the privileged sign of progress. Taken as the most visible marker of tradition and religion, the veil provided the benevolent Western woman with what she had desired: a clinching example that interlocks "woman" and "tradition/Islam" so that it could be morally condemned in the name of emancipation. The veil is taken as the sign of the inherently oppressive and unfree nature of the entire tradition of Islam and Oriental cultures and by extension it is used as a proof of oppression of women in these societies. When the necessity to modernize these cultures was taken for granted, there was no hesitation in morally condemning the practice of veiling, for it was regarded as an impediment to modernization.

It is no coincidence that the desire to unveil the Oriental woman coincided with the broader agenda of "progress" and belief in the incompatibility of Islam with Western models of modernity and reason. Within this continual quest for a modern and civilized identity for Oriental women, Islam gained centrality in debates concerning the "woman question." The subordination of Oriental women was read off mainly from the Islamic cultural practices. Conceived as the indisputable emblem of Islamic culture's essential traditionalism, the veil was consistently seen as a problem and its lifting as the most important sign of reform and modernization. Within this constructed imagery of Muslim cultures, the harem, veil, and polygamy were highly charged symbols and they all functioned as synonyms of female oppression and nourished the colonial female desire with a most exquisite example for designating the target of change.[20] Grace Ellison, an English woman writing in the early twenties, expresses this very widespread trend in her representation of Turkish women: "the slavery of ages cannot be set aside in a few months, and the ladies continue to wear their thick black canvas veils over their faces."[21]

The privileged place accorded to woman within such discourses reveals what Lata Mani has convincingly demonstrated in the context of the debates on sati in colonial India: "women . . . became the site on which tradition was debated and reformulated. Thus, what was at stake was not women but tradition";[22] she is constructed as representing the inner, sacred, spiritual, and inviolable locus of the true, authentic identity of the culture. And it is precisely by being such a locus that she embodies the tradition and represents the nation's innermost essence.[23] Therefore, if a fundamental rupture from this traditional identity is to be achieved, then the ideals of progress and modernization have to be meticulously inscribed onto her; she has to be remade.

It is from this modernist position that Ruth Frances Woodsmall speaks in *Woman in the Changing Islamic System*. The book's main focus is on Muslim women's adjustment to the modern world. In a chapter typically entitled "Lifting the Veil," after declaring the veil as "the barometer of social change in the Moslem world," she identifies the progress and achievement of freedom with women's unveiling: "although there is no concerted move to discard the veil, one is conscious of a very strong urge for freedom which is symbolized by unveiling[24] . . . although there is little unveiling as individuals, there is a growth in freedom in collective unveiling."[25]

Among all the "signs of advancement," it is the native's conviction of the necessity of abandoning traditional customs which is regarded as the indisputable way to foster social "progress." Woodsmall regards women's and men's recognition of veiling as a problem more important than the unveiling itself: "that purdah is recognized by men and women alike as a national problem is the most helpful sign of advancement."[26] Such a recognition is fundamental not simply because its ensures that the desired change will be achieved, but it has also the power of bestowing an illusive agency onto the native herself and thereby making her the agent of her own subjection to Western norms of progress.

The association between the unveiling of women and the modernization of the Orient recalls the inner/outer distinction Chatterjee talks about.[27] The veil represents for the colonial gaze the Orient's/woman's mask; it is an exterior surface which is assumed to conceal the site of interiority, the essence of the culture, i.e. femininity as the embodiment of culture's authentic core. Like the female sphere of domesticity, which connotes "interiority," the veil signifies the true self of the Islamic culture, its spirituality, its quintessential and unchanging essence. I am referring here to a colonial fantasy structured or (over)determined by binary oppositions of the inside and outside or veiled and unveiled. And it is within such a condensed totality of signifiers that woman becomes, to borrow a phrase from Radhakrishnan, "the mute but necessary allegorical ground" for the discursive operations of imperial feminists. In turning woman to a signifier of interiority through associating her with tradition and by advocating the necessity of transforming the oppressive Islamic cultural practices by unveiling her, the discourse of imperial feminism in turn generates the divided topography of inside versus outside, and tradition versus modernity.

Allegedly, it is Western feminists who have, with their achievements of freedom, inspired and prepared the ground for the liberation of Oriental women. Woodsmall is a typical example of the attitude which takes Western feminist ideals as the norm:

In this movement towards the freer life of to-day, Eastern women have received much from the West. Social freedom, educational advance, economic independence, political privilege and participation in public life, the widening range of interests and activities of Eastern women – in short, the whole forward movement towards a free life for women has been inspired by the advance of women in the West. The feminist struggle in the West, to establish the principle of equality, has in no small measure prepared the way, so that men of affairs, nationalist leaders of the East to-day, have accepted equal opportunity for women as an inseparable element of Western progress.[28]

What is at stake in the unequivocal acceptance of Western feminists' lives and achievements as democratic, advanced, emancipated, in short as the *norm*, is the positing of a universal subject status for themselves, for after all it is their condition which represents the highest achievement of humanity. For example, despite her "awareness" of the possible dangers of Eurocentrism, Juliet Minces wants to retain the Western feminist ideal as a universal one:

Can the evolution of the condition of women in the Arab world be evaluated by the same criteria as in the West? Is it not Eurocentric to put forward the lives of Western women as the only democratic, just and forward-looking model? I do not think so. The demands of Western feminists seem to me to represent the greatest advance towards the emancipation of women as people. Ideally, the criteria adopted, like those for human rights generally should be *universal*.[29] (emphasis added)

Minces declares Western feminist achievements as the universal ideal without any further discussion of the content and context of specifically Western feminist ideals. This desire for a direct expression of universal feminist ideals in Western feminism is typical. The question here is not simply to criticize this, but also to understand what is at stake in such bold, dogmatic assertions. What kind of discursive or ideological mechanism is operating here? As Spivak suggests, it is by erasing his/her role as an investigator that the imperialist subject denies his/her own worlding and renders his/her own position transparent.[30] This preempting of their particular position provides the discursive ground for the constitution of the universality of the Eurocentric subject. The assertion of a universal norm could not have been possible without designating the achievements of Western women as the yardstick against which one can measure and define the goal other women must achieve. In other words, the declaration of an emancipated status for the Western woman is contingent upon the representation of the Oriental woman as her devalued other and this enables Western woman to identify and preserve the boundaries of self for herself. The deliberate confusion of their particularity and specificity with universalist norms has crucial implications for the subject status these women occupy. To be Western here implies feeling that one is entitled to universalize one's particular achievements and interests. The effacement/erasure of the particularity of Western women in the name of universality has the effect of legitimizing the colonial-feminist discourse as an act of generosity and as an act of conferring upon Middle East women the privilege of participating in Western women's universalism rather than a denial and negation of difference. As Spivak puts it, "if there is one universal, it cannot be inclusive of difference."[31] The attribution of a universal subject status to Western women should be understood as nothing but a "particular becoming dominant";[32] it is a particular that masquerades as universal. But it should be emphasized that not any particular has the power to enforce itself as universal. Nor is the command of the universal simply a result of prior attainment of such a status, but it is a consequence of an oppositional and hierarchical ordering of the universal and the particular. And, as Joan Scott points, it is important to recognize the effect of power in this ordering. Relegation to the status of the particular does not happen because difference and otherness is discriminated against. Rather, in following Scott, we can suggest that such discrimination occurs precisely because difference is relegated to the status of particularity and, more importantly, the particularity of difference is a product or effect of power and discrimination. It is "a process that establishes the superiority or the typicality or the universality of some in terms of the inferiority or atypicality or particularity of others." [33] This is a process which not only establishes a standard to exclude those who are different by defining them as other-than the norm, but operates first and foremost as a means of registering the relationship of difference and thereby as a means of securing a sovereign status to the subject of representation in a relation of contrast. It is a process that allows setting the self off from the particular and this is nothing other than centering oneself as universal. As David Lloyd cogently describes, the alleged neutrality and universality is at the same time a process that secures a sovereign status for the subject:

the position occupied by the dominant individual is that of the Subject without properties. This Subject with 'unlimited properties' is precisely the undetermined subject . . . Its universality is attained by virtue of literal indifference: this Subject becomes representative in consequence of being able to take anyone's place, of occupying any place, of a pure exchangeability. Universal where all others are particular, partial, this Subject is the perfect, disinterested judge formed for and by the public sphere.[34]

A similar universalizing gesture can be found in the collaborative work of Nicki Keddie and Louis Beck. In a striking statement, Keddie and Beck explicitly state that they are not interested in whatever satisfactions and positive aspects Middle Eastern women's lives may contain. In advance of a possible objection, they insist that they will keep the West as standard:

there is, by current Western standards and possibilities, something lacking in the lives of most Middle Eastern women, whatever satisfactions and positive features these lives may often contain . . . What most Middle Eastern women lack when compared either with their wealthier and better educated compatriots or with Western women of many social classes, is freedom of choice regarding basic life decisions.[35]

It is not surprising that such an ethnocentric representation reveals itself as the illusion of freedom of choice. It is always the "absence" of Western principles of progress and freedom which marks the Orient. What is lacking in Oriental women is indicative of a general deficiency in the culture at large. The result is not only the identification of what is Western with what is universal, but also the creation of an essentialist typology in which the distinction between East and West is conceived of as constitutively contrary and profoundly different. It is this absolute and systematic difference between the West and the Orient that is repeated (and evidenced) in the respective positions of their women.[36] In Woodsmall's words:

> The social systems of the East and West are established on *diametrically different principles*. The pivotal difference is the difference in the position of woman. In the *East* society has always been *based on the separation of the sexes and seclusion of women*, limiting their sphere to the home. Perhaps their power within this limited world has been considerable, but there are boundaries beyond which they have not been free to go. The *West* has *not sharply differentiated between the world of women and that of men*. Western society is built on the basis of unity, which may not mean equality, but which does not definitely place women in a sphere apart.[37] (emphasis added)

Woodsmall's discourse exemplifies here a typical feature of Orientalism, the creation of an absolute or radical difference between the West and East (what Said calls "epistemological and ontological distinction") in a way in which the East is seen as the negative opposite (characterized by lack, absence, etc.) of the West. This is indeed a *profoundly phallocentric* gesture, if we see phallocentrism not simply as "men oppressing women" but understand from it *a particular structuring of discourse where the law of the One operates*. The association of the West with modernity, progress, development, and freedom and the East with the opposites of these features is indeed a phallocentric gesture which is characterized by a binary logic of oppositions. Such a gesture, which associates the Orient with negativity, simultaneously construes it as that which is other-than the established norm. In this respect the actual content of the terms of the opposition is less important than the logic that posits the two as contrary and profoundly different. Within this oppositional structure, the Orient and the condition of its women are represented as the sites of devalued difference. Such a gesture provides the ground for the production and legitimation of a normative discourse where the West and the "free" and "liberated" condition of its women are taken as the norm. If the position of the Orient and its women are represented within such a dualist logic, then it follows that the colonial nature of this "feminist" discourse is not an exception but rather part of a system that requires the representation of difference as negativity to be able to posit the positivity of the norm. *Therefore, the colonial and phallocentric nature of such a feminist discourse is not an aberration, but rather a structural necessity of a discourse that represents otherness and difference as negativity*. The representation of the other as negativity, as devalued difference, remains a constant in Western thought. The logic that is operative here can be understood as the law of the one. There is a paradoxical mixture of "the same and yet different" in the logic that recognizes the Eastern woman's difference in so far as it is other-than the Western woman as the norm. In other words, the law of the one, the phallocentric gesture *par excellence*, is operative as long as a norm is erected.

Imperial self, colonial woman, and subjectivity

In an era where the intellectual and political scene is marked by attempts at dismantling the universalizing gesture of the Enlightenment project, all variants of difference remain a predominant preoccupation for academics, minority groups, and women. Ardent debates in the field of post-colonial criticism reveal universalism's origin in the European Enlightenment and make it harder for the notion of the universal to continue to serve as an alibi for a renewed imperialism. On the other hand, feminist criticism, particularly French feminist theory, has revealed the liaison between universalism and masculinism. It is man who claimed himself to be the sole inhabitant of it; women are excluded from this domain. As Monique Wittig notes, "the abstract form, the general, the universal – that is what the so-called masculine gender means . . . The universal has been and is continually at every moment, appropriated by men."[38] Since the universal is conceived of on the basis of one and access to it is restricted, the only possible way for women to enter into this privileged space and enjoy its benefits is through *imitating the masculine gesture*. In other words, they are allowed to enjoy the benefits of universality only if they assume a male position. The strange paradox here is that women's acceptance of a share in the universality simultaneously implies a denial of their difference. There is then no affirmative entry to the universal for women as women.

If, as I argued above, the universalizing operation is at the same time a phallocentric gesture, can we then remain comfortable in the belief that the appeals to Muslim women's emancipation along the allegedly universal achievements of Western women is simply an expression of benevolence, and that this benevolence is easily separable and distinct from the process of construction of an imperial subject status for Western women? It is important to note at this point that, although feminist theory has successfully revealed the phallocentric bind of the claims for neutrality and universality, it has nevertheless, by privileging sexual difference to other forms of difference, itself remained blind to the imperialist and ethnocentric bind of such a gesture.[39] The relegation of the pretensions of universality only into the domain of sexual difference carries the risk of dismissing the

phallocentric gesture in representations of cultural difference and the ethnocentric bind of phallocentrism. In fact, as my reading of the above
anthropological texts demonstrates, Western women's discourse on Middle
East women was enabled and fortified by an undeclared entanglement and
articulation with imperialism and phallocentrism. The apparently benign
appeals to a common good for universal womanhood and the presumption
that all women are being spoken for in the name of global sisterhood are
not free from colonial and masculinist fantasies of attaining a sovereign
subject status.

The sub-text of the desire to liberate Muslim women from the atrocities
perpetrated by Islamic culture was to attain a particular self-representa-
tion. As Antoinette Burton suggests, these "feminists deliberately cultivated the civilizing responsibility as their own modern womanly burden
because it affirmed an emancipated role for them in the imperial nation
state."[40] The attribution of an emancipated role to themselves helps these
women to disavow their own position at home, for "by thinking of themselves as all powerful and free *vis-à-vis* Egyptian women, Western women
could avoid confronting their own oppression at home."[41] In other words,
the failure of Western women, as the devalued others of men, to assume the
universal has motivated them to look for other means of claiming universality.

The modern notion of individual was one of the fundamental values valorized by Enlightenment ideology. This was a historical period in which
there was an incitement for women to desire a share in the emerging definitions of human and the individual. This was, in other words, a specific
moment in which profound transformations in economic as well as in traditional social and symbolic structures were taking place. During this period,
concomitant with the escalation of capitalist development in Western
Europe, the desire to be an autonomous, free, rational, and liberated
subject was in ascendance. However, despite the valorization of this new
vision of subjectivity, the social, political, economic, and symbolic conditions that were enforced by patriarchal power were far from granting
women a share in this emerging norm, for they functioned as the necessary
ground upon which men were able to erect their sense of sovereign subjectivity. In conflating the masculine (and Western) with the universal, the
Enlightenment discourse embarked on mechanisms of exclusion and
domination and thereby confined the feminine to a secondary position of
difference. In other words, the grand narrative of the Enlightenment relied
on the intrinsic and implicit linkage established between reason, individuality, and masculinity. The assumptions that govern Enlightenment notions
of individual imply a subject that is *rational, universal,* and, by extension,

male. In this respect, the Enlightenment marks the constitution of the subject/human/individual (in the political, ideological, and epistemological sense of the term) as *male*. However, the "false" universality claimed by and for the masculine cannot be separated from the colonization of the space of subjectivity by phallocentrism. The Enlightenment was able to posit its values by excluding women and racially and culturally different groups who were devalued in its hierarchical scale of power relations. For this reason, in order to be able to consolidate their sense of subjectivity women had to look for alternative avenues outside their own culture. The colonies in the nineteenth and twentieth centuries were deemed a suitable site for this endeavor, for such sites marked difference that was compatible for othering in the light of the prevalent dualistic logic where the marking of the different as other-than the norm was central in creating a sense of authoritative selfhood. In this respect, there was a *simulation of sovereign masculine discourse* by Western women. It is in the East that Western woman was able to become a full individual, which was the goal desired and promoted by the emerging modernist ideology. Hence, for Western women it was possible to achieve the desired subject status against a devalued *cultural difference*. Rosemary M. George, in examining the impact of imperialism on women's attainment of an authoritative selfhood, notes that the "modern individual woman was first and foremost an imperialist."[42] The invention of the new vision of woman-as-subject was therefore built upon and took off from the dualistic model of phallogocentric logic which identified the male as the referent of the universal subject and thereby installed the mechanism of exclusion as the ground of (Western) feminist discourse. Hence, it is not far-fetched to argue that Western woman's recognition of herself as a subject was possible only outside national boundaries, in the encounter of a *sexually same yet culturally different other*. Gayatri Spivak's comment on the impact of imperialism on feminist individualism is insightful here:

what is at stake, for feminist individualism in the age of imperialism, is precisely the making of human beings, the constitution and "interpellation" of the subject not only as individual but as "individualist." . . . As the female individualist, not quite/not male, articulates herself in shifting relationship to what is at stake, the "native female" as such (within discourse *as* a signifier) is excluded from any share in this emerging norm.[43]

The scopic regime of colonialism

If the colonial feminist discourse on Muslim women can be read in the light of Enlightenment ideology, then we also need to explain the reasons why it was specifically the *unveiling* of women which was taken as one of the fundamental signs of progress and emancipation. What does the myth of liberation through unveiling have to do with the predominant rationalist epistemological paradigm and the assumptions that govern the production of knowledge which were historically and conceptually coextensive with or built into the Enlightenment project?

How is the *discourse of Enlightenment* (characterized by the privileging of reason, truth, and progress) and the *scopic regime of modernity* (characterized by the valorization of the visual) articulated? What are the points of intersection between the episteme of the Enlightenment and the regimes of visibility? How do these two orders act upon each other? If modernity and Enlightenment mark the triumph of the will to possess, master, and control with the correlative privileging of a disinterested, invisible, disembodied, objectively observing and recording subject, then how are the desire to know, desire to unveil, desire to see linked in the quest for colonial mastery? If the project of Enlightenment is inseparable from the privileging of visibility, can it then be argued that there was a connection between the imperial feminist gesture's desire to unveil the Muslim woman and the desire to master, control, and reshape that body by making it available for vision and thereby for knowledge?

Modern disciplinary power wove together knowledge, vision/seeing, and the techniques of rational control and productive domination. In other words, as Foucault's discussion of the panopticon demonstrates, the age of modernity/Enlightenment was an age marked by a desire for total control and mastery (of the body) based on the notion of perfect visibility. In the light of this Foucauldian insight, the political rationality that shaped the logic behind the colonial feminist project's concern with the unveiling of women can best be made sense of if we can locate it within the context of principles of modern disciplinary power which is concerned with actively shaping individual minds and bodies based on the knowledge acquired by rendering them perfectly visible. As I suggested above, the ethnographic discourse on Middle East women was part and parcel of the Enlightenment project which was predicated upon the constitution of a sovereign subject status for the subject of representation. Can we also understand the expression of the desire to unveil as a resurfacing of the same modernist/Enlightenment project which is characterized by its adamant ocularcentrism?

Vision, with its accompanying imagery of the unveiling of truth, is figured as the key instrument of knowledge. The privileging of the visual in Western culture has surfaced in a wide variety of spheres. In philosophy it is expressed as the "mirror of nature" as demonstrated by Richard Rorty,[44] or in the "society of surveillance" exemplified by the panoptic gaze, which is examined by Foucault,[45] or as Luce Irigaray[46] demonstrates, in the privileging of the phallic gaze which can be discerned in Freud's and Lacan's scenarios of sexual curiosity and difference. Despite these sophisticated attempts to examine the role and privileging of vision in the field of philosophy, in the emergence of modern forms of power and psychoanalytic theory, the problematic of seeing and the consequent attempts to master and control the colonial other have not been addressed in the context of colonialism. It is this connection that I would like to bring to the fore in this section.

As Martin Jay shows, the dominant visual model of the modern era is characterized by the combination of Renaissance notions of perspective and by the Cartesian ideas of subjective rationality in philosophy, which he calls Cartesian perspectivalism.[47] The valorization of the visual in Cartesian perspectivalism implies a certain epistemological project in which the gaze is considered as the central agent in the acquisition of knowledge of the world of nature in the most objective way possible. Hence the gaze was aimed at recording the observable. However, in nature not everything is observable; it is at the same time a world where *truth is concealed by appearances*. It is the role of the gaze to penetrate the hidden essence by piercing the veil that is assumed to cover it. The investigative gaze that is directed at the object is a particularly detached one. This means that the observer's entanglement in his emotions has to be withdrawn; this is the gaze of, as Jay puts it, the dispassionate eye of the neutral observer. What this implies is a "privileging of an ahistorical, disinterested and disembodied subject entirely outside of the world it claims to know only from afar."[48] As Jay further notes, the subject position created for this scrutinizing gaze in the Cartesian perspectivalist epistemology is one that is construed as universal and transcendental, i.e. the characteristic subject position of the Enlightenment paradigm. Within the modernist problematic of vision, the point from which vision is directed is assumed to be male in all its disembodiedness. As I suggested above, this disembodied universal subject is the prototype of masculine subject and in all its disembodiedness it is a panoptically positioned observer, an omnipotent eye that is positioned as invisible and can see without being seen.

A similar dialectic of visuality can be seen operating in the nineteenth-century realist tradition. In his *Body Work*, Peter Brooks demonstrates the inextricable link between the scopophilic and the epistemophilic projects, that is, between the desire to see and the erotic investment in knowing.[49] Suggesting that the desire to know is inseparable from sexual desire and curiosity, Brooks demonstrates how the desire to see is simultaneously a desire to possess and and a desire to know. As they are closely intermingled, it can be suggested that any desire for knowledge is closely tied to the desire for mastery. The object that is subjected to such an appropriating gaze is both an object of hostility and an object of fascination and these are expressed as a continual quest for knowledge. The convergence of the erotic investment in seeing and the epistemic principles of realist vision has manifested itself most notably in the narratives of the body. The model of intellectual inquiry, curiosity, and research is characterized by a visual inspection of reality. While positivist sciences were aiming to achieve a mastery over the world of nature through a scrutinizing and objectivizing gaze, there was a simultaneous proliferation of discourses trying to master the body through visual inspection. Vision has thus been construed as the central instrument and metaphor in the search for truth that is presumed to be veiled. The uncovering of truth thus becomes a process of unveiling, and revelation, and a process of stripping the obstacle that prevents its immediate comprehension. Brooks refers to Barthes's characterization of the nineteenth-century tradition as a strip-tease narrative to further illustrate how the visual has been valorized as the privileged instrument in attaining the truth.[50] According to Barthes the realist narrative is predicated upon the hope of knowing the end of the story. What allows the reader to experience pleasure is not simply the point of arrival or what is finally to be unveiled but the promise of an eventual unveiling of the truth. For Barthes, the desire to know the end of the story coalesces with the hope of seeing the genitals. Hence a fetishistic attention on articles of clothing, accessories as objects of fascination that need eventually to be pulled down. In his reading of Gustave Flaubert's (as the realist *par excellence*) *Emma Bovary*, Brooks demonstrates that the pursuit of truth implies an erotic pursuit of nudity, as nudity implies an act of exposing and laying bare the body that is considered to be the ultimate object of knowledge. In a tradition governed by a patriarchal economy, the body that needs to be unveiled is always the body of a woman and the gaze is a masculine one. The desire for knowledge and the secrets of that body becomes the means of mastering the feminine and the truth.[51]

In harmony with the dominant Western speculative or scopic tradition,[52] the colonial imagery of this period was governed by the same epistemology and the scopophilic imagination, by the desire for mastery through the knowledge acquired by vision. The project of liberating the Oriental woman through unveiling her is inseparable from the mechanism of a subjectifying gaze that is supported by the desire to know her. The visual/scopic drive implicit in all representation is brought out with particular intensity in the field of colonial power. As Bhabha notes, "in order to conceive of the colonial subject as the effect of power that is productive . . . one has to see the *surveillance* of colonial power functioning in relation to the regime of the *scopic drive.*"[53]

The imperial feminist desire to unveil is enabled and conditioned by such a social, epistemological, scientific, and cultural milieu. It is in a culture where the entire epistemology is characterized and dominated by a speculative or scopic tradition that the desire to unveil the Oriental woman can emerge as the precondition of her liberation. In this regard it is not an exaggeration to say that the body of the veiled Oriental woman is very much in the field of vision; she is the object of a look that turns her into a particular object of fascination and fixation. As Barthes's strip-tease metaphor reminds, the dress and all other obstacles that prevent the colonial gaze from obtaining knowledge about these women need to be removed.

Looking where there is nothing to see, the imperial women's desire to know becomes disoriented when she looks at the other/woman ("they are everywhere and nowhere" as the French general puts it during the Dahar insurrection in North Africa), for it is a knowledge that can only ever actualize itself by yielding the other visible. The unveiling of the Oriental woman thus ensures a "panoptic" position for the colonial subject. Such a visibility ensures a system of surveillance which is the precondition of interventive and "corrective" practices of colonial governmentality. By rendering the veiled body perfectly visible, the colonial, observing subject assures his/her own invisible, unmarked and thereby universal position, for as Peter Brooks suggests, "the body [is] relentlessly presented by an invisible observer who can be variously situated in the place of observing characters . . . but *in his very mobility and lack of identity is also panoptical.*"[54] The position of the panoptic subject of the colonial discourse correlates with the "universal" (i.e. unmarked and invisible) position of the sovereign subject of colonial discourse. For this reason, the imperial feminist desire to emancipate the Muslim woman is part of a system based on the disciplining and normalizing gaze of modern colonial disciplinary power. It is therefore a desire which implies an investment of power which is at the same time a subjective investment: while the other woman's body, life, subjectivity is rendered visible, this imperial gesture has the implicit function of making the Western woman's sovereign subject status entirely invisible. Therefore, it is important to point out how knowledge and vision are part of an interlocking desire for modern, disciplinary colonial governing, for such a desire is also part of the sadistic desire to physically master the object of gaze by ripping it apart.[55] Thus Western woman's relation to her Oriental counterpart was conditioned and nourished by the occulocentrism of the whole rationalist and epistemological tradition of Enlightenment. As several feminist philosophers have emphasized, this scopic desire also needs to be read as a masculine gesture, for within the established conviction of visibility, it is the woman's sexual organ that is taken to be illustrative of what is unseeable and hidden.

As Braidotti notes, "seeing is the prototype of knowing. By elaborating a scientific technique for analyzing the bodily organs, Western sciences put forward the assumption that a body is precisely that which can be seen and looked at . . ."[56] Unveiling (both literal and figurative) guarantees that the Muslim woman's body becomes knowable, mainly, as I suggested before, because within the modernist tradition knowing means rendering the object observable, visible, and thereby manipulable. If the target of territorial imperialism is to de-territorialize and then re-territorialize the land of the native, the target of the imperial feminist project, directed towards unveiling, is to *alter the embodiment of the other woman by inscribing it according to different cultural, social, symbolic codes*. Before I elaborate this point further let me discuss how embodiment needs to be conceptualized and why it is important to posit the notion of a *bodily materiality* to be able to understand that it is the body that is located at the center of the techniques of colonial control and domination. The acknowledgment of the corporeal roots of the subjectivity is also crucial in another sense, for understanding the body as the mark of the embodied nature of subjectivity is essential not only for a *materialist* but also for the *culturally specific* nature of the body and bodily difference.

The veiled embodiment: sartorial fabric-ation of the Muslim woman's body

How can we think of the veil and embodiment together? Can we read veiling simply as an instrument of oppression? Or should we conceive of veiling and unveiling in terms of the bodily affects such practices imply? How should we conceptualize the relationship between discourses, practices, norms about dressing and the embodiment? What kind of an understanding of the body can enable us to understand corporeality in culturally and sexually specific terms, in their concrete specificities? What kind of presumptions about subjectivity and body need to be scrutinized and challenged so as to posit the bodily roots of subjectivity?

Feminist theory is witnessing heated discussions about the status of the body. Increasingly, emphasis is placed upon the need for a materialist conception of the body, for the embodied nature of subjectivity and sexual difference. Feminist theorists who emphasize the usefulness of post-structuralism for feminist theory, such as Elizabeth Grosz, Judith Butler, Rosi Braidotti, Vicki Kirby, and others, point to the need for understanding the body as an effect of historically specific technologies of power. Foucault's analysis shows how the body does not stand in an external relation to power, but is marked, stamped, invested, acted upon, inscribed, and cultivated by a historically contingent nexus of power/ discourse; that is how it is brought into being by power.[57] Power is the productive principle through which the materiality of the subject is constituted. Such a constitution takes place through processes of training, shaping, cultivation, and investment of the body by power. Power takes the body as its target, the object, the medium to extract information so as to transform, remake, reinscribe, and subject it to the functioning of power. However, the subjection and control of the body within the field of power must not be understood through a model of repression. The Foucauldian approach challenges the understanding of subjection of the body to power as a simple process of subordination or as a repression of its desires and instincts. As Butler, following the Foucauldian insight puts it, "this 'subjection', or *assujettisement*, is not only a subordination but a securing and maintaining, a putting in place of a subject, a subjectification."[58] Therefore, the formation and regulation of bodies in their materiality cannot be understood separately from their subjectification, for subjectification implies both a creative and a coercive process simultaneously. As Foucault argues:

the body is also directly involved in a political field; power relations have an immense hold upon it; they invest it, mark it, train it, torture it, force it to carry tasks, to perform ceremonies, to emit signs. This political investment of the body is bound up, in accordance with complex reciprocal relationships, with its economic use; it is largely as a force of production that the body is invested with relations of power and domination; but on the other hand, its constitution as labor power is possible only if it is caught up in a system of subjection . . . the body becomes a useful force only if it is both a productive body and a subjected body.[59]

Understanding power as a productive and formative process requires a questioning of the presumptions of the paradigms which conceive of the subject in terms of the primacy of mind and the concomitant assumption of the body's naturalness and precultural status. As Elizabeth Grosz persuasively argues, bodies are not ahistorical, precultural, or presocial: they are in no way natural, but always-already marked, inscribed, and engraved by social pressures.[60] In emphasizing that bodies cannot be adequately understood if they are seen as impregnable by cultural, social, and historical factors, Grosz's aim is to underline the fact that power produces bodies always as a *determinate* type; bodies are neither universal nor neutral, but always culturally, sexually, racially specific. To liberate the body from its colonization by the paradigms which privilege the mind in understandings of subjectivity will not only enable us to posit its *materiality* but also foster an understanding of bodies in their sexual, cultural, and racial *specificities*. In a way, raising the question of the *specificity* of the body requires simultaneously raising the question of its *materiality*, for questions regarding the differences between bodies can only be meaningfully asked if the corporeality of bodies is no longer seen as biological, natural, and neutral, but always as a product, an effect of power relations which constitutes them in their specificities.

To be able to develop a materialist conception of the body, the body as an affect of power/knowledge nexus, we need to formulate theories that have the force and capacity to overcome the various dualisms through which the body is traditionally envisioned. As Grosz shows, among the most pertinent oppositions that need to be displaced for exploring and developing an understanding of the body other than that offered by-traditional philosophical and phallogocentric understanding are the body–mind, nature–culture, and discourse–referent.[61] Following Grosz, we can suggest that the constituted nature of the body does not imply that the effectivity of discourses (among all of them medicine and biology occupy a privileged place) on the body should be seen as limited to the shaping and influencing of the mind, for such an understanding implies that there is a biological, natural, real, material body on the one hand, and there are various cultural and historical representations of it. The controlling, making, and marking of bodies are not realized through the control of ideas. Such inscriptions are not merely added to a body that is naturally and biologically given. If a materialist notion of corporeality implies that power operates by constituting the subject's biological make-up, then positing the body's naturalness as prior to its inscription needs to be seen as an effect of power. As Butler notes, the representation of the body as preceding signification is itself an effect of signification and of power: "the body posited as prior to the sign, is always *posited* or *signified* as *prior*. This signification produces as an *effect* of its own procedure the very body that it nevertheless and simultaneously claims to discover as that which *precedes* its own action."[62] The notion of a biological or natural body is the very discourse which neutralizes and universalizes the cultural, racial, sexual specificity of different bodies. In fact such a universalizing and neutralizing gesture is the gesture of phallogocentrism which preempts the embodied nature of the masculine subject, a gesture which conflates the human with masculine and thus marks women as the site of embodiment. As Braidotti notes:

Simone de Beauvoir observed fifty years ago that the price men pay for representing the universal is a kind of loss of embodiment; the price women pay, on the other hand, is a loss of subjectivity and the confinement of the body. The former are disembodied and through this process gain entitlement to transcendence and subjectivity, the latter are overembodied and thereby consigned to immanence.[63]

The notion of the body as the stuff of inscription of social norms, practices, and values can be extended to the discussion of veiling and the positioning of Muslim women's bodies within Western representations. We can bring a different perspective to the taken-for-granted presumption about the cruelty and primitiveness of veiling when we recognize the possibility of the inscription of bodies through various practices of adornment, clothing, cosmetics, and so on. If veiling can be seen as a specific practice of marking and disciplining the body in accordance with cultural requirements, so can unveiling. In other words, the practice both of veiling and unveiling are culturally specific procedures of corporeal inscriptions, conditioned by specific cultural histories. What needs to be examined here is the presumption of the truth and naturalness of the unveiled body that the discourse of colonial feminism is predicated upon. However, if veiling is a specific practice of situating the body within the prevailing exigencies of power, so is unveiling. Therefore, the unveiled body is no less marked or inscribed; rather a whole battery of disciplinary techniques and practices have produced Western women's bodies and therefore not-to-veil needs to be seen as one among many practices of corporeal inscriptions. In other words, there is nothing natural about unveiling and therefore not-to-veil is no less inscriptive than being veiled. Not-to-veil is also another way of turning the flesh into a particular type of body. However, the body that is not veiled is taken as the norm for specifying a general, cross-culturally valid notion of what a feminine body is and must be. Hence the presumption of the naturalness of not-to-be-veiled has come to secure the truth of bodies and is used as the universal norm to yield Muslim woman as a knowable and comprehensible entity for the West. In other words, it is the naturalness and truth of the unveiled body which legitimates and endorses colonial feminist sentiments and certitude in the necessity of interventionist action against Muslim women's veiling. Although the beliefs and values about not veiling are also incorporated in the existential and embodied being of Western women, the fact that this is a culturally specific inscription is effaced in colonial feminist representations. Such an effacement ensures that the beliefs and values that produce Western women's bodies stand in for the truth of women universally. They are used as the explanatory norm to unravel the desires and pleasures of bodies that are located in other histories and cultures: one culture's coding of bodies becomes the template through which all bodies are conjured. Veiling is one of those practices that irritates the Western, especially feminist cognizance; it is one of those practices, like incision and various other body markings, that incite anxiety. Practices and processes by which other bodies are marked have appeared to the Western eye to be excessively violent, barbaric, and indisputable proof of the cruelty to which Muslim women are subjected. The disciplinary techniques and procedures that inscribe, control, and train other-Muslim bodies are distinguished from the "civilized," Western techniques and practices by the degree of barbarism inflicted upon the former. Emphasizing the culturally specific nature of embodiment reveals, however, that the power exercised upon bodies by veiling is no more cruel or barbaric than the control, supervision, training, and constraining of bodies by other practices, such as bras, stiletto heels, corsets, cosmetics, and so on.

If bodies are produced through various cultural practices, then their desires, pains and pleasures must be specific to particular cultures. If this is so, then the truth of veiled women and their bodies cannot easily be retrieved within the terms of the colonial feminist discourse, for it is a discourse which is already a cultural product, enabled and conditioned by dominant discourses. The foreignness of the veiled body is assumed to be deciphered by being translated and neutralized within an economy of universal truth.

The body is the medium through which power operates and functions and knowledge is the major instrument power utilizes for this operation. It is also through the exercise of power that knowledge from bodies can be extracted, and this knowledge in turn functions as the main instrument in the control, inscription, and training of bodies. Following Foucault on the issue of the power/knowledge nexus, we can suggest that power and knowledge are the condition of existence of each other. Power is transformed, altered, modified, intensified in accordance with the diversification and alterations in the order of knowledges.

The intertwined relation between power and knowledge can be extended to the ways in which Muslim women's bodies are positioned within colonial discourse. The exercise of colonial control implied in unveiling was a way of seizing hold of Muslim bodies. This seizure required knowledge and information to be extracted about them. But this knowledge required rendering them visible in the first instance, for, as I have argued above, visibility in the Enlightenment ideology is regarded as the precondition of the possibility of true knowledge. It was only by rendering Muslim women's bodies visible that they became capable of being recodified, redefined, and reformulated according to new, Western codes. The regime and control involved in colonial power needs the creation of docile, obedient subjects.

This is indeed a fundamental characteristic of colonial power which the commanders of the French army articulated in their own way. The following are the words of a French general in his study of the lessons of the Dahar insurrection in North Africa in the nineteenth century:

In effect the essential thing is to gather into groups this people which is everywhere and nowhere; the essential thing is to make them something we can seize hold of. When we have them in our hands, we will then be able to do many things which are quite impossible for us today and which will perhaps allow us to capture their minds after we have captured their bodies.[64]

Although the general's body–mind distinction is rather non-Foucauldian, the essence of his argument can only be understood through a Foucauldian approach. In his discourse, the people appear to be veiled indeed, they are visible and invisible, everywhere and nowhere. The fundamental question is to "seize hold of them," and the capture which the general articulates does not aim at repression in a simple sense, but at the *production* of "minds" and of course "bodies." By conceptualizing the interlocking of bodies and discursive regimes, Foucault enables us to understand the process of subject constitution in modern society. As a body subject to modern, colonial technology of power-knowledge, the colonized should be produced as a new body and mind with certain skills, characteristics, and form; she/he needs to be re-made. But to understand this re-mapping and re-territorialization, we need to position the body of the other within a frame which can account for it as a historical and cultural effect of power. The other's particular mode of corporeality is an important site for colonial inscriptions of power, as the desire to get hold of the native woman's body is evoked as the metaphor of colonial occupation (hence French colonialism's obsession with unveiling the Algerian women). If veiling is one of the instruments of coding Muslim women's bodies and their embodied nature of subjectivity, then what bodily implications might unveiling have for these women? The following quotation from Frantz Fanon is worth citing here as he describes the bodily transformations an Algerian woman undergoes when she is unveiled:

The body of the young Algerian woman in traditional society is revealed to her by its coming to maturity and by the veil. The veil covers the body and disciplines it, tempers it, at the very time when it experiences its phase of greatest effervescence. The veil protects, reassures, isolates. One must have heard the confessions of Algerian woman or have analyzed the dream content of certain recently unveiled women to appreciate the importance of the veil for the body of the woman. Without the veil she has an impression of her body being cut up into bits, put adrift; the limbs seem to lengthen indefinitely. When the Algerian woman has to cross a street, for a long time she commits errors of judgment as to the exact distance to be negotiated.

The unveiled body seems to escape, to dissolve. She has an impression of being improperly dressed, even of being naked. She experiences a sense of incompleteness with great intensity. She has the anxious feeling that something is unfinished, and along with this a frightful sensation of disintegrating. *The absence of the veil distorts the Algerian woman's corporal pattern. She quickly has to invent new dimensions for her body, new means of muscular control.* She has to create for herself an attitude of unveiled-woman-outside. She must overcome all timidity, all awkwardness . . . and at the same time be careful not to overdo it, not to attract notice to herself. *The Algerian woman who walks stark naked into the European city relearns her body, reestablishes it in a totally revolutionary fashion.*[65] (emphasis added)

Fanon draws our attention to one of the most striking instances of the cultural violence of colonialism. He also suggests that the veil is not simply attire that covers the woman's body, but it is what transforms a little girl into a woman in Muslim society. It is because her mature female body is made by the veil that unveiling her is not simply an uncovering, or change of dress, but *peeling her skin off.* In this sense, the so-called dream hallucinations which she experiences are very real sensations which have parallels in the everyday, "normal" experiences of crossing a street or simply walking out in the street. As Kaja Silverman notes, clothing (and veiling should be seen as one particular style among many) has the force of constituting identity and corporeality: "clothing exercises as profoundly determining an influence upon living, breathing bodies . . . affecting contours, weight, muscle development, posture movement and libidinal circulation. Dress is one of the most important cultural implements for articulating and territorializing human corporeality – for mapping its erotogenic zones and for affixing a sexual identity."[66]

Following Silverman, then, we can see the veil, that sartorial matter, as not something that is external to the identity of Muslim women, but as a fundamental piece conjoined with the embodied subjectivity of Muslim woman. If we cannot comfortably assume that her body is inside the veil or the veil is something that is outside of her body and hence does not function merely as a body cover, can we then think of bringing this body outside the veil (as colonial or imperial feminism desires) without at the same time exercising another form of power? If the veil is part of her body, *part of her being-in-the-world,* then it differs from a simple cover that has an inside and an outside; its "function" cannot be captured by such categorical oppositions. The veil can indeed be understood as the Derridean reading of hymen which has "the structure of *and/or,* between *and* and *or.*"[67] As a "confusion" between a set of opposites, the veil or hymen embraces both terms; it is in-between them. As Derrida puts it, "it is an operation that *both* sows confusion *between* opposites *and* stands *between* the opposites 'at once.' What counts here is the *between,* the in-between-ness of the hymen. The hymen 'takes place' in the 'inter-,' in the spacing between desire and fulfillment, between perpetration and its recollec-tion."[68]

As the in-between of outside and inside, the veil makes both inside and outside possible. There would indeed be no inside-outside without the veil. It is what constructs a before and a behind. But there would also be no veil without the inside and outside that it makes possible by separating and con-structing. In the ambiguous position it occupies, the veil is not outside the woman's body. Nor is she the interior that needs to be protected or pene-trated. *Her body is not simply the inside of the veil: it is of it; "she" is con-stituted in (and by) the fabric-ation of the veil.* Being an undecidable text-ile, the veil interweaves the woman's skin with its threads; as the sign of fusion it stitches together the epidermus of woman with cultural codings. It is both her identity and her difference, or it is what makes her identity different. The veil is that which produces woman, or difference; it is spacing, *différance.*[69]

By assuming an interiority that is concealed by the veil, colonial gesture articulates itself in terms of the Western metaphysical or philosophical oppositions between origin and representation, essence and appearance, identity and difference. A number of writers have pointed to the funda-mental continuity and homology between the structure of Western meta-physics and phallocentric order.[70] There is thus a fundamental affinity or a chain of equivalence among Western philosophical, colonial and patriar-chal discourses. This implies that any serious challenge to patriarchy can not overlook questions of colonial discourse, for both are placed within a larger cultural project whose fundamental philosophical assumptions need to be questioned. To assume that these questions are separate from each other is the very illusion that the categorical-analytic discourse of Reason produces. A feminist discourse which tries to emancipate others should in the first place learn how to question this very process of other-ing, and what this implies for its "own" "identity" (that is to say, whether a discourse can be both a discourse of identity and sameness under the governance of Reason and Progress and a feminist one at the same time). Such a ques-tioning should of course include the questioning of the very opposition between inside and outside as one of the fundamental cultural oppositions which constructs femininity itself.

The veil is dress, but a dress which we might consider as articulating the very identity of Muslim women. Only if we see the veiling of woman in Muslim culture as a unique cultural experience, we can then actually learn about what it is to veil or unveil as woman, rather than simply re-setting the liberal scene and repeating commonsensical and clichéd standards in the name of universal emancipation. I want to argue here that such commonsensical and clichéd standards may not be so commonsensical and clichéd after all. They may, on the contrary, be part of a colonial gesture that is hard to define as colonial because, especially in a now de-colonized world, it articulates itself as a universal, and politically and morally correct task.

5

The battle of the veil: woman between Orientalism and nationalism

> Nationalism . . . seeks to represent itself in the image of the Enlightenment and fails to do so. For Enlightenment itself, to assert its sovereignty as the universal ideal, needs its Other; if it could ever actualize itself in the real world as the truly universal, it would in fact destroy itself.
>
> Partha Chatterjee, *Nationalist Thought and the Colonial World*

Nationalism as Orientalism and the question of gender

Whenever I evoked, in various scholarly meetings and conversations in the US, the power of Orientalism to understand the place the veil occupies in such constructions I have consistently encountered the somewhat suspicious remark as to whether, by locating the question of the veil within the problematic of Orientalism, I am not overlooking the question of Muslim women's oppression at "home" by Islam and indigenous patriarchy. Such remarks are usually followed by a set of questions which demand that I deliver the "truth" about women in Muslim societies, the conditions under which they live, and so on. In other words, what the Western audience desires to hear is the native's own voice, the true and authentic story of the situation of women in Muslim societies, as opposed to the negative Orientalist stereotypes. This liberal desire to turn me into a native informant and thereby re-value the weak and the subjugated is the very gesture by which the sovereign Western subject constructs himself/herself as considerate and benevolent. More importantly, such a quest implies that the question of Orientalism is not fully grasped, for the unspoken assumption in such questions is that indigenous patriarchal domination and Orientalist hegemony are two separate issues. But although the notions of authenticity and nativism appear to be the opposite of Orientalism, they are in fact the very product of Orientalist hegemony. To understand the interconnections between the two, we need to remember two crucial axioms of Said's work: "Orientalism Orientalizes the Orient" and "Orientalism is based upon an epistemological and ontological distinction between the Orient and the Occident." I will argue in this chapter that if we follow the spirit of Said's analysis we can no longer treat the oppression of women by indigenous patriarchy and by colonialism as two separate issues. As Said himself comments: "imperialism is after all a cooperative venture."[1] To pose the "truth" of the Orient as distinct from the Orientalist discourse and to construct a nativist position outside Orientalism is indeed to reproduce the division imposed by Orientalism. In what follows, I will attempt to illustrate how Orientalist discourse has reproduced itself in the Orient via nationalist projects whose fundamental principle was based upon the imperial divide between the Westerner and the native. In doing so I will examine how the veil has been articulated to the nationalist projects in Algeria and Turkey. I hope to show how, in the battle between nationalism and imperialism, it is the question of woman which is "doubly in shadow," as Spivak puts it.[2] In the light of these concerns, I hope my reluctance to satisfy the benevolent subject's desire to hear the "native's" voice will be seen as my resistance to participate in the Orientalist divide between the "truth of the native" and the Western construction of it.

In the essay I have referred to above, Said shows how the search for an authentic national origin that characterizes nationalist/nativist anti-imperialist discourse is itself dictated by the colonial history and thus "the cultural horizons of nationalism are fatally limited by the common history of the colonizer and the colonized assumed by the nationalist movement itself . . . Both the master and the slave participate in it, and both grew up in it, albeit unequally."[3] The Orientalization of the Orient can be read in the modernization attempts undertaken by the indigenous elites which aim to "develop" and "civilize" the native population. For Said, such modernizing trends are in fact the resurfacing of the nineteenth-century imperial division between the native and the Westerner. Thus speaking the language of authenticity or resorting to national origins in no way guarantees that the colonized is outside the structure of imperialism. On the contrary, as Said puts it:

The colonized may . . . speak and write in the dominant language even as he or she tries simultaneously to recover a native original, may even act in ways that directly conflict with the over-all interests of his/her people, and still the divide remains. This it seems to me has always been the case in every colonial relationship, because it is the first principle of imperialism that there is a clear-cut and absolute hierarchical distinction between ruler and ruled.[4]

The fundamental homology and complicity between the nationalist and Orientalist discourses have also been cogently demonstrated by Partha Chatterjee in his *Nationalist Thought and the Colonial World*. According to Chatterjee, in trying to approximate the characteristics of modernity, nationalist thought reveals a basic contradiction that lies at its core: the attainment of those values implies its subjugation to the Western hegemony that it wants to combat. This explains why one of the characteristic features of nationalism is a basic split that divides it: while it aspires to become modern and achieve the "valued" qualities of Enlightenment, at the same time it asserts its autonomous identity by claiming an authentic, pure, and uncontaminated origin. It therefore simultaneously accepts and refutes the epistemic and moral dominance of the West. It is precisely this split character of nationalist ideology, Chatterjee argues, which could explain why non-European countries constantly try to approximate to Western modernity in spite of the fact that such an approximation implies their subjugation. The distinction Chatterjee makes, by utilizing the conceptual tools provided by Althusser, Merleau-Ponty, Sartre, and Said, between the *thematic* and the *problematic*, illustrates more fully how nationalism is complicit with the project of imperialism and thereby sustains the legacies of Orientalism and Eurocentricism. According to Chatterjee, "the thematic refers to an epistemological and ethical system which provides a framework of elements and rules for establishing relations between elements; the problematic, on the other hand, consists of concrete statements about possibilities justified by reference to the thematic."[5] By applying this distinction to the question of nationalism, Chatterjee observes that "the problematic in nationalist thought is exactly the reverse of that of Orientalism," in the sense that the object still remains the Oriental except that he or she is now endowed with subjectivity; he/she is not passive and non-participating. Being just a reverse of the passive subject, the native continues to retain the same essential characteristics depicted in Orientalism, but nevertheless imagines himself as autonomous, active, and sovereign. Concerning the thematic, Chatterjee argues that "nationalist thought accepts and adopts the same essentialist conception based on the distinction between 'the East' and 'the West,' the same typology created by a transcendent studying subject, and hence the same 'objectifying' procedures of knowledge constructed in the post-Enlightenment age of Western science."[6] While nationalist thought rejects the immediate political implications of colonialist thought and interrogates its knowledge and truth claims and refutes its moral claims, it still remains hostage to the categories of Eurocentric thought by continually aspiring to modernize and progress. It thus inhabits two antagonistic discursive spaces at once. This implies that nationalist thought is inherently contradictory, because the framework upon which it builds itself is at the same time the framework of colonial power which it wants to renounce. Despite the structural homology between the two it is misleading to assume that nationalist thought is nothing but a mere duplication of Orientalist discourse. Chatterjee warns us that the relation between the two is not one of mere correspondence. Rather, "nationalist thought is selective about what it takes from Western rational thought."[7] Since its immediate political target is to object to colonial rule, it therefore has to be selective about what it takes from the West. It also needs to assert its difference from the colonialist thought that seeks to dominate it. As Chatterjee puts it: "a different discourse, yet one that is dominated by another."[8] Understanding what nationalism selects from colonialist thought and why it selects what it selects will also help us to understand how the signifier "woman" is employed in nationalist discourse.

In supplying an ideological principle of selection, the nationalist paradigm in fact utilizes the distinction between the material and the spiritual. It is through the mapping of this opposition onto the distinction between outside and inside that the woman's question is articulated to nationalist discourse. In another essay Chatterjee suggests that one of the principles upon which nationalism is built is the separation of the domain of culture into material and spiritual spheres.[9] The material sphere is construed as the site which the nationalist project needs to rationalize and thereby reform the vestiges of traditional culture, for if it wants to defeat colonialism it must have the knowledge of the superior techniques of the West. Moreover, Chatterjee argues, it is not a question of dismissing modernity but of making it compatible with the project of nationalism. This implies that the incorporation of Western principles of rationality and technological development need to be limited to the material world; the spiritual essence of culture must remain uncontaminated by the West, otherwise the features that make the East superior and distinct from the West would disappear and the self-identity of the nation would be threatened. In answering the question of what to take from the West and what to reject, the material/spiritual opposition provided a useful framework of selection for nationalists. The material domain is deemed less important; it is the spiritual, inner side where the true self of the nation resides. The West succeeded in subjugating the outer world of the natives. However, they remained undominated in the spiritual, inner side; their essential identity remained intact. The opposition between the material and the spiritual has been mapped onto the gender question. Chatterjee explains this mapping in the following manner:

Now apply the inner/outer distinction to the matter of concrete day-to-day living and you get a separation of the social space into *ghar* and *bahir*, the home and the world. The world is external, the domain of the material; the home represents our inner spiritual self, our true identity. The world is a treacherous terrain of the pursuit of material interests, where practical considerations reign supreme. It is also typically the domain of the male. The home in its essence must remain unaffected by the profane activities of the material world – and woman is its representation. And so we get an identification of social roles by gender to correspond with the separation of the social space into *ghar* and *bahir*.[10]

Chatterjee describes how this division between the outside and the inside has been articulated to the question of woman in nationalist thought as follows: "once we match this new meaning of the home/world dichotomy with the identification of social roles by gender, we get the ideological framework within which nationalism answered the women's question."[11] More importantly, Chatterjee elaborates in great depth how it is woman who becomes the ground upon which nationalism builds its discourse to construct a national identity. As he illustrates in his discussion of Indian nationalist discourse, when home, and by extension woman, are regarded as the principal site for expressing the nation's culture, controversies about woman's dress, manners, food, education, her role at home and outside become intensified. The outcome of this controversy was the emergence of a new definition of woman which was not only contrasted with modern Western society, but also distinguished from the indigenous patriarchal tradition. The nationalist image of the woman was deliberately separated from the degenerate condition of woman in Western societies; she was culturally superior to the excessively Westernized women of wealthy families who had colonial connections. However, she was also not vulgar, coarse, devoid of superior moral sense, sexually promiscuous, etc., like the lower-class women were. It was emphasized that she could achieve a healthy balance between being refined by modern Western methods of education and at the same time retaining her place at home safely. In this respect she was superior to the Western woman who has achieved education mainly to compete with men in the outside world, but she was also superior to the previous generation of women who lacked freedom and were oppressed by traditional culture. In this new ideology, her characteristic role, the guardianship of the spiritual qualities of the nation, was thought not to restrain the new woman from "moving out of the physical confines of the home."[12] Rather, it became possible to have woman in the "outside" world in a manner that would not threaten her essential feminine qualities. Her sexuality was erased by a successful portrayal of her as a mother, symbolizing the motherland, so that her new place in the outside world would not constitute a significant challenge for the care and protection of the nation's true self, its genuine and essential identity. Chatterjee goes on to suggest that the new patriarchy which was nourished by nationalism, by associating female emancipation with "the historical goal of sovereign nationhood, bound them to a new, and yet entirely legitimate, subordination."[13]

Although Chatterjee's object of analysis is the particular instance of Indian nationalism, his framework can be usefully applied to many other Third World countries, whether or not subjected to territorial imperialism. Of course, each cultural and historical context is unique and thus requires its own specific analysis. But I believe we can safely suggest that in all cases it is always the question of sexual difference which is successfully effaced in the discursive battle between nationalism and imperialism. It is this effacement that I want to address in this chapter. I aim to do this through a discussion of the ways in which the veil is articulated in two different nationalist projects, namely Algerian and Turkish nationalisms. It is my contention that, in both cases, it is the woman who disappears by being transformed into a battleground in the struggle between nationalism and imperialism (Algeria) and between Islamism and secular/Westernist nationalism (Turkey). It is the veil which becomes one of the most effective and convenient instruments of this battle. The visible cultural effects one can induce by veiling or unveiling woman makes it a convenient signifier for the contending parties to fight out their differences through manipulating this highly charged symbol. The veil is thus transformed into a medium through which the male subjects of the nation can articulate their desires and fears, but, more importantly, can assert "national" difference. However, the very construction of national difference is possible only through the mediation of woman, a mediation which nevertheless has to be repressed.

Turkish nationalism

The Ottoman period

The Turkish nationalist project which was developed through successive waves of modernization and secularization attempts took Westernization as its predominant ideology. The nationalist project in the late nineteenth and early twentieth centuries was heavily under the influence of Western models of modernity. Emphasis on the principles of Western European Enlightenment thought such as science, rationality, and progress came to dominate the discourse of the Westernized indigenous elite who were in the business of developing a new national identity for the emerging secular Turkish state. The women's question gained its vitality in such a context. It was one of the main reference points of the ideological debates and arguments that characterized this complex historical process of transformation of a feudal world empire into a nation-state. As Kandiyoti suggests, "the 'woman question' in both the Ottoman Empire and later in the Turkish Republic has served as a vocabulary to debate questions of cultural and national integrity, notions of order and disorder, and finally conceptions of the indigenous relative to foreign."[14] Since what was at stake was the question of national identity via the discussion of woman, it is important to examine the critical turning moments in the discourse on woman, for as Kandiyoti points out, these moments "coincide with the critical junctures in the transition from the Ottoman Empire to the Turkish Republic."[15] It is therefore important to examine how the tensions between Westernism, nationalism, and Islam have been played out in two crucial historical moments in the Turkish history, namely, the period of Ottoman reforms which were started by the Tanzimat movement in the early nineteenth century, and then instituted mainly by the Young Turks during the early twentieth century, and second, the process of intense Westernization which was attempted through the set of reforms instituted by Mustafa Kemal during the early years of the establishment of the Turkish Republic. Kandiyoti remarks that the transition from Ottoman Empire to Republic is characterized by a "progressive shift from enlightened 'modernist' Islamic positions to a feminism grounded in Turkish nationalism."[16] What characterizes this shift with regard to the woman's question is the "progressive distancing from Islam as the only form of legitimate discourse on women's emancipation, in favor of a cultural nationalism appropriating such emancipation as an indigenous pattern."[17] I will now discuss the discursive contours of this shift.

It was basically after the Tanzimat period that the "woman's question" appeared in the public political discourse of the Ottoman Empire. This discursive domain was largely constituted by the polarization between modernist reformists and religious traditionalists. The fundamental aspects of the woman's question were set during the second constitutional period (the period of reforms instituted by Young Turks), in the first half of the twentieth century, a period which also witnessed the rapid development of Turkish nationalism. Indeed, the essential features of the debate concerning women were fundamentally inspired by the questions and concerns that shaped the nationalist discourse. During these debates, issues like family, responsible motherhood, and the education of citizens were all articulated as parts of the woman's question in the discourses of contending parties whose primary and common concern was to "save" the declining empire. It was the Enlightenment ideals of reason and progress which provided a framework for the progressivists who emphasized the emancipation of women as an indispensable precondition for the nation's civilization – a powerful signifier which came to be identified with modernization and Westernization. They argued that women, as mothers and wives, have a crucial role to play in the rejuvenation of the nation by actively participating in the creation and education of enlightened citizens. It was thus deemed important to educate women, for if they remained within the shackles of Islam and tradition they could not fulfill such a role. The Islamic divorce law was regarded as an impediment in the way of women's emancipation, because it was held responsible for the easy repudiation of wives, the segregation of sexes, and arranged marriages.[18] It was religion which was held responsible for keeping women in the "dark ages" and for the debased position they occupied in society. Thus the denunciation and condemnation of traditional Islamic values went hand-in-hand with the valorization of the ideals of humanism and Enlightenment, such as rationality, progress, and freedom. On the other side of the debate, it was the destruction and abandonment of Islamic institutions and the laws of Islam and the consequent incorporation of Western culture which were held responsible for the decline of the empire. It was believed that the utilization of Western technology might be necessary, but that this should not lead to the contamination of Islamic values by Western culture. Women came to symbolize the site which needed to be protected from such contamination. Consequently, issues of veiling, polygamy, and divorce became objects of intense debate. For example, Musa Kazım, a leading figure of the conservative faction in the *Ulema* encouraged punitive measures against those who violated the Islamic rules of veiling.[19]

As Kandiyoti's analysis of the novels of the Tanzimat period demonstrate, one of the privileged themes is the attack on the traditional Ottoman family system and the position women occupy in it.[20] Alongside this, we witness a perpetual critique of "excessive" Westernization. In both these critiques, the inside/outside distinction and the concomitant association of women with the domain of the inside, home and the spiritual essence of the national culture can be seen operating in the Ottoman/Turkish novel. Despite the desire to Westernize and modernize the nation, there is a tenacious concern with "excessive" Westernization. Therefore, Westernization needs to be implemented without really eroding women's place in the home, and also the moral and spiritual values of the family. In other words, the overall moral fabric of society had to be protected while it was being Westernized. The entrance of the "foolish and feckless young men and fashionable loose women" to home is used to illustrate the measure of utmost degradation.[21] The excessively Westernized woman was accorded responsibility in the moral decadence into which Ottoman culture fell. On the other hand, these novels also reflect a desire to mark a difference from tradition, and consequently we witness endless attempts to distinguish the "new woman" from the old one who had been victimized by institutions and practices of unwanted marriage, polygamy, unilateral divorce, and slavery. Thus, by distinguishing itself both from Islamic tradition and from "extreme" Westernization, the early nationalist ideology in Turkey attempted to create an authentic cultural Turkish identity. The writers of this period, such as Namık Kemal, Ahmet Mithad Efendi, and Şemseddin Sami were all critical of the condition of women and by extension of the institutions of slavery, marriage, and divorce customs that sustain women's degraded position in society. However, as Kandiyoti rightly suggests, these "modernist reformers could easily identify with her to voice their own restiveness with the more oppressive aspects of Ottoman society."[22] But the Tanzimat novel is not as clear cut as the later novels in identifying the emancipation of women with Westernization. The writers of this period express an anxiety with "women's emancipation which came to be identified with licentiousness rather than 'enlightened' Westernization, more explicitly"[23] – a theme which will become more explicit in the republican period. However, in this period too, despite the emphasis on "emancipation" of women through Westernization, the critiques of "excessive" Westernization continued: in the nationalist language such excess was seen as the ultimate source of moral corruption. For example, the women in modern households who neglected the duties of childhood, homemaking, and who led an idle existence in decadent Europeanized İstanbul, represented the corruption caused by "excessive" Westernization. Moreover, the woman who is too liberated and denies her essential nature and duties in the name of civilization is the theme of several novels. Woman thus became a convenient signifier for the representation of the moral decay caused by "excessive" Westernization.

As I suggested above, the women's question was used as a point of leverage through which different positions were able to forge their nationalist projects; women thus became the medium through which other issues, such as those that pertain to national identity, were contested. As Kandiyoti puts it, "there is one persistent concern which unites the nationalist and Islamic discourses on women: an eagerness to establish that the behavior and position of women, however defined, are congruent with the 'true' identity of the collectivity and constitute no threat to it."[24] This meant that, when women attempted to speak, they did not have an autonomous subject position from which they could articulate their question as *women*. On the contrary, their subject position as women was always subjected to other priorities constructed in the public domain. This does not mean that it was only men who spoke in the name of women; on the contrary, women took part in the debate, but always within terms and contexts which were already established by the discursive polarization in the political domain. For example, the desire for the education of women was voiced *by women*, in one of the progressive journals of the time (*Terakki*), as a necessary means for transforming women into useful citizens (as the medium through which a successful nation could be established). The liberation of women was thus identified with the nation's progress and education was put forward as the means to achieve it. To follow the spirit of Spivak's argument,[25] there was no position of enunciation from which women could speak and be heard as women. On the contrary, as the few examples of this period illustrate, they were only heard if they took up positions on one or the other side of the debate. Perhaps this can also be seen as women's instrumental use of these public discourses spoken by men. However, this does not invalidate the argument that the woman was constructed as the very ground of such debates. It points to the tension and ambiguity which characterize such discursive struggles, especially from the point of view of the oppressed. The conditions which make women's speech possible need to be examined so that we come to see how the same conditions which enable this speech also make it an impossible one.

Another group of women writers explicitly criticized the subordination of women independently of such instrumental uses. However, these women were firm believers in the idea that women's ignorance was the cause of all sorts of evils in the country. The fundamental structure of their discourse was thus the same as men's. Many of the articles published by women during this period speak of women mainly as mothers and wives – the primary signifiers of the progressivist discourse on women – who would participate in a fully-fledged manner in the sustenance of the nation. Yet another group of women voiced the view that Islam granted women many rights and therefore their freedom was not in danger under Islamic law, as was suggested by the progressivist argument. By supporting their arguments with the examples they brought from the prophet's life and the condition of women during his time, they claimed that the debasement of women does not necessarily stem from Islamic precepts, but from the specific ways in which customs like polygamy have been adapted by various Arab cultures. Kandiyoti brings Fatma Aliye, a well-known woman writer of this period who engaged in a debate with conservative Mahmut Esat Efendi over the issue of polygamy, as an example of an early feminist who voiced her concerns only by making her desire compatible with the dictates of Islam. The early feminists' inscription of their own voices within the existing official positions can also be seen in the aspirations of one of the women's weeklies, *The Ladies' Gazette,* which was expressed as serving the principles of "being a good mother, a good wife and a good Muslim."[26]

The republican reforms and the question of veiling

Among the successive waves of modernization and secularization, the series of reforms instituted by Mustafa Kemal were the most drastic ones and had the effect of consolidating the project of Enlightenment within Turkish nationalist ideology. With the establishment of the Republic of Turkey at the end of World War I, the magnitude of already existing preoccupation with Europeanization was intensified and broadened. Secular modernization became the official ideology and, concomitantly, to be civilized was measured according to the degree of Westernization achieved in different areas of social life. Progress was identified with breaking away from Ottoman backwardness, symbolized in the distance achieved from Islam. Kemal's discourse can thus be seen in terms of Chatterjee's notion of the thematic, as it depended on a clear-cut distinction between the East and West, and the natural superiority of the latter as representing the level of civilization to be attained. In the various speeches he delivered, Mustafa Kemal insisted on these two points:

The Turkish nation has perceived with great joy that the obstacles which constantly, for centuries, had kept Turkey from joining the civilized nations marching forward on the path of progress, have been removed.[27] . . . The nation has finally decided to achieve, in essence and in form, exactly and completely, the life and the means that contemporary civilization assures to all nations.[28]

In this attempt to establish a new identity for the nation and reach the desired level of progress on the path of Westernization, the abolition of the Caliphate was a necessary but insufficient step. As Bernard Lewis observes, "a further shock was necessary – a traumatic impact that would shake every man in the country into the realization that the old order had gone, and a new one come into its place."[29] It is in this context that Mustafa Kemal installed what Lewis calls his "great symbolic revolutions" which marked the transformation of the nation from a backward to a "civilized" identity. In achieving the desired fundamental leap from backward to civilized nationhood, the figure of woman played a significant role. As Kandiyoti remarks, "the new woman of the Kemalist era became an explicit symbol of the break with the past, a symbolism which Mustafa Kemal himself did much to promote."[30] The emancipation of women "from the rigid shackles of orthodoxy" thus became one of the constitutive elements of Mustafa Kemal's vision of modernized Turkey.[31] This is clear in the various speeches he delivered throughout the country. In these speeches, Kemal adhered strongly to the premises of European Enlightenment thought: the ideals of progress, freedom, and equality. In the new ideal to be striven for, the education of women for the well-being of the nation and for reaching the desired level of civilization was emphasized time and again. The linking of modernization to women was clear in Kemal's Izmir speech in 1923: "A civilization where one sex is supreme can be condemned, there and then, as crippled. A people which has decided to go forward and progress must realise this as quickly as possible. The failures in our past are due to the fact that we remained passive to the fate of women."[32]

In his Kastamonu speech it was the ideal of equality between the sexes which was deemed necessary for achieving the desired level of progress:

Let us be frank: society is made of women as well as men. If one grants all the rights to progress to the one and no rights at all to the other, what happens? Is it possible that one half of the population is in chains for the other half to reach the skies? Progress is possible only through a common effort, only thus can the various stages be by-passed.[33]

Viewed from the perspective of Kemal's reforms, it was the women's dress and men's hats which were considered as the most visible and outward indicators of allegiance to the "civilized" West or "barbaric" East. Although the veil was not legally abolished with the series of reforms which had great significance for women (the introduction of a new civil code based on the Swiss model, giving equal rights to women in matters of divorce, custody of children, and inheritance), it nevertheless remained an issue of regulation and control, indeed an issue which had strategic value in the construction of the nationalist ideology. It might not be an exaggeration to suggest that the fundamental contours of the project of nationalism can be established by examining the discursive articulation of the veil. The veil functioned, to borrow a phrase from Lacan, as a *point de capiton* (quilting point), a point of condensation of the modernist discourse. The unveiling of women became a convenient instrument for signifying many issues at once, i.e. the construction of modern Turkish identity as opposed to backward Ottoman identity, the civilization and modernization of Turkey and the limitation of Islam to matters of belief and worship.[34] During this period, the veil carried connotations of Muslim backwardness and it was argued that a true Turkish woman had never been covered.[35] In various speeches he delivered throughout the country, Kemal talked about the practice of veiling as particularly backward and thus targeted it as an issue needing immediate "remedy." The regulation of the existing codes of dressing was an indispensable element in Kemal's attempt for modernization:

In some places I have seen women who put a piece of cloth or a towel or something like it over their faces, and who turn their backs or huddle themselves on the ground when a man passes by. What is the meaning and sense of this behaviour? Gentlemen, can the mothers and daughters of a civilized nation adopt this strange manner, this barbarous posture? It is an object of ridicule. It must be remedied at once.[36]

One of the defining features of Kemal's reforms was the Orientalist divide between the East/West, and primitive/civilized. In fact, as I have argued above through a discussion of Chatterjee and Said's texts, it was through such modernization attempts that the imperial divide was reproduced *within* the Third World and hence sustained the legacies of Eurocentric thought. The Orientalization of the Orient can be traced back to the ways in which such a fundamental divide took over the discourse of the indigenous elite. Kemal's speeches are in fact a perfect illustration of what Chatterjee calls the *problematic* and *thematic* of nationalist thought, because not only was the Oriental retained as the object but also the essentialist typology and the imperial distinction between the East and West was reproduced in a subtle manner. For example, in Mustafa Kemal's discourse, what gives Western dressing (which is not marked as Western) its legitimacy is its civilized and international (read universal) quality:

Gentlemen, the Turkish people who founded the Turkish republic are civilized; they are civilized in history and in reality. But I tell you as your own brother, as your friend, as your father, that the people of the Turkish Republic, who claim to be civilized, must show and prove that they are civilized, by their ideas and their mentality, by their family life and their way of living. In a word, the truly civilized people of Turkey . . . must prove in fact that they are civilized and advanced persons also in outward aspect. I must make these last words clear to you, so that the whole country and the world may easily understand what I mean. I shall put my explanations to you in the form of a question. Is our dress national? (cries of no!); Is it civilized and international? (cries of no, no!); I agree with you. This grotesque mixture of styles is neither national nor international . . . My friends, international dress is worthy and appropriate for our nation, and we will wear it. Boots or shoes on our feet, trousers on our legs, shirt and tie, jacket and waistcoat – and, of course, to complete these, a cover with a brim on our heads. I want to make this clear. This head-covering is called "hat".[37]

However, while trying to modernize the nation, Mustafa Kemal was wary of "going too far." In an effort to soften the impact, he did not neglect to assert an autonomous identity for the nation by reclaiming the authentic and the traditional. Hence, the West should be taken as a model but the original native culture must be preserved and remain intact. Such an ambivalent double gesture exemplifies the split character of nationalist thought that Chatterjee explains. Again, it was women who were called upon to achieve a "healthy" balance between the two; while abandoning their veils in the path of achieving a modern identity, they should be careful not to overdo it by copying the Western women in every respect: they were ordered to retain their original traditions and maintain the spirit of the nation, and thereby its essential, authentic core. It was possible for women to acquire the cultural refinements afforded by the modern West without actually jeopardizing the authentic culture:

Those who go to extreme in the form of dressing by exactly imitating the European women should know that each nation has its own traditions and customs, its own national characteristics. No nation can entirely copy another. Such a nation can neither be the same as the one it imitates, nor can it stay as itself. This is obviously a sad consequence. What we need to take into account on the subject of dressing is to think of the spirit of the nation on the one hand, the requirements of modern life on the other. We can meet these two requirements by getting rid of extreme attitudes.[38]

This "new" woman was supposed to be educated, Westernized, and unveiled but still retain the essential "feminine" virtues. That is, she should not have been over-Westernized. As the above quote illustrates, the "spirit of the nation" must not be neglected while "new" women are fulfilling the requirements of modern life: they should continue to be good mothers and wives. After all is it not in women that the essential identity and the spirit of the nation is embodied? In his speech in 1923 Kemal expressed this in the following manner:

History shows the great virtues shown by our mothers and grandmothers. One of these has been to raise sons of whom the race can be proud. Those whose glory spread across Asia and as far as the limits of the world have been trained by highly virtuous mothers who taught them courage and truthfulness. I will not cease to repeat it, woman's most important duty, apart from her social responsibilities, is to be a good mother. As one progresses in time, as civilisation advances with giant steps, it is imperative that mothers be enabled to raise their children according to the needs of the country.[39]

There was now a new dimension added to this modern woman: she had to be a good, patriotic citizen. As Kandiyoti illustrates in her reading of Halide Edip's novels of this period, the heroines, usually political activists in the nationalist cause, appeared as the new image for women to aspire to.[40] The figure of the self-sacrificing "comrade-woman" was particularly desirable because she participated in the national struggle together with her man; in Kandiyoti's words, she was an "asexual sister-in-arms."[41] This patriotic citizen is devoid of all sexual traces: she is the virtuous, chaste, and honorable woman. It was precisely this asexualization which guaranteed that "letting her go" to the outside world would not impede the chances of women fulfilling their "essential" feminine duties, nor, for that matter, threaten the responsibility of maintaining the nation's essential culture that was conferred upon them.

During the War of National Liberation, women's, particularly peasant women's, participation in the national cause was highly glorified and commended in patriotic discourse. Here is Kemal talking about peasant women:

> The Anatolian woman has her part in these sublime acts of self-sacrifice and must be remembered with gratitude, by each one of us. Nowhere in the world has there been a more intensive effort than the one made by the Anatolian peasant woman.
>
> Woman was the source of a vital dynamism: who ploughed the fields? She did. Who sowed the grain? She. Who turned into a woodcutter and wielded the axe? She. Who kept the fires of home burning? She. Who, notwithstanding rain or wind, heat or cold, carried the ammunition to the front? She did, again and again. The Anatolian woman is divine in her devotion.
>
> Let us therefore honour this courageous and self-sacrificing woman. It is for us to pledge ourselves to accept woman as our partner in all our social work, to live with her, to make her our companion in the scientific, moral, social and economic realm. I believe that is the road to follow.[42]

Modelled on the project of Enlightenment, the nationalist discourse in Turkey established a tense relationship with Islam. It construed its identity by progressively distancing itself from Islam, which thus became its constitutive outside. In a sense, Islam, by being pushed outside the identity of the emerging secular, modern Turkish identity, helped the nationalist discourse to create the identity and authority of the Turkish nation-state in a reverse manner. Islam was increasingly marginalized as the negative of the civilized national self; it represented a threat to the emerging secular, modern, enlightened Turkish nation. The nationalist discourse established a clear-cut border and an opposition between what belonged to its interior and what needed to be pushed outside in an effort to construct its own authority. Islam thus functioned as the other of the new national self, modelled on the Reason of Enlightenment. Timothy Mitchell explains this dialectical relationship, which he describes as "the paradoxical method of ordering" in a succinct way. This method

> helps to produce, for instance, the identity and authority of an "individual" nation-state. One could think of a particular case in the modern Middle East, of a state whose existence is contingent upon maintaining a radical difference between itself and the identity of those outside it. The outside must be represented as negative and threatening, as the method of maintaining meaning and order within. The outside,

in this sense, is an aspect of the inside. On closer inspection, moreover, the same opposition is found at work within the state, between what belongs within. The authority and self-identity of the nation-state, like that of the city and the colonial world are not stable, circumscribed conceptions but internal boundaries of hierarchical separation which must constantly be policed.[43]

It is precisely this policing which was exercised in the nationalist project. The oppositions deployed in the nationalist discourse between backward and civilized, religious and secular, veiled and unveiled, national and international, East and West are all examples of such a border policing and re-territorialization. It was women who were constructed as the discursive instrument of this border-drawing and nation-building, and it was through regulating their bodies and subjectivities that the borders were maintained and the nation was built.

However, the intense process of Westernization which characterizes the Turkish nationalist discourse should not be seen as a historical "mistake" that the Turkish indigenous elite has committed and which can be corrected simply through a refusal of the project of Enlightenment. With all its emphasis on progress, development, and modernization, the nationalist project in Turkey was an offspring of global interactions and the discourses such as Orientalism which accompanied the increasing imperialist domination of Europe over the Ottoman Empire.

From a feminist point of view, there seem to be two major aspects of the production of an elite nationalist discourse in Turkey: first of all, it is women who become the ground for the transactions between the contending parties and who are turned into a medium which allows the indigenous elite to discern their differences; second, the process of the production of nationalism requires an involvement with the major element of the traditional culture, the religion of Islam. These two aspects can also be observed in similar processes in many other Muslim Third World societies.[44] The unveiling of Turkish women thus came to symbolize the nation's distance from Islam and thereby its progress and development, whereas, as I will discuss in the following pages, the re-veiling of the Algerian women, in response to French colonialism's desire to unveil them, represented the Algerian nation's affirmation of its authentic and true culture. However, although the veiling and unveiling of women appear to be reverse strategies of responding to Western hegemony they are both in fact conditioned by and therefore the products of Orientalist hegemony.

Algerian nationalism and the re-veiling of women

In order to comprehend why, for the Algerian people, Islam became such a prominent discursive element during decolonization and why they resorted to Islam as their authentic tradition and identity with such intensity, we need to explain how the French colonial administration attempted to demolish Islam, its cultural institutions, and its economic structure in their entirety as part of its "civilizing mission." Religion gained the utmost importance in the eyes of the French colonial administration as a way of controlling the subject population, for Islam was seen as the most stubborn obstacle in the "acculturation" of the Algerian people. As part of this process, the French converted many mosques into barracks, abolished Koranic schools, discouraged pilgrimage to Mecca, and so forth. As Marnia Lazreg suggests, in the eyes of the French, the colonization of Algerian society was a "successful crusade against Islam."[45] In this "crusade" the whole of Algerian society was endowed with a religious character; Islam was seen as the distinguishing feature of the Algerian culture. That is, in the French imagery, Islam was construed as the essence of Algerian society. French colonists using the name Muhammad (prophet's name) for all men, and Fatma (prophet's daughter's name) for all women is indicative of such an essentializing imagery.

In a context where Islam was constituted as the fundamental source of difference between Algerians and French, the Algerian people's resort to their Islamic identity should not be surprising. Hence, as Lazreg describes, the relationship between the colonizer and the colonized was ingrained with a dialectical interplay: the French picked up Islam as the essence of Algerians and hence directed their policy of annihilation towards it. In a similar vein, "Algerians responded by making Islam the bastion of their resistance to colonialism."[46] While formerly Islam was one element among others, it suddenly became a *nodal point* around which all the other signifiers condensed. It thus arrested the flow of other signifiers and dominated the colonized's field of discursivity by becoming the focus of their identity, and it was articulated in their effort to maintain their difference from the colonial oppressor. As Peter Knauss argues, the French, by negating everything that was regarded as authentically Islam, in fact cultivated the desire to affirm what is deemed to be an authentic Algerian culture/religion.[47]

Within the Manichean world created as a result of colonization, Algerian women occupied a dubious place. In the struggle over capturing or preserving the essence of the Algerian culture, women came to symbolize, both for the French and for the Algerians, the embodiment of this essence. Hence the struggle over this authentic essence was fought over women's bodies; it was onto her veiled body that both French colonialism and Algerian patriarchy projected their fears, desires, and policies. The veil became a potent symbol in this battle. I will return to the discussion of the battle over the veil during decolonization in the following pages, but let me first briefly discuss how the women's question was handled during the reform movements in Algeria before the liberation struggle started.

The reforms of the young Algerians and the Ulema

The set of reforms which were instituted at the turn of the century were also developed as part of the strategy of resistance to colonial order. It is possible to identify two reform movements during this period: one secular, which was inspired by the French and the Young Turks and the other religious and inspired by the Arabs. Those who advocated secular reforms were French educated and were referred as the "Young Algerians," recalling the famous reformists in Turkey, the Young Turks, who led the reform movement in the Ottoman Empire. Like the Turkish reformists, the Young Algerians, established in 1912, did not advocate a radical break with Islam. They argued that Islam was not necessarily incompatible with Western models of development and progress. Despite their careful relationship with Islam, their non-radical reforms were not met with an enthusiastic response in general, mainly because they were seen by the popular masses as advocating the adoption of the colonial culture which dominated Algeria. Consequently, not many people embraced the call for a Western type of progress; instead their discourse was seen as anti-Muslim, an ideology which was identified with the colonizer.

However, nationalism's relationship to colonial ideology should not be regarded as one of simple reiteration. In this sense, neither Young Turks nor Young Algerians were simply imitators of Western culture. For example, the leader of the Young Algerians, Emir Khaled, was known for his total compliance with Mustafa Kemal's reforms. Not only did he support the reforms Atatürk instituted concerning women, but also he particularly admired him for his nationalistic opposition to the Western powers during the World War I. In Journals like *La voix des humbles* and *La voix indigéne*, the secular reformists of Algeria not only talked in positive terms about the radical changes that were taking place in Turkey, but defended the idea that women's emancipation was in harmony with Islamic traditions.[48] Like the Young Turks, Khaled did not endorse the idea of total assimilation into French culture; he wanted Algerians to maintain their Algerian culture and roots, while simultaneously suggesting secular reforms. As Knauss notes, the reforms Khaled proposed were part of the reformist syndrome (or what might be called "colonial episteme" in another register) that was taking place in the Middle East during this period. The defining characteristics of this trend can be traced in the endorsement of the following three "isms": secularism, nationalism, and modernism. For

Khaled, women's rights was a prime example of the internal virtues of Western modernity and secularism, which were themselves the cornerstones of the very idea of the "nation."

On the other hand, the religious reforms of the Ulema, led by Ibn Badis, were successful in reaching and responding to the problems and concerns of the Algerians whose religion and customs were under threat due to colonization. Badis advocated the improvement of women's status and defended their education. However, although he strongly argued for the education of children and particularly of girls, he specified that such education could take place only in strictly religious schools. It was assumed that this would help them to become the moral guardians of their families and was offered by the Ulema as a way of resolving the problems Algerians were experiencing. It was in the context of this moral guardianship that the veiling of women was promoted: it would assure protection for women from the lustful looks of foreigners and also from the temptations of French fashions. Ulema was particularly conservative on the issue of education. Such conservative emphasis on education was a response to the French administration's attempt to open French Lycées and encourage the education of Algerian women and discourage them from wearing veils. The protection of women from such French "assimilation" symbolized for the Ulema the protection of their true identity. What was at stake was the coherence and stability of national identity. Likewise, the rights and well-being of women were discussed and the critique of customs that pertain to women, such as dowry, were articulated to the anti-colonial discourse. As Lazreg shows, what was at stake in Ibn Badis's critique of the high price of dowry is in fact the preservation of the authentic culture of Algeria. Here is one such example: "Fathers, make things easier not more difficult! . . . measure the consequences of such a situation [expensive dowry] and return to the spirit of charity, and natural simplicity of our religion. Be warned that our youth might fall prey to the kind of 'colonialism' which draws strength from its 'weakness.'"[49]

Lazreg suggests that Badis's target in criticizing the high dowries was to prevent young Algerian men marrying French women (who did not request any dowry at all) and thereby avoid the danger of cultural assimilation due to mixed marriages. The ills and problems that Algerian society was experiencing, such as alcoholism, drugs, and prostitution were all attributed to the foreign presence. In response to this the revitalization and restoration of the native culture was promised. It was in the context of this program of revitalization that a call for a return to original Islam gained significance. As Peter Knauss observes, it was the Muslim national patriarchal consciousness which emerged as the political and cultural anti-thesis of totalitarian French colonial domination which was exercised through an intense effort of *la mission civilisatrice*.[50] The development of such a response can be read in the Ulema's credo: "Arabic is my language, Algeria is my country, Islam is my religion."[51]

In this political and social construction, the subject position of the Algerian people can be defined as a "popular subject position" in Laclau and Mouffe's terms; that is to say, a subject position that is constructed on the basis of a clear division of political space into two antagonistic poles. According to Laclau and Mouffe, this political subject position is more likely to develop in the Third World where there are more direct, brutal, and centralized forms of domination, which permit an identification of a single and clearly defined enemy.[52] Hence the emergence of the opposition between the loyal and disloyal, the believer and the infidel was the consequence of this division of the political space into two. But, as I have pointed above, this clear-cut and absolute division between the Western and Oriental, the foreign and native is the division created by Orientalist/colonial discourse. How, then, does nationalism differ from Orientalism? Following Chatterjee, we can see the difference in the respective positions of the native in colonial and nationalist discourses: in the former, the native is passive, whereas in the latter, he/she is constructed or imagined as autonomous, active, and sovereign. In other words, the fiction of the nation means that the native is imagined as the *subject* of his/her own history. However, despite endowing the native with some sort of subjectivity, the nationalist discourse of the Ulema unavoidably reproduced the epistemological structure of Orientalist hegemony: the distinction between West and East is retained. Nationalism was therefore a "reverse Orientalism." But the important point that needs to be kept in mind is that such a reversal was a product of colonial/Orientalist hegemony: embracing Islam in response to a civilizing mission, emphasizing religious education in response to promotion of *lycée* education, the veiling of women in response to the colonial desire to unveil them, revitalization of the native tradition in response to the dissemination of Western mores and culture. As Lazreg notes, before the colonial conquest, the Algerians perceived their Muslimness not very differently from the way French conceived of themselves as Christian.[53] However, with colonial subjugation, Islam achieved the utmost importance in defining the Algerian identity. In this sense, the nationalist project of the Ulema is not simply a unique and independent creation of its own, but is an effect of colonialism.

The nationalism of the FLN and the contest over the veil

The nationalist movement gained momentum in 1950s. The leading force in the anti-colonial struggle was the National Liberation Front (FLN) founded by urban petty bourgeois intellectuals. Despite the more urban class nature of the leadership, the same reversal of the native position operated in the discourse of the FLN, though it was not as strongly religious in terms of its content as it had been in the prior discourse of Ulema. The most important consequence of the passage to armed resistance and the increasing pace of the struggle was that the nationalist construction of the native as an autonomous and sovereign subject gained an increasing reality and force. Islam thus continued to be the predominant ideological element in the FLN's interpellation of the popular masses, indeed a major element which connected the urban leadership to the peasant masses. Ben Bella explains why and how Islam characterized their nationalism as follows:

The peasants have always been very attached to Islam. It was they who gave us the combatants of the liberation struggle, not the workers. And not in the name of a national union, but in the name of Islam. It's an error to believe that our nationalism is the nationalism of the French Revolution. Ours is a nationalism fertilized by Islam. Our principal journal, *El Mujahid*, is a Koranic name as is the name for the resister, *musebbin*. All of our political formulation is Koranic formulation. Thus Algerian nationalism and Arab nationalism is a cultural nationalism essentially based on Islam.[54]

In so far as women are concerned, there were some differences between the FLN and the Ulema. But they did not differ in signifying women as always subject to nation. For instance, even though the FLN was in favor of the "emancipation" of women, it nevertheless insisted that it was women who maintained the indigenous culture by the traditional roles they performed. Within the nationalist discourse of the FLN, women were regarded as the true guardians of their authentic traditions and identity. As David Gordon states, "with the rise of nationalism and then the outbreak of the revolution, Algerian nationalists were generally in favor of emancipation, but they also insisted that women in their traditionalist role had preserved the native traditions (being less polluted than men by French influence), and that what they wanted was a free Algerian woman not a free French woman."[55]

As I have noted above, the French colonialists also perceived Algerian women as embodying the true and authentic self of Algerian culture. As Winifred Woodhull suggests, the women were the point of contact in so far as Algeria is concerned.[56] Since they represented the "essence" of the culture that was colonized, having access to them and their bodies symbolized the means for a successful penetration to the heart of the colonized culture. They were, in Woodhull's words, the "living symbols of both the colony's resistance *and* its vulnerability to penetration."[57] I have suggested, in chapter 2, that the battle over women's veiling became the locus of contest between the indigenous patriarchy and the French colonial administration. The unique text-ile of the veil made it all the more important for the colonial administration to insist on its regulation, for the veil was seen as the concrete manifestation of the colonized's resistance to an imposed reciprocity: veiled women are able to see without being seen. Orientalist desire was thus articulated as the desire to unveil the colony, for women's insistence on wearing the veil really meant the colony's resistance to being colonized. In other words, for the colonial gaze, just wearing the veil was a sufficient sign of resistance. Consequently, as Knauss rightly observes, by unveiling the women, and exposing their bodies, the colonist was indicating the ultimate attempt of pacification.[58]

The campaign against the veil was intensified in the 1930s with the French administration's campaign to encourage the education of women. On May 13, 1958, a coup by a group of colonial generals displaced the civilian governor of Algeria. The same day, they organized a rally in front of the governor's palace and featured the unveiling of a group of Algerian women. The staging of such a performance was meant to symbolize the conquest of the last but foremost obstacle in the total capitulation of Algerian culture.[59] Such a performance was supposed to symbolize, in Bourdieu's words, that "the whole of Algerian society was offering itself, naked and willingly, to the embrace of the European society."[60] Hence this demonstration is significant in another sense: it illustrates, rather pointedly, how, within the colonial unconscious, the other culture and other sex are closely connected.

In response to the colonialist's attempt, the nationalistically oriented patriarchy restored the veil even more forcefully than before to resist the invasion of Algerian culture. The veil was reclaimed in an effort to resuscitate the authentic/traditional culture which was under threat of extinction. Islamic identity, which had been spontaneously accepted by every Algerian as an natural aspect of their life in pre-colonial times, was now transformed into one of the most salient aspects of their identity. The veil gained a new vitality and was articulated entirely differently in the colonial context. Bourdieu describes this process as the replacement of *traditionalism of the traditional* society with *colonial traditionalism*. Consequently, elements of culture which signified different meanings and function were furnished with new meanings:

The veil and the *chechia* . . . had been in the traditional context mere vestimentary details endowed with an almost forgotten significance, simple elements of an unconsciously devised system of symbols. In the colonial situation, however, they take on the function of signs that are being consciously utilized to express resistance to the foreign order and to foreign values as well as to pledge fidelity to their own system of values.[61]

Algerians' strong adherence to the veil should thus be seen in the context of resistance to colonialism. The veil came to signify not only the Algerian people's refusal to subscribe to the dictates of French mandate and thereby to colonial subjugation, but also "their will to affirm their radical and irreducible difference from the Europeans, their resistance to any attempt to make them deny their own way of life and their desire to defend their besieged identity."[62] It was the presence and force of the existing colonial system which produced the Algerians' discovery of their "essence" in their traditions. In this regard, the veil which gained such vitality during the liberation struggle has to be seen as a totally new dress: it was not a mere continuation of old habits and customs, but a Western product in the sense of the creation of a "colonial traditionalism" as described by Bourdieu. Since, within the colonial imagery, the veil was constructed as symbolizing Algeria's refusal to reciprocate, "all attempts at assimilation have taken the discarding of the veil to be their primary objective."[63]

Although women occupied such a central place, they occupied it in so far as they were the objects of a discursive struggle. The very building of a *national* subject position and authority, which was indispensable for the anti-colonial struggle, required the effacement of women's own question. Thus any attempt to bring the question of women on to the agenda was perceived as a threat to the goal of restoring national identity and sovereignty. As Knauss describes, "what had emerged during the 1920s, as the Muslim program, evolved by the end of the 1930s into the Muslim consensus. Socialism and the emancipation of women were either rejected outright or deferred until national sovereignty was restored. Islam, Arabic, and the reaffirmation of patriarchy were the central tenets of the Muslim consensus."[64]

The erasure of the question of sexual difference can be observed in the speech of one of the militant women, Djamilah. It illustrates how there was no position other than that of the nationalist project available to her:

The young Algerian women of Algeria don't have time to discuss the problems of sex right now. We are still in a struggle to make our new country work, to rebuild the destroyed family, to preserve our identity as a nation. In the future, perhaps, we will arrive at a kind of life where men and women relate on a more friendly, equal, and open basis. I hope so.[65]

In other words, what was lost in this battle over the veil was the women's question. The question is not whether there was female participation in insurgency or not, but the double effacement of sexual difference. Within the struggle between colonialism and nationalism women were turned into, in Peter Knauss's words, double prisoners. Although the Algerian women were the objects of an intense struggle between the French administration, Ulema, and the FLN, they were not participants in this battle as subjects. Gayatri Spivak's description of the position of Third World women has its place here: "between patriarchy and imperialism, subject-constitution and object-formation, the figure of the woman disappears, not into a pristine nothingness, but into a violent shuttling which is the displaced figuration of the 'third-world woman' caught between tradition and modernization."[66]

Notes

Introduction

1 Jacques, Derrida. "'Eating Well' or the Calculation of the Subject," in *Who Comes After the Subject*, Eduardo Cadva, Peter Connor and Jean-Luc Nancy (eds.) (New York and London: Routledge, 1991), p. 99.
2 Derrida reminds us of the necessity of retaining the category "subject" while at the same time resituating it in the following way: "I have never said that the subject should be dispensed with. Only that it should be deconstructed. To deconstruct the subject does not mean to deny its existence. There are subjects, operations, or effects of subjectivity. This is an incontrovertible fact. To acknowledge this does not mean, however, that the subject is what it says it is. The subject is not some meta-linguistic presence; it is always inscribed in language. My work does not therefore destroy the subject; it simply tries to resituate it." "Deconstruction and the Other," in *Dialogues with Contemporary Continental Thinkers – The Phenomenological Heritage*, ed. Richard Kearney (Manchester: Manchester University Press, 1984), p. 125.
3 For an illuminating analysis of the nation as a social-imaginary/fantasy and the process of ontologizing individuals as members belonging to a national community, see Stathis Gourgouris, "Tarih ve Rüya Arasında Ulus-Biçimi," *Toplum ve Bilim* 70 (Fall 1996).
4 I offer here a cautionary remark about who this Western subject is. The individuals who inhabit this position need not necessarily be limited to individuals who are citizens of a Western nation, who live in the West or who have Western identity cards. Since I refer here to a position, positioning, a certain imaginary that constitutes individuals, it is equally viable to have a "woman of color," "a man of color" to be positioned as Western. In a similar vein, my above remarks about the Western subject pertains to the subject position I call "masculine," which I discuss in the following section.
5 G. W. F. Hegel, *Phenomenology of Spirit*, trans. A. V. Millar (Oxford: Oxford University Press, 1977).

6 Homi Bhabha, "Of Mimicry and Man: The Ambivalence of Colonial Discourse," *October*, 23 (Spring 1984).

1 Mapping the field of colonial discourse

1 Edward Said, *Orientalism* (Harmondsworth: Penguin, 1978).
2 Lata Mani and Ruth Frankenberg, "The Challenge of Orientalism," *Economy and Society*, 14/2 (May 1985), p. 178.
3 Robert Young, *White Mythologies: Writing History and the West* (London and New York: Routledge, 1990), p. 129.
4 James Clifford, "On Orientalism," in *The Predicament of Culture: Twentieth-Century Ethnography, Literature and Art* (Cambridge, Mass.: Harvard University Press, 1988), p. 268.
5 Variations of such a position can be found in Abdul R. JanMohamed, "The Economy of Manichean Allegory: The Function of Racial Difference in Colonialist Literature," in *"Race," Writing and Difference*, Henry Louis Gates (ed.) (Chicago: University of Chicago Press, 1986), and in Aijaz Ahmad, *In Theory: Classes, Nations, Literatures* (London and New York: Verso, 1992). Also, several critics have misinterpreted this aspect of Said's text. For example Young, in *White Mythologies*, who in many other ways offers a rather succinct explication of *Orientalism*, falls into the same mistake of conceiving the power and knowledge relationship in terms of an "instrumentalist" conception of power. He argues that Said's analysis shows us that "Orientalism has close ties to enabling socio-economic and political institutions to the extent that it can be seen to have justified colonialism in advance as well as subsequently facilitating its successful operation," p. 129. A more striking example of this kind of reading is JanMohammad's reading of colonialist literature as a Manichean allegory. He argues that the "real function of these texts" is "to justify imperial occupation and exploitation." Throughout the text he distinguishes the material and discursive practices and the covert and overt purposes of colonialism; the covert purpose refers to the exploitation of natural resources and the overt aim is exemplified by the colonial discourse whose function is presented as the "civilization" of natives . However, I do not wish to collapse these two quite different pieces of work, which are guided by two rather radically different theoretical approaches into one unified position.
6 Said, *Orientalism*, p. 86.
7 Judith Butler, *Bodies That Matter: On the Discursive Limits of Sex* (London and New York: Routledge, 1993).
8 Said, *Orientalism*, p. 72.
9 Ibid., p. 72.
10 Ibid., pp. 5–6.
11 Ibid., p. 40.
12 Ibid.
13 Ibid., p. 94.
14 For a succint discussion of the relationship between "representation" and

"reference" in Said's analysis of orientalism, see Mahmut Mutman, "Under the Sign of Orientalism: the West vs. Islam," *Cultural Critique*, 23 (Winter 1992–3).

15 Clifford, "On Orientalism," p. 260.

16 Said, *Orientalism*, p. 322.

17 Ibid., p. 322.

18 Ibid., p. 87.

19 Ibid., p. 21.

20 Ibid., p. 5.

21 Ibid., p. 273.

22 Ibid., p. 203.

23 Ernesto Laclau and Chantal Mouffe, *Hegemony and Socialist Strategy: Towards a Radical Democratic Politics* (London: Verso, 1987), p. 108. See also Mutman, "Under the Sign of Orientalism."

24 Young, *White Mythologies*, p.129.

25 Derrida's remarks are illuminating here: "It is totally false to suggest that deconstruction is a suspension of reference . . . deconstruction tries to show that the question of reference is much more complex and problematic than traditional theories supposed." Jacques Derrida, "Deconstruction and the Other: An Interview with Richard Kearney," in *Dialogues with Contemporary Continental Thinkers: The Phenomenological Heritage*, ed. Richard Kearney (Manchester: Manchester University Press, 1984), p. 123.

26 Butler, *Bodies That Matter*, Elizabeth Grosz's and Vicki Kirby's works can be cited as other important examples in the field of feminist theory: Elizabeth Grosz, *Volatile Bodies: Toward a Corporeal Feminism* (Bloomington: Indiana University Press, 1996); Vicki Kirby, "Corporeal Habits: Addressing Essentialism Differently," *Hypathia*, 6/3 (Fall 1991).

27 Butler, *Bodies That Matter*.

28 Ibid., p. 11

29 Ibid., p. 15.

30 Ibid., pp. 7–8. For a critical assesment of this point see Elizabeth Grosz, "Experimental Desire: Rethinking Queer Subjectivity," in *Space, Time and Perversion* (New York and London: Routledge, 1995).

31 Butler, *Bodies That Matter*, p. 10.

32 Said, *Orientalism*, p. 73.

33 Ibid., p. 206.

34 Ibid., pp. 221–22.

35 Ibid., p. 222.

36 Homi Bhabha: "The Other Question," *Screen*, 24/6 (December 1983), p. 24.

37 There are number of reasons why one should crtiticize psychoanalytic theory. For example both Lacan's and Freud's theory of sexuality, in which the Law of the Father is regarded as the founding principle of all cultures and languages needs to be criticized. The assumption about the cross-cultural relevance or universalism of psychoanalytic accounts of the constitution of subjectivity and of sexuality and the explicit Eurocentrism involved in such an assumption

poses serious problems for scholars working in the field of colonial discourse. Similarly, the privileging of phallus as the founding signifier leaves feminist critics uneasy (and rightfully so) about an uncritical use of psychoanalysis. Being aware of such perils and traps in psychoanalysis, I nevertheless feel uneasy about disclaiming psychoanalysis in toto also.

38 Young, *White Mythologies,* p. 141.

39 Homi Bhabha: "Difference, Discrimination and the Discourse of Colonialism," *The Politics of Theory*, ed. Francis Baker *et al.* (Colchester: University of Essex, 1983), pp.199–200.

40 Said, *Orientalism*, p. 207.

41 Ibid., p. 184: "The Orient symbolizes Nerval's dream quest and the fugitive woman central to it, both as desire and as loss. Vaisseau d'Orient – vessel of the Orient – refers enigmatically either to the woman as the vessel carrying the Orient, or possibly, to Nerval's own vessel for the Orient, his prose *voyage*. In either case, the Orient is identified with commemorative *absence*."

42 Ibid., p. 188.

43 It is only in his article, "Orientalism Reconsidered," *Cultural Critique*, 1 (Fall 1985) that Said makes a rather rudimentary attempt to engage with the problem of why and how Orientalist discourse was projected onto various sexual and feminine metaphors. He argues, for example, that Orientalism is a praxis of male gender dominance or patriarchy which defines the Orient in feminine terms: "its riches as fertile, its main symbols the sensual woman, the harem, and the despotic – but curiously attractive – ruler." He goes on to argue that these are "connected to the configurations of sensual, racial, and political asymmetry underlying mainstream modern Western culture" (p. 104). However, these were left as brief assertions begging further analysis and development.

44 Bhabha, "Difference, Discrimination and the Discourse of Colonialism," p. 207.

45 Bhabha, "The Other Question," p. 27.

46 Young, *White Mythologies*, p. 154.

47 Francis Parker, Peter Hulme and Margaret Iversen, eds., *Colonial Discourse/Postcolonial Theory* (Manchester: Manchester University Press, 1994).

48 Nicholas Thomas, *Colonialism's Culture: Anthropology, Travel and Government* (Cambridge: Polity Press, 1994).

49 Robert Young, *Colonial Desire: Hybridity in Theory, Culture and Race* (New York and London: Routledge, 1995).

50 See Thomas, *Colonialism's Culture*, pp. 3, 15

51 See Young, *Colonial Desire*, p. 164.

52 Ibid., p. 5.

53 Benita Parry: "Resistance Theory/ Theorizing Resistance or Two Cheers for Nativism," in *Colonial Discourse/Postcolonial Theory*, ed. F. Parker, P. Hulme, and M. Iversen, p. 173.

54 See Young, *Colonial Desire*, pp. 159–60.

55 See Benita Parry, "Resistance Theory/ Theorizing Resistance," p. 176.
56 See Thomas, *Colonialism's Culture*, p. 105.
57 Young, *Colonial Desire*, p. 165.
58 Thomas, *Colonialism's Culture*, p. 59.
59 Ibid., p. 68.
60 Ibid., p. 69.
61 Ibid., pp. 69–70.
62 Young, *Colonial Desire*, p. 164.
63 Ibid., p. 164.
64 Ibid., p. 163.
65 Gilles Deleuze and Felix Guattari, *Anti-Oedipus: Capitalism and Schizophrenia*, trans. Robert Hurtley, Mark Seam, and Helen Lana (Minneapolis: University of Minnesota Press, 1990).
66 Young, *Colonial Desire*, p. 166.
67 Ibid., pp. 173–75
68 Ibid., p. 260
69 Ibid., p. 162.
70 Ibid., p. 180.
71 Ibid., p. 94
72 I borrow this formulation from Butler, *Bodies that Matter*, p. 3.
73 Ibid., p. 3.
74 Parker *et al.*, "Introduction" in *Colonial Discourse*, pp. 10–11.
75 Vicki Kirby, "Corporeal Habits: Addressing Essentialism Differently," *Hypatia*, 6/3 (Fall 1991), p. 10.
76 Ibid., p. 9.
77 Gayatri Chakravorty Spivak, "Neocolonialism and the Secret Agent of Knowledge," interview with Robert Young, *Oxford Literary Review*, 13/1–2 (1991), p. 222.
78 Bruce Robbins, "Comparative Cosmopolitanism," in *Social Text*, 31/32 (1992), pp. 174–75.
79 Jacques Derrida, "White Mythology: Metaphor in the Text,' in *Margins of Philosophy*, trans. Alan Bass (Chicago: University of Chicago Press, 1982), p. 213.
80 Bhabha, "Difference, Discrimination"; "Of Mimicry and Man: The Ambivalence of Colonial Discourse," *October*, 28 (1984); "Signs Taken for Wonders: Questions of Ambivalence and Authority Under a Tree Outside Delhi, May 1817," *Critical Inquiry*, 12: 1 (1985).

2 Veiled fantasies: cultural and sexual difference in the discourse of Orientalism

1 Hayden White, *Tropics of Discourse: Essays in Cultural Criticism* (Baltimore and London: The Johns Hopkins University Press, 1982), p. 1.
2 Olivier Richon, "Representation, the Despot and the Harem: Some Questions Around an Academic Orientalist Painting by Lecomte-Du-Nouy (1885)," in

Europe and its Others, Proceedings of the Essex Conference on the Sociology of Literature, vol.I, ed. F. Barker *et al.* (Colchester: University of Essex, 1985), p. 8.

3 Frantz Fanon, *A Dying Colonialism*, trans. Haakon Chevalier (New York: Grove Press, 1965), p. 36.

4 Ibid., pp. 37–38.

5 As Said shows this is evident in a speech by Lord Balfour in which he spends a lot of effort in denying such a superiority, while at the same time proposing it. Edward Said, *Orientalism* (Harmondsworth: Penguin, 1978), p. 32.

6 Theodor Adorno and Max Horkheimer, *The Dialectic of Enlightenment*, trans. John Cumming (London and New York: Verso, 1979), p. 3.

7 Michel Foucault, *Discipline and Punish: The Birth of the Prison*, trans. A. Sheridan (New York: Vintage Books, 1979), pp. 200–1; See also the interesting article by Jacques-Alain Miller, "Jeremy Bentham's Panoptic Device," trans. Richard Miller, *October*, 41 (Summer 1987).

8 Michel Foucault, *Power/Knowledge: Selected Interviews and Other Essays 1972–1977*, ed. Colin Gordon (New York: Pantheon Books, 1977), pp. 152–54. Foucault talks about this emergent modern formation as an "opinion society." Of course, we are reminded of de Amicis' cry to Turks whose silence must be the result of a secret agreement or of some malady: "Come, more like other men, for once! tell us who you are, what you are thinking of, and what you see in the air before you, with those glassy eyes!" Turks seem to be a people without opinions, or worse, a people who hide their opinions. See Edmondo de Amicis, *Constantinople*, trans. Caroline Tilton (New York: Putnam's Sons, 1878), p. 305.

9 Jean Starobinski, *Jean-Jacques Rousseau: Transparency and Obstruction*, trans. A. Goldhammer (Chicago: University of Chicago Press, 1988), pp. 65–80.

10 Foucault, *Discipline and Punish*, p. 191.

11 I am employing Michel de Certeau's definition of "strategy" here. See his *The Practice of Everyday Life*, trans. Steven Rendall (Berkeley: University of California Press, 1988), pp. 35–36. For a similar application of the concept of strategy, and an astute analysis of the employment of the trope of veil in Iraqi war, see Mahmut Mutman, "Under Western Eyes" in *Prosthetic Territories: Politics and Hypertechnology,* ed. Gabriel Brahm Jr. and Mark Driscoll (Boulder, Colo.: Westview Press, 1995). In an admirable study of the colonization of Egypt, Timothy Mitchell has shown for instance, how Foucauldian power/knowledge technologies were employed by the French and British colonizers in the so-called model villages, in the military barracks and in the educational apparatus. Mitchell argues that the aim of these strategies was to suppress, marginalize or transform the native culture in order to establish a new one which constructs "the world as picture." Timothy Mitchell, *Colonizing Egypt* (Cambridge, Cambridge University Press, 1988).

12 Gayatri Chakravorty Spivak, "Can the Subaltern Speak?" in *Marxism and the Interpretation of Culture*, ed., Cary Nelson and Lawrence Grossberg (Urbana: University of Illinois Press, 1988), pp. 280–81.

13 Gilles Deleuze, *The Fold: Leibniz and the Baroque*, trans. Tom Conley (Minneapolis: University of Minnesota Press, 1993), p. 38.
14 Ibid., p. 94.
15 Ibid., p. 33.
16 Malek Alloula, *The Colonial Harem*, trans. Myrna Godzich and Wlad Godzich (Minneapolis: University of Minnesota Press, 1986).
17 Fanon, *A Dying Colonialism*, p. 35.
18 Jacques Lacan, *The Four Fundamental Concepts of Psychoanalysis*, trans. Alan Sheridan (New York and London: Norton & Company, 1981), p. 103.
19 Ibid., pp. 118–19.
20 Ibid., pp. 72–74.
21 Fanon, *A Dying Colonialism*, pp. 45–46.
22 Lacan, *Four Fundamental Concepts of Psychoanalysis,* p. 84.
23 de Amicis, *Constantinople*, p. 208.
24 Théophile Gautier, *Constantinople*, trans. Robert H. Gould (New York: Henry Holt and Company, 1875), pp. 193–94.
25 de Amicis, *Constantinople*, p. 206.
26 Ibid., pp. 206–8.
27 Ibid, p. 207.
28 Irene Szyliowich, *Pierre Loti and the Oriental Woman* (Hong Kong: Macmillan, 1988), p. 97.
29 Joan Copjec, "The Sartorial Superego," *October*, 50 (Fall 1989), p. 87.
30 Lacan, *Four Fundamental Concepts of Psychoanalysis*, p. 105.
31 Slavoj Zizek, "Looking Awry," *October*, 50 (Fall 1989), p. 34.
32 Stephen Heath, "Joan Riviere and the Masquerade," in *Formations of Fantasy,* ed. V. Burgin, J. Donald, and C. Kaplan (London and New York: Methuen, 1986), p. 52.
33 Jacqueline Rose, "Introduction II," in *Feminine Sexuality, Jacques Lacan and the École Freudienne*, ed. Juliet Mitchell and Jacqueline Rose (London: Macmillan, 1987), pp. 35, 47–48.
34 I adapt Lacan's formulaic statement. See, Lacan, *Four Fundamental Concepts of Psychoanalysis*, pp. 80–82.
35 Jacques Lacan, *The Seminar of Jacques Lacan II: The Ego in Freud's Theory and in the Technique of Psychoanalysis 1954–1955*, ed. Jacques-Alain Miller, trans. Sylvana Tomaselli (New York and London: Norton and Company, 1991), p. 223.
36 *The Oxford English Dictionary*, The Compact Edition (New York: Oxford University Press, 1988).
37 Gerard de Nerval, *The Women of Cairo, Scenes of Life in the Orient*, vol. I, (London: George Routledge and Sons, 1929), pp. 3–4.
38 Mary Harper, "Recovering the Other: Women and the Orient in Writings of Early Nineteenth-Century France," *Critical Matrix*, 1/3 (1985), p. 11.
39 The figure of veil is a well-known trope of Western metaphysics, especially in the texts of Hegel (dialectic of essence and appearance), Nietzsche (woman as the untruth of truth), and Heidegger (alethia or unconcealment). I will have to

say more on this below. The employment of this figure in orientalist discourse should be taken as a sign of the complex relationship between Western philosophy (Reason) and the production of (West's) cultural difference.

40 Richon, "Representation, the Despot and the Harem," p. 9.
41 Slavoj Zizek, *The Sublime Object of Ideology* (London and New York: Verso, 1989), p. 193.
42 Teresa Brennan,"History After Lacan," *Economy and Society*, 19/3 (August 1990), p. 299.
43 de Certeau, *The Practice of Everyday Life*, pp. 35–36.
44 Mitchell, *Colonising Egypt*, p. 166.
45 de Amicis, *Constantinople*, pp. 304–5.
46 Ibid., p. 307.
47 Stephen Heath's reading of Nietzsche's representation of femininity as masquerade is very illuminating. See "Joan Riviere and the Masquerade."
48 Friedrich Nietzsche, *The Will to Power*, trans. Walter Kaufmann and R. J. Hollongdale (New York: Vintage Books, 1968), p. 425.
49 Friedrich Nietzsche, *Beyond Good and Evil,* trans. Walter Kaufman (New York: Vintage Books, 1974), p. 163.
50 For a discussion of the figuration of woman in Nietzsche's texts see Eric Blondel, "Nietzsche: Life as Metaphor," in *The New Nietzsche*, ed. D. Allison (Cambridge and London: The MIT Press, 1988).
51 Nietzsche, *Beyond Good and Evil*, p. 163.
52 Mary Ann Doane, "Veiling Over Desire," in *Feminism and Psychoanalysis*, ed. R. Felstein and J. Roof (Ithaca: Cornell University Press, 1989), pp. 118–19.
53 Friedrich Nietzsche, *The Gay Science*, trans. Walter Kaufman (New York: Vintage Books, 1974), p. 38.
54 Doane, "Veiling Over Desire," p. 121.
55 Ibid., p. 122.
56 Luce Irigaray, *Speculum of the Other Woman*, trans. Gillian Gill (Ithaca: Cornell University Press, 1985), p. 270.
57 Joan Riviere, "Womanliness as Masquerade," in *Formations of Fantasy*, ed. V. Burgin, J. Donald, and C. Kaplan (London and New York: Methuen, 1986), p. 43. I have benefited greatly from Stephen Heath's reading of Riviere's article: "Joan Riviere and the Masquerade" in the same collection.
58 Heath, "Joan Riviere and the Masquerade," p. 51.
59 Riviere, "Womanliness as Masquerade," p. 53.
60 Heath, "Joan Riviere and the Masquerade," p. 50.
61 de Amicis, *Constantinople*, p. 206.
62 Sigmund Freud, *Three Essays on the Theory of Sexuality,* trans. James Strachey (New York: Basic Books, 1975), p. 17. I would like to thank Stephen Heath for bringing this to my attention.
63 Doane, "Veiling Over Desire," p. 107
64 Jacques Derrida, *Spurs: Nietzsche's Style*, trans. Barbara Harlow (Chicago: University of Chicago Press, 1979), p. 51.
65 Ibid., p. 71.

66 Gayatri Chakravorty Spivak, "Displacement and the Discourse of Woman," in *Displacement: Derrida and After*, ed. Mark Krupnick (Bloomington: Indiana University Press, 1987), p. 184.

67 Ibid., p. 186.

68 See the quotation from Karl Marx in ibid., p. 191.

69 Homi Bhabha, "The Other Question," *Screen*, 24/6 (December 1983), p. 26.

70 The reader will notice that I use the pronoun "he" to refer to the Western/colonial subject. This is not a mere slippage, but a conscious effort on my part to highlight the claim, as developed most notably by Irigaray, that the subject is always-already masculine, and constitutes himself and retains his autonomy at the expense of the feminine, but disavows this dependence.

71 Riviere, "Womanliness as Masquerade," p. 38.

72 Luce Irigaray, *Marine Lover*, trans. Gillian Gill (New York: Columbia University Press, 1991), p. 110.

73 Karl Marx quoted in Spivak: "Displacement and the Discourse of Woman," p. 191. My thanks go to Mahmut Mutman for drawing my attention to this important quote and sharing his ideas with me.

74 See Zizek, *Sublime Object of Ideology*, p. 114.

75 There are a number of theoretical approaches one might use to explain the process of the constitution of the subject, such as Foucault's. The reason for my emphasis on the psychoanalytic theory of desire in understanding this constitution is that it enables us to grasp the process of exclusion and differentiation through which the Western Subject constitutes itself.

76 Homi Bhabha, "Interrogating Identity: The Postcolonial Prerogative," in *Anatomy of Racism*, ed. D. T. Goldberg (Minneapolis: University of Minnesota, 1990), p. 193.

77 The concept of ambivalence, as developed by Bhabha, has been very useful in my understanding of the structure of colonial discourse. However it is a concept that has been misread by many. For instance, Abdul JanMohamed argues that "by dismissing the 'intentionalist' readings of such discourse (colonial) as 'idealist' quests, Bhabha is able to privilege its 'ambivalence' and thereby, to imply that its authority is genuinely and innocently *confused*, unable to choose between two equally valid meanings and representations", see Abdul JanMohamed: "The Economy of Manichean Allegory: The Function of Racial Difference in Colonialist Literature," in *"Race", Writing, and Difference*, ed. Henry L. Gates (Chicago: University of Chicago Press, 1986), p. 83 . This is rather an inaccurate conclusion that one can draw from the concept of ambivalence, for Bhabha does not refer to a confusion, but the inevitable split that governs the colonial authority. It is with the concept of ambivalence that Bhabha is able to understand the nature of colonial stereotyping which is based upon simultaneous recognition and disavowal of difference. As such, the concept of ambivalence does not indicate the confusion of colonial authority (a notion of authority which is predicated upon the notion of intentional human subject as the originating source of power), but rather indicates how the mastery of otherness is never complete, but ceaselessly displaced. See Homi

Bhabha, "Difference, Discrimination and the Discourse of Colonialism" and "Of Mimicry and Man: The Ambivalence of Colonial Discourse," *October,* 28 (Spring 1984).

78 Bhabha,"Interrogating Identity," p. 195.

79 Bhabha, "The Other Question," p. 25 (emphasis added).

80 For a keen analysis which places the question of reversal in the historical context of Orientalist hegemony, see Mahmut Mutman, "Under the Sign of Orientalism: The West vs, Islam," *Cultural Critique*, 23 (Winter 1993).

81 I borrow these terms from Gayatri Chakravorty Spivak. She points to the desire invested by benevolent humanism to hear the "authentic voice of the native." See, "Naming Gayatri Spivak," Interview with Maria Koundoura, *Stanford Humanities Review*, (Spring 1989), pp. 91–93. More importantly, with these notions, she alludes to the process by which the subject renders itself transparent or invisible. As she claims, "To render thought or the thinking subject transparent or invisible seems, by contrast, to hide the relentless recognition of the Other by assimilation. It is in the interest of such cautions that Derrida does not invoke "letting the other(s) speak for himself" but rather invokes an "appeal" to or "call" to the "quite-other" (*tout autre* as opposed to a self-consolidating other), of "rendering *delirious* that interior voice that is the voice of the other in us." See, "Can the Subaltern Speak," p. 294. In response to imperialism's benevolent attempt to restore the lost authentic colonial self, Spivak's project is to document and theorize "the itinerary of the consolidation of Europe as Sovereign subject, indeed sovereign and subject." See Gayatri C, Spivak: "Rani of Sirmur," in *Europe and Its Others*, ed. F. Barker *et al.* (Colchester: University of Essex, 1985), p. 128.

82 Note that I have said "might", for the veil is neither necessarily subversive nor necessarily oppressive in itself. As Trinh T. Minh-ha suggests, "if the act of unveiling has a liberating potential, so does the act of veiling. It all depends on the context in which such an act is carried out, or more precisely, on how and where women see dominance . . . when women decide to lift the veil, one can say that they do so in defiance of their men's oppressive rights to their bodies; but when they decide to keep or put back on the veil they once took off, they may do so to reappropriate their space or to claim a new difference, in defiance of genderless hegemonic standardization," "Introduction," *Discourse*, 8 (Winter 1986–87), p. 5. A similar suggestion regarding the necessity of recognizing the specific cultural and historical contexts in which the meaning of the veil is articulated has also been made by Chandra Mohanty in her stimulating article examining the complicity between Western feminist representations of the non-Western women and colonial discourse. See "Under Western Eyes: Feminist Scholarship and Colonial Discourses," *Feminist Review*, 30 (Autumn, 1988). Such specific articulations of the veil have been demonstrated rather well in Fanon's analysis of what he calls the "historic dynamism of the veil." Fanon's analysis of the Algerian women's removing and reassuming the veil goes one step further than what Trinh T. Minh-ha and Chandra Mohanty claim. He demonstrates, for example, how the veil can be transformed into a

means of struggle and how there was "a whole universe of resistance around this particular element of the culture." I will further discuss the issue of resistance as it relates to veil in the following pages.

83 Homi Bhabha, "Of Mimicry and Man: The Ambivalence of Colonial Discourse," *October*, 28 (Spring 1984), p. 126.

84 Frantz Fanon, *Black Skin, White Masks* (New York: Grove Press, 1967), p. 218.

85 Michel Foucault, *The History of Sexuality*, vol. I, trans. Robert Hurley (New York: Vintage Books, 1990), p. 96.

86 Christian Metz quoted in Mary Ann Doane: "Film and the Masquerade: Theorizing the Female Spectator," *Screen*, 23/3–4 (September–October 1982), p. 78.

87 Bhabha, "Interrogating Identity," p. 195.

88 Ibid., p. 195.

89 This is a persistent and unfortunately not a very substantiated criticism that has been advanced by the critiques of post-structuralist theory and psychoanalysis. Such charges of determinism have been brought time and again in the name of defending the notion of agency. What is overlooked in such criticisms is the assumption of a rigid alternative between, to borrow a formulation from Ernesto Laclau and Chantal Mouffe, total autonomy and absolute subordination. See, "Post-Marxism Without Apologies," in *New Reflections on the Revolution of Our Time* (London and New York: Verso, 1990).

90 Judith Butler, "The Imperialist Subject," *Journal of Urban and Cultural Studies*, 2/1 (1991), p. 77.

91 Fanon, *A Dying Colonialism*, pp. 46–47.

92 Ibid., p. 63.

93 Ibid., p. 44.

94 When French colonial power identified the veil as a problem and constructed it as an exterior target, it was involved in a reading and writing (or re-writing) of the veil which is different from that of the native culture. In his influential *Outline of a Theory of Practice*, Pierre Bourdieu provides an ethnographic study of the native Muslim patriarchal culture. The historical precondition of such a study is of course the French colonization of Algeria. Bourdieu's observation of the binarisms which make the native culture is instructive in this sense. Bourdieu does not mention the veil, but he observes that the opposition between male and female is associated with a number of other oppositions between the outside and inside. In the mythical structure of the native society, woman is associated with the inside, the house and the land. The veiled woman represents an "inside" that needs to be protected. Pierre Bourdieu, *Outline of A Theory of Practice,* trans. Richard Nice (Cambridge: Cambridge University Press, 1989), pp. 44–45, 90–94, 122–26. The only place where Bourdieu mentions the veil is a native proverb reserved for the son-in-law, "the veil cast over shame" (ibid., p. 44). Since woman is associated with evil acts, the lesser evil can only be produced by the protection of a man, etc. Despite his apparent criticism of "legalism," and his recognition of different interests of men and

women, Bourdieu re-inscribes the same mythical patriarchal structure based on sexual difference. In Spivak's words, "the figure of the exchanged woman still produces the cohesive unity of a clan . . ." Introduction, *Selected Subaltern Studies,* ed. Ranajit Guha and Gayatri Chakravorty Spivak (New York and Oxford: Oxford University Press, 1988), p. 30.

95 Alloula, *The Colonial Harem*, p. 7.

96 Fanon, *A Dying Colonialism*, p. 44.

97 For this formulation see Christian Metz quoted in Paul Willemen, "Voyeurism, The Look and Dwoskin," *Afterimage*, 6 (Summer 1976), p. 41.

98 Even Edward Lane, who stands as one of the solemn and least "masculine" Orientalists, almost confesses this desire to see: "A man may also occasionally enjoy opportunities of seeing the face of an Egyptian lady when she really thinks herself unobserved; sometimes at an open lattice, and sometimes on a house-top," *An Account of the Manners and Customs of the Modern Egyptians* (New York: Dover Publications, 1973), p. 177.

99 Willemen, "Voyeurism, The Look and Dwoskin," p. 48.

100 Mary Ann Doane suggests a similar structure of reversal for understanding the difficulty the masculine subject experiences when woman appropriates the gaze and turns herself from being a passive object of look to a subject of active looking, from spectacle to spectator. See "Film and the Masquerade."

101 Bhabha, "Interrogating Identity," p. 190.

102 Fanon, *A Dying Colonialism*, p. 61.

103 Ibid., p. 62.

104 Ibid., p. 62.

105 To identify Muslim women's gaining her agency and subjectivity by "moving" outside the home and equating her veiling with confinement implies an unquestioned acceptance of the assumptions of the liberal Western feminism which advocates the unveiling of Muslim women as a means of "liberation."

106 Luce Irigaray, *This Sex Which is Not One*, trans. Catherine Porter (Ithaca: Cornell University Press, 1985), p. 76.

107 Rosi Braidotti, *Nomadic Subjects: Embodiment and Sexual Difference in Contemporary Feminist Theory* (New York: Columbia University Press, 1994), p. 7.

108 Jacques Derrida, *Of Grammatology*, trans. Gayatri Chakravorty Spivak, (Baltimore: Johns Hopkins University Press, 1976), p. 24.

109 Naomi Schor, "This Essentialism Which is Not One: Coming to Grips with Irigaray," *differences*, 1/2 (1989), p. 48.

110 Irigaray, *Marine Lover*, p. 118.

3 Supplementing the Orientalist lack: European ladies in the harem

1 See Sara Mills, *Discourses of Difference: An Analysis of Women's Travel Writing and Colonialism* (New York and London: Routledge, 1991); Reina Lewis, *Gendering Orientalism: Race, Femininity and Representation* (London and New York: Routledge, 1996); Lisa Lowe, *Critical Terrains: French and*

British Orientalisms (Ithaca: Cornell University Press, 1991). I will focus my discussion in this chapter on Lowe. The common thread in these books is that they all contest Orientalism's totalizing and homogenizing gesture by way of examining women's writings which are claimed to display diversity within Orientalist discourse .

2 See Rana Kabbani, *Europe's Myths of Orient* (Bloomington: Indiana University Press, 1986). However, it is important to distinguish Kabbani's work from those above as the focus of her book is not limited to women's travel writings, but is concerned with exploring the use of masculine discourse at the service of Orientalism. Examining British and French Orientalist art and literature, Kabbani points to the eroticization of colonialism and to the feminization of the Orient. Malek Alloula's *The Colonial Harem* (Minneapolis: University of Minnesota Press, 1986) has a similar point of emphasis. Sarah Graham Brown, *Images of Women: The Portrayal of Women in Photography of the Middle East, 1860–1950* (New York: Columbia University Press, 1988) investigates how Orientalist photographs of women are a surfacing of Western men's sexual fantasies, defining otherness in such a way as to justify colonialism.

3 Edward Said, *Culture and Imperialism* (New York: Alfred Knoff, 1993), p. xxiv.

4 Edward Said, *Orientalism* (Harmondsworth: Penguin, 1978), p. 206.

5 Ibid., p. 206.

6 Ibid., p. 222

7 Ibid., p. 222.

8 Timothy Mitchell, *Colonising Egypt* (Cambridge: Cambridge University Press, 1988), p. 31.

9 Said, *Orientalism*, p. 177.

10 Ibid., p. 176.

11 Gayatri Chakravorty Spivak, "Imperialism and Sexual Difference," *Oxford Literary Review*, 8/1–2 (1986), p. 225.

12 Mitchell, *Colonising Egypt*, p. 31.

13 Mary Harper, "Recovering the Other: Women and the Orient in Writings of Early Nineteenth-Century France," *Critical Matrix*, 1/3 (1985), p. 2.

14 Jean Jacques Ampere quoted in Harper, "Recovering the Other," p. 11.

15 Ibid., p. 12.

16 Théophile Gautier, *Constantinople,* trans. Robert H. Gould (New York: Henry Holt and Company, 1875), p. 192.

17 Ibid., p.192.

18 Théophile Gautier quoted in Reina Lewis, p. 132.

19 Jean Jacques Ampere quoted in Harper, "Recovering the Other," p. 11.

20 Sophia Poole, *EnglishWoman in Egypt*, vol. II (London: Charles Knight, 1844), p. 94.

21 Jacques Derrida, *Of Grammatology*, trans. Gayatri Chakravorty Spivak (Baltimore: Johns Hopkins University Press, 1976), p. 144.

22 Ibid., p. 145.

23 Ibid., p. 145.

24 Jonathan Culler, *On Deconstruction: Theory and Criticism After Structuralism* (Ithaca: Cornell University Press, 1986), p. 105.

25 For Derrida "metaphysics consists of excluding non-presence by determining the supplement as *simple exteriority*, pure addition or pure absence. The work of exclusion operates within the structure of supplementarity. The paradox is that one annuls addition by considering it a pure addition. *What is added is nothing because it is added to a full presence to which it is exterior.* Speech comes to be added to intuitive presence; writing comes to be added to living self-present speech; masturbation comes to be added to so-called normal sexual experience; culture to nature, evil to innocence, history to origin and so on," Derrida, *Of Grammatology*, p. 167.

26 Christopher Norris, *Derrida* (Cambridge, Mass.: Harvard University Press, 1987), p. 67.

27 Lady Mary Wortley Montagu, *The Complete Letters 1708–1720*, vol. I, ed. Robert Halsband (Oxford: Clarendon Press, 1965).

28 Lisa Lowe is not alone in arguing against such totalizations. As she also observes, other critics agree, such as James Clifford, "On Orientalism," in *The Predicament of Culture* (Cambridge, Mass.: Harvard University Press, 1988); and B. J. Moore-Gilbert, in *Kipling and Orientalism* (London: Croom Helm, 1986).

29 As I suggested above, we run into serious difficulties when we posit the unity and hegemony of Orientalism, and multiplicity and heterogeneity as alternatives, for, as Said's observations regarding the latent and manifest content of Orientalism imply, we need to see them as two sides of the same coin. But this is not to suggest that the structure of Orientalism is simple. Indeed, it is precisely by comprehending its voluminous character, expressed in and constituted by its manifest content that we can begin to understand the complexity in the *unity* of Orientalism. In other words, what I am advocating is not to locate the complexity of Orientalism by pluralizing it, for the narrative of Orientalism implies *one* hegemonic story of the world.

30 Montagu, *The Complete Letters,* vol. I, p. 368.

31 Ibid., p. 405.

32 Ibid., p. 385.

33 Ibid., pp. 396–97.

34 For example, Grace Ellison in *An English Woman in a Turkish Harem* (London: Methuen, 1915), describes her task as "to correct the errors, prejudice and hatred" developed in earlier texts towards Turkey. Throughout the book, she alludes to the falsehoods of the representations of the Orient and its women. In my reading of this and several other similar texts, I try to show how, despite the "contradictory" position these texts may occupy, they reveal not only the Western provenance of modernist discourse, but also demonstrate how libertarian feminism, as it expresses an interest in Third World women, is embedded within a benevolent imperialist ideology. I will discuss this point further in chapter 4.

35 Lowe, *Critical Terrains*, p. 31.

36 Ibid., p. 31.
37 Indeed, Orientalism starts way before the act of anthropological representations of the cultures and peoples of the Orient, for it is embedded in the very desire to go to the Orient, to be "there" and in the very desire to name and mark the distinction between the West and the Orient.
38 Homi Bhabha, "The Other Question," *Screen*, 24/6 (December 1983), p. 18.
39 Lowe, *Critical Terrains*, p. 32.
40 Ibid., p. 40.
41 Ibid., p. 42.
42 Ibid., p. 42.
43 Ibid., p. 45.
44 Ibid., p. 45.
45 Spivak, "Imperialism and Sexual Difference," p. 225.
46 Gayatri Chakravorty Spivak, "Can the Subaltern Speak," in *Marxism and the Interpretation of Culture*, eds. C. Nelson and L. Grossberg (Urbana: University of Illinois Press, 1988), p. 294.
47 Spivak, "Imperialism and Sexual Difference," p. 235.
48 Edward Said, "Representing the Colonized: Anthropology's Interlocutors," *Critical Inquiry*, 15 (Winter 1989).
49 For an excellent reading of Luce Irigaray see, Elizabeth Grosz, *Sexual Subversions: Three French Feminists* (Sydney: Allen and Unwin, 1989) and Margaret Whitford, "Luce Irigaray and the Female Imaginary: Speaking as a Woman," *Radical Philosophy*, 43 (1986).
50 Luce Irigaray, *Speculum of the Other Women*, trans. Gillian Gill (Ithaca: Cornell University Press, 1985), pp. 26–27.
51 Lowe, *Critical Terrains*, p. 51.
52 Ibid., p. 51.
53 Montagu, *The Complete Letters*, pp. 328–29.
54 Ibid., p. 328.
55 Lowe, *Critical Terrains*, p. 44.
56 Ibid., p. 45.
57 Ibid., pp. 43–44.
58 Gerard de Nerval, *The Women of Cairo: Scenes of Life in the Orient* (London: George Routledge and Sons, 1929), p. 148.
59 Montagu, *The Complete Letters*, p. 313.
60 Ibid., p. 314.
61 Ibid., p. 313.
62 In Ingres' case the citationary process becomes much starker given that he has, as Lowe also mentions, never travelled to North Africa or Middle East.
63 Mitchell, *Colonising Egypt*, p. 32.
64 Harper, "Recovering the Other," p. 6.
65 Ibid., p. 6.
66 Irigaray, *The Speculum of the Other Women*, p. 42.
67 Ibid., p. 42.
68 Gayatri Chakravorty Spivak, "Rani of Sirmur," in *Europe and Its Others*:

Proceedings of the Essex Conference of the Sociology of Literature, ed. Francis Baker *et al.* (Colchester: University of Essex, 1985), p. 128.

4 Sartorial fabric-ations: Enlightenment and Western feminism

1 See Homi Bahbha, "'Race', Time, and the Revision of Modernity," *Oxford Literary Review*, 13/1–2 (1991); "Sly Civility," *October*, 34 (1985); "Representation and the Colonial Text: A Critical Exploration of Some Form of Mimeticism," in *The Theory of Reading*, ed. Frank Gloversmith (Sussex: Harvester Press, 1984); Partha Chatterjee, "Colonialism, Nationalism and Colonized Women: The Contest in India," *American Ethnologist,* 16/4 (1989); *Nationalist Thought and the Colonial World: A Derivative Discourse* (London: Zed Books, 1986); David Lloyd, "Race Under Representation," *Oxford Literary Review*, 13/1–2 (1991); Chandra Talpade Mohanty, "Feminist Encounters: Locating the Politics of Experience," *Copyright* 1, (1998); S. P. Mohanty, "Us and Them: On the Philosophical Bases of Political Criticism," *The Yale Journal of Criticism*, 2/2 (1989); Gayatri Chakravorty Spivak, "Subaltern Studies: Deconstructing Historiography," in *In Other Worlds,* (New York and London: Routledge, 1988); Robert Young, *White Mythologies: Writing History and the West* (London and New York: Routledge, 1990).
2 Jean-Paul Sartre quoted in Young, *White Mythologies*, p. 125.
3 Spivak, "Subaltern Studies," p. 202.
4 For a fuller discussion of the use of temporal devices in anthropology in the construction of its object, see Johannes Fabian, *Time and the Other: How Anthropology Makes Its Object* (New York: Columbia University Press, 1983).
5 Cornellius Castoriadis, "Reflections on 'Rationality' and 'Development'," *Thesis Eleven*, 10/11 (November/March 1984–85), p. 22.
6 R. Radhakrishnan, "Nationalism, Gender, and the Narrative of Identity," in *Nationalisms and Sexualities*, ed. Andrew Parker *et al.* (New York and London: Routledge, 1992), p. 87.
7 Homi Bhabha, "'Race', Time, and the Revision of Modernity," p. 198.
8 Lloyd, "Race Under Representation," p. 69.
9 Fabian, *Time and The Other.*
10 Bhabha, "Representation and the Colonial Text," p. 98.
11 Mohanty, "Us and Them," p. 6.
12 The best-known figures of this critique are Talal Asad, "Two European Images of Non-European Rule," in *Anthropology and the Colonial Encounter* (New York: Humanities Press, 1973); Fabian, *Time and the Other.*
13 Fabian, *Time and the Other,* pp. 143–44. The complicity between colonialism and anthropology has also been noted by Said in the following way: "It will be said that I have connected anthropology and empire too crudely, in too undifferentiated a way; to which I respond by asking how – and I really mean *how* – and when they were separated. I do not know when the event occurred, or if it occurred at all." Edward Said, "Representing the Colonized: Anthropology's Interlocutors," *Critical Inquiry*, 15 (Winter 1989), p. 214.

14 Asad, "Two European Images of Non-European Rule," p. 115.

15 Ruth Francis Woodsmall, *Woman in the Changing Islamic System* (Delhi: BILMA Publishing House, 1983; 1st edn 1936), p. 48.

16 Edward Said, *Orientalism* (Harmondsworth: Penguin, 1978), p. 269.

17 Ruth Frances Woodsmall, p. 39.

18 Juliet Minces, *The House of Obedience* (London: Zed Press, 1980), p. 14.

19 Chatterjee, "Colonialism, Nationalism, and Colonized Women," p. 622.

20 Leila Ahmed, "Western Ethnocentricism and Perceptions of the Harem," *Feminist Studies*, 8/3 (Fall 1982), p. 523.

21 Grace Ellison, *An Englishwoman in a Turkish Harem* (London: Methuen, 1915), pp. 61–62.

22 Lata Mani, "The Contentious Traditions: The Debate on *Sati* in Colonial India," *Cultural Critique*, 7 (Fall 1987), p. 151.

23 For an excellent discussion of this question see, R. Radhakrishnan: "Nationalism, Gender."

24 Woodsmall, *Women in the Changing Islamic System*, p. 48.

25 Ibid., p. 49.

26 Ibid., p. 42.

27 Partha Chatterjee: "The Nationalist Resolution of the Women's Question", in *Recasting Women: Essays in Colonial History*, ed. Kum Kum Sangari and Sudesh Vaid (New Brunswick: Rutgers University Press, 1990).

28 Woodsmall, *Women in the Changing Islamic System,* p. 413.

29 Minces, *House of Obedience*, p. 25.

30 Gayatri C. Spivak, "Imperialism and Sexual Difference," *Oxford Literary Review*, 8/1–2 (1986), p. 229.

31 Gayatri Chakravorty Spivak, "French Feminism Revisited: Ethics and Politics," in *Feminist Theorize the Political*, ed. J. Butler and J. Scoat (New York and London: Routledge, 1992), p. 75.

32 Ernesto Laclau, "Universalism, Particularism and the Question of Identity," *October*, 61 (Summer 1992).

33 Joan Scott, "Multiculturalism and the Politics of Identity," *October*, 61 (Summer 1992), pp. 14–15.

34 Lloyd, "Race Under Representation," p. 70.

35 Nikkie Keddi and Lois Beck, *Women in the Muslim World* (Cambridge, Mass.: Harvard University Press, 1978), p. 18.

36 However, there is a fundamental assymetry here. The possibility of inferring the characteristics of a culture from the position of its women seems to be valid only for cultures that are other-than the West. This is such a taken for granted belief that, for instance, the large numbers of raped or beaten women found everyday in the West are not taken as typical or essential features of a specifically Western culture. There is no metonymic relationship established between *Western* culture and rape or wife-beating. The differences between the two cultures is not complexly articulated, rather they are seen as absolute, radical, essential, profound.

37 Woodsmall, *Woman in the Changing Islamic System*, p. 39.

38 Monique Wittig, cited in Naomi Schor, *Bad Objects: Essays Popular and Unpopular* (Durhan: Duke University Press, 1995), p. 8.

39 The question of women's relation to other Others remains a blindspot in Irigaray's analysis as she regards the exclusion of the feminine as the most fundamental form of othering. While using Irigaray, we should keep alive the question as to who remains excluded in her analysis.

40 Antoinette M. Burton, "The White Woman's Burden: British Feminists and the Indian Woman, 1865–1915," *Women's Studies International Forum*, 13/4 (1990), p. 295. The same article also appeared in *Western Women and Imperialism: Complicity and Resistance*, ed. Nupur Chaudri and Margaret Strobel (Bloomington: Indiana University Press, 1992).

41 Mervat Hatem, "Through Each Other's Eyes: The Impact on the Colonial Encounter of the Images of Egyptian, Levantine-Egyptian, and European Women, 1862–1920," in *Western Women and Imperialism*.

42 Rosemary Marangoly George, "Homes in the Empire, Empire in the Home," *Cultural Critique*, 26 (Winter 1993–94), p. 97.

43 Gayatri Chakravorty Spivak, "Three Women's Texts and a Critique of Imperialism," in *"Race", Writing, and Difference*, ed. Henry Louis Gates (Chicago: University of Chicago Press, 1986), pp. 263–64.

44 Richard Rorty, *Philosophy and the Mirror of Nature* (Princeton: Princeton University Press, 1979).

45 Michel Foucault, *Discipline and Punish: The Birth of the Prison*, trans. Alan Sheridan (Harmondsworth: Penguin, 1977).

46 Luce Irigaray, *Speculum of the Other Woman*, trans. Gilliam Gill (Ithaca: Cornell University Press, 1985).

47 Martin Jay suggests that although this is claimed to be the dominant model, his concern is to demonstrate the internal tension of Cartesian perspectivalism and thereby show how the scopic regime of modernity is not a harmoniously integrated complex of visual theories and practices, but a contested terrain where there are several and even competing ones. Hence he acknowledges the plurality of scopic regimes of the period which is characterized by a differentiation of subcultures. What can be concluded from Jay's essay is that although acknowledging Cartesian perspectivalism as a dominant model, he contests its characterization as a hegemonic one. Martin Jay: "Scopic Regimes of Modernity," in *Modernity and Identity*, ed. Scott Lash and Jonathan Friedman (Oxford and Cambridge: Blackwell, 1992).

48 Ibid., pp. 182–83.

49 Peter Brooks, *Body Work: Objects of Desire in Modern Narrative* (Cambridge, Mass.: Harvard University Press, 1993).

50 Ibid., p. 104.

51 The association of truth with woman has been a well-elaborated theme in the phallogocentric logic of Western thought. The privileging of vision as the fundamental source of knowledge has also been a crucial component of the narrative of sexual difference in the discourse of psychoanalysis. It is gaze which appears as the key device for providing the first knowledge of sexual

difference in Freud's and Lacan's theory of sexuality. The importance attributed to vision in Western culture is also demonstrated in Foucault's discussion of Jeremy Bentham's project. The panopticon is a perfect apparatus of surveillance which secures invisibility for the observing eye while at the same time yielding the subject perfectly visible. The omnipotent and omnipresent eye, located centrally, can see without being seen. For relevant literature see Toril Moi, "Patriarchal Thought and the Drive for Knowledge," in *Between Feminism and Psychoanalysis*, ed. Teresa Brennan (London and New York: Routledge, 1989); Sigmund Freud, *Three Essays on the Theory of Sexuality*, trans. James Strachey (New York: Basic Books, 1975); Irigaray, *Speculum of the Other Woman*; Jacques-Alain Miller: "Jeremy Bentham's Panoptic Device," *October*, 41 (Summer 1987), p. 4.

52 I in no way imply that there are no discontinuities or ruptures within the hegemonic construction of the reign of this visual tradition. For an examination of such ruptures see Jonathan Crary, "Modernizing Vision," in *Vision and Visuality, Dia Art Foundation: Discussion in Contemporary Culture*, ed. Hal Foster (Seattle: Bay Press, 1988).

53 Homi Bhabha, "The Other Question," *Screen*, 24/ 6 (December 1983).

54 Peter Brooks, "The Body in the Field of Vision," *Paragraph*, 14/1 (1991), p. 47.

55 Braidotti relates the desire to go and see how things work to the primitive sadistic drive: the child's pulling apart his/her favorite toy to see how it is made inside, *Nomadic Subjects: Embodiment and Sexual Difference in Contemporary Feminist Theory* (New York: Columbia University Press, 1994), p. 90. We should at this point remember Frantz Fanon's reading of the colonial fantasy: the fantasy of penetration to Algerian women is indistinguishable from the military desire to conquer the foreign territory.

56 Ibid., p. 90.

57 Michel Foucault, *Language, Counter-Memory, Practice: Selected Essays and Interviews*, ed. Donald Bouchard (Oxford: Blackwell, 1977); *The History of Sexuality*, vol. I, *An Introduction*, trans. Robert Hurley (New York: Vintage, 1990). For a useful incorporation of Foucault's analysis for feminist discussions of embodiment see Elizabeth Grosz, *Volatile Bodies: Toward a Corporeal Feminism* (Bloomington: Indiana University Press, 1994) and Judith Butler, *Bodies That Matter: On the Discursive Limits of "Sex"* (New York and London: Routledge, 1993); Rosi Braidotti, *Nomadic Subjects: Embodiment and Sexual Difference in Contemporary Feminist Theory* (New York: Columbia University Press, 1994); Vicki Kirby, "Corporeal Habits: Addressing Essentialism Differently," *Hypatia*, 6/3 (Fall 1991).

58 Judith Butler, *Bodies That Matter*, p. 34.

59 Foucault, *Discipline and Punish*, pp. 26–27.

60 Grosz, *Volatile Bodies*, p. x.

61 Ibid., p. 3.

62 Butler, *Bodies That Matter*, p. 30.

63 Rosi Braidotti, *Patterns of Dissonance*, trans. Elizabeth Guild (New York: Routledge, 1991), p. 153.

64 Charles Richard, *Etude sur l'insurrection du Dahra (1845–1846)*, quoted in Timothy Mitchell, *Colonising Egypt* (Cambridge: Cambridge University Press, 1988), p. 95.
65 Frantz Fanon, *A Dying Colonialism,* trans. Haakon Chevalier (New York: Grove Weidenfeld, 1965), pp. 58–59.
66 Kaja Silverman: "Fragments of a Fashionable Discourse," in *Studies in Entertainment: Critical Approaches to Mass Culture,* ed. Tania Modleski (Bloomington: Indiana University Press, 1986), p. 146.
67 Jacques Derrida, *Dissemination,* trans. Barbara Johnson (Chicago: University of Chicago Press, 1981), p. 261.
68 Ibid., p. 212.
69 Carole Naggar describes the veil as a second skin. Although I would certainly agree to see the veil as a skin, I would also argue that to see the veil as a *second* skin, is still to assume that there is a "first," i.e. "natural" skin that comes *before* the cultural skin. My reading of the veil aims to question precisely this kind of binary opposition between nature and culture, body and mind. See Carole Naggar, "The Unveiled Algerian Women, 1960," *Aperture* (Summer 1990), p. 4.
70 Jacques Derrida and Christie V. McDonald, "Choreographies," *Diacritics,* 12/2 (1982); Irigaray, *Speculum of the Other Woman.*

5 The battle of the veil: women between Orientalism and nationalism

1 Edward Said, "Yeats and Decolonization," *Nationalism, Colonialism and Literature*, A Field Day Pamphlet, 15 (1988), p. 9.
2 Gayatri C. Spivak: "Can the Subaltern Speak?" in *Marxism and the Interpretation of Culture*, ed. Cary Nelson and Lawrence Grossberg (Urbana and Chicago: University of Illinois Press, 1988), p. 288.
3 Said: "Yeats and Decolonization," p. 9.
4 Ibid., p. 14.
5 Partha Chatterjee, *Nationalist Thought and the Colonial World: A Derivative Discourse* (London: Zed Books, 1986), p. 38. For a discussion of Chatterjee's text, see R. Radhakrishnan, "Nationalism, Gender and the Narrative of Identity," in *Nationalisms and Sexualities*, ed. Andrew Parker *et al.* (New York and London: Routledge, 1992).
6 Ibid., p. 38.
7 Ibid., p. 41.
8 Ibid., p. 42.
9 Partha Chatterjee, "The Nationalist Resolution of the Women's Question," in *Recasting Women: Essays in Colonial History*, ed. KumKum Sangari and Sudesh Vaid (New Brunswick: Rutgers University Press, 1990).
10 Ibid., pp. 338–39.
11 Ibid., p. 239.
12 Ibid., p. 249.
13 Ibid., p. 248.

14 Deniz Kandiyoti, "Women as Metaphor: The Turkish Novel From the Tanzimat to the Republic," in *Urban Crises and Social Movements in the Middle East: Proceedings of the C.N.R.S.: E.S.R.C. Symposium,* ed. Kenneth Brown *et al.* (Paris, Harmattan, 1989), p. 140.

15 Ibid., p. 140.

16 Ibid., p. 140.

17 Deniz Kandiyoti, "End of Empire: Islam, Nationalism, and Women in Turkey," in *Women, Islam and the State,* ed. Deniz Kandiyoti (Philadelphia: Temple University Press, 1991), p. 23.

18 Bernard Caporal, *Kemalizm ve Kemalizm Sonrasında Türk Kadını* (Ankara: İş Bankası Yayınları, 1982).

19 Kandiyoti, "End of Empire," p. 32.

20 Kandiyoti, "Women as Metaphor," 140.

21 Ibid., p. 142.

22 Ibid., p. 144.

23 Ibid., p. 145.

24 Ibid., p. 140.

25 Spivak, "Can the Subaltern Speak"; "Rani of Sirmur," in *Europe and Its Others,* vol. I, ed. Francis Baker *et al.* (Colchester: University of Essex, 1985).

26 Deniz Kandiyoti, "Women and the Turkish State: Political Actors or Symbolic Pawns?," in *Woman-Nation-State,* ed. Nira Yuval-Davis and Floya Anthias (New York: St. Martin's Press, 1989), p. 132.

27 Kemal Atatürk, *Atatürk'ün Söylev ve Demeçleri* (Collected Speeches), quoted in Bernard Lewis, *The Emergence of Modern Turkey* (London, Oxford and New York: Oxford University Press, 1961), p. 266.

28 Ibid., p. 268.

29 Lewis, *Emergence of Modern Turkey,* p. 268.

30 Kandiyoti, "End of Empire," p. 41.

31 Kumari Jayawardena, *Feminism and Nationalism in the Third World* (London and New Jersey, Zed Books), 1986.

32 Mustafa Kemal Atatürk quoted in Jayawardena, *Feminism and Nationalism in the Third World,* p. 36.

33 Ibid., p. 36.

34 Lewis, *Emergence of Modern Turkey,* p. 412.

35 Emelie Olson, "Muslim Identity and Secularism in Contemporary Turkey: 'The Headscarf Dispute,'" *Anthropological Quarterly,* 58/5 (1985).

36 Mustafa Kemal Atatürk, *Atatürk'ün Türk Kadını Hakkındaki Görüşlerinden Bir Demet,* ed. Türkan Arıkan (Ankara, T.B.M.M. Yayınları, 1984), p. 19.

37 Mustafa Kemal, quoted in Lewis, *Emergence of Modern Turkey,* pp. 268–69.

38 Atatürk, *Atatürk'ün Türk Kadını Hakkındaki Görüşlerinden Bir Demet,* p. 21.

39 Mustafa Kemal quoted in Jayawardena, *Feminism and Nationalism in the Third World,* p. 36.

40 Kandiyoti, "Women as Metaphor," pp. 148–49.

41 Kandiyoti, "Women and the Turkish State," p. 143.

42 Jayawardena, *Feminism and Nationalism in the Third World,* pp. 35–36.

43 Timothy Mitchell, *Colonising Egypt* (New York: Cambridge University Press, 1988), pp. 66–67.
44 Kumari Jayawardena refers to similar developments in Egypt and Iran, *Feminism and Nationalism in the Third World*, pp. 43–72. For Egypt, see also Margot Badran: "Competing Agenda: Feminists, Islam and the State in 19th and 20th century Egypt," ed. Deniz Kandiyoti, *Women, Islam and the State*, pp. 201–36.
45 Marnia Lazreg, "Gender and Politics in Algeria: Unravelling the Religious Paradigm," *Signs,* 15/4 (Summer 1990), p. 758.
46 Ibid., p. 759.
47 Peter Knauss, *The Persistence of Patriarchy: Class, Gender, and Ideology in Twentieth Century Algeria* (New York: Praeger, 1987).
48 Ibid., p. 50.
49 Quoted in Lazreg, "Gender and Politics in Algeria," p. 764.
50 Knauss, *The Persistence of Patriarchy,* p. 57.
51 Ibid., p. 57. Knauss reads this reaction as follows: "because of the power of French culture, in its subtle and seductive appeals to Algerians and because of the potency of *la mission civilisatrice* there, the traditionalist Algerian reaction was necessarily a total rejection of the "other" and the other's culture. This reaction was also necessarily a total and complete reaffirmation of the judgement of one's own traditions.
52 Ernesto Laclau and Chantal Mouffe, *Hegemony and Socialist Strategy: Towards a Radical Democratic Politics* (London and New York: Verso, 1987), p. 131.
53 Lazreg, "Gender and Politics in Algeria," p. 758.
54 Quoted in Knauss, *The Persistence of Patriarchy*, p. 57.
55 David Gordon, *Women of Algeria: An Essay on Change* (Cambridge: Mass.: Harvard Middle Eastern Monograph Series, 1968), p. 36.
56 Winifred Woodhull, "Unveiling Algeria," *Genders*, 10 (Spring 1991), p. 117.
57 Ibid., p. 119.
58 Knauss, *The Persistence of Patriarchy*, p. 29.
59 Lazreg, "Gender and Politics in Algeria," p. 766.
60 Pierre Bourdieu, *The Algerians* (Boston: Beacon Press, 1961), p. 158.
61 Ibid., p. 156.
62 Ibid., p. 155.
63 Ibid., p. 158.
64 Knauss, *The Persistence of Patriarchy,* p. 69.
65 Quoted in ibid., p. 83.
66 Spivak, "Can the Subaltern Speak," p. 306.

Bibliography

Adorno, Theodor and Horkheimer, Max. *The Dialectic of Enlightenment*, trans. John Cumming (London and New York: Verso, 1979).

Ahmad, Aijaz. *In Theory: Classes, Nations, Literatures* (London and New York: Verso, 1992).

Ahmed, Leila. "Western Ethnocentricism and Perceptions of the Harem," *Feminist Studies*, 8/3 (Fall 1982).

Alloula, Malek. *The Colonial Harem*, trans. Myrna Godzich and Wlad Godzich (Minneapolis: University of Minnesota Press, 1986).

Amicis, Edmondo de. *Constantinople*, trans. Caroline Tilton (New York: Putnam's Sons, 1878).

Arıkan, Türkan (ed.). *Atatürk'ün Türk Kadını Hakkındaki Görüşlerinden Bir Demet* (Ankara: T.B.M.M. Yayınları, 1984).

Asad, Talal. "Two European Images of Non-European Rule," in *Anthropology and the Colonial Encounter* (New York: Humanities Press, 1973).

Atatürk, Mustafa Kemal, *Atatürk'ün Türk Kadını Hakkındaki Görüşlerinden Bir Demet*, ed. Türkan Arıkan (Ankara, T.B.M.M. Yayınları, 1984).

Badran, Margot. "Competing Agenda: Feminists, Islam and the State in 19th and 20th Century Egypt," in *Women, Islam and the State*, ed. Deniz Kandiyoti (Philadelphia: Temple University Press, 1991).

Barker, Francis, Hulme, Peter, and Iversen, Margaret (ed.). *Colonial Discourse/Postcolonial Theory* (Manchester: Manchester University Press, 1994).

Bhabha, Homi. "Difference, Discrimination and the Discourse of Colonialism," in *The Politics of Theory*, ed. Francis Baker *et al.* (Colchester: University of Essex, 1983).

"The Other Question . . ." *Screen*, 24/6 (December 1983).

"Of Mimicry and Man: The Ambivalence of Colonial Discourse," *October*, 28 (Spring 1984).

"Representation and the Colonial Text: A Critical Exploration of Some Form of Mimeticism," in *The Theory of Reading*, ed. Frank Gloversmith (Sussex: The Harvester Press, 1984).

"Sly Civility," *October*, 34 (1985).

"Interrogating Identity: The Postcolonial Prerogative," in *Anatomy of Racism*, ed. D. T. Goldberg (Minneapolis: University of Minnesota, 1990).

"'Race', Time, and the Revision of Modernity," *Oxford Literary Review*, 13/1–2 (1991).

Blondel, Eric. "Nietzsche: Life as Metaphor," in *The New Nietzsche*, ed. D. Allison (Cambridge, Mass. and London: The MIT Press, 1988).

Bourdieu, Pierre. *The Algerians* (Boston: Beacon Press, 1961).

Braidotti, Rosi. *Patterns of Dissonance*, trans. Elizabeth Guild (New York: Routledge, 1991).

Nomadic Subjects: Embodiment and Sexual Difference in Contemporary Feminist Theory (New York: Columbia University Press, 1994).

Brennan, Teresa. "History After Lacan," *Economy and Society*, 19/3 (August 1990).

Brooks, Peter. "The Body in the Field of Vision," *Paragraph*, 14/1 (1991).

Body Work: Objects of Desire in Modern Narrative (Cambridge, Mass.: Harvard University Press, 1993).

Brown Graham, Sara. *Images of Women: The Portrayal of Women in Photography of the Middle East, 1860–1950* (New York: Columbia University Press, 1988).

Burton, Antoinette M. "The White Woman's Burden: British Feminists and the Indian Woman, 1865–1915," *Women's Studies International Forum*, 13/4 (1990).

Butler, Judith. "The Imperialist Subject," *Journal of Urban and Cultural Studies*, 2/1 (1991).

Bodies That Matter: On the Discursive Limits of "Sex" (London and New York: Routledge, 1993).

Caporal, Bernard. *Kemalizm ve Kemalizm Sonrasında Türk Kadını* (Ankara: İş Bankası Yayınları, 1982).

Castoriadis, Cornelius. "Reflections on "Rationality" and "Development,"" *Thesis Eleven*, 10/11 (November/March 1984–5).

Certeau, Michel de. *The Practice of Everyday Life*, trans. Steven Rendall (Berkeley: University of California Press, 1988).

Chatterjee, Partha. *Nationalist Thought and the Colonial World: A Derivative Discourse* (London: Zed Books, 1986).

"Colonialism, Nationalism and Colonized Women: The Contest in India," *American Ethnologist*, 16/4 (1989).

"The Nationalist Resolution of the Women's Question," in *Recasting Women: Essays in Colonial History*, ed. KumKum Sangari and Sudesh Vaid (New Brunswick: Rutgers University Press, 1990).

Clifford, James. "On Orientalism," in *The Predicament of Culture: Twentieth-Century Ethnography, Literature and Art* (Cambridge, Mass.: Harvard University Press, 1988).

Copjec, Joan. "The Sartorial Superego," *October*, 50 (Fall 1989).

Culler, Jonathan. *On Deconstruction: Theory and Criticism After Structuralism* (Ithaca: Cornell University Press, 1986).

Deleuze, Gilles. *The Fold: Leibniz and the Baroque* (Minneapolis: University of Minnesota Press, 1993).

Derrida, Jacques. *Of Grammatology*, trans. Gayatri Chakravorty Spivak (Baltimore: Johns Hopkins University Press, 1976).

Spurs: Nietzsche's Style, trans. Barbara Harlow (Chicago: University of Chicago Press, 1979).

Dissemination, trans. Barbara Johnson (Chicago: University of Chicago Press, 1981).

"White Mythology: Metaphor in the Text," in *Margins of Philosophy*, trans. Alan Bass (Chicago: University of Chicago Press, 1982).

"Deconstruction and the Other: An Interview with Richard Kearney," in *Dialogues with Contemporary Continental Thinkers – The Phenomenological Heritage*, ed. Richard Kearney (Manchester: Manchester University Press, 1984).

"'Eating Well' or the Calculation of the Subject," in *Who Comes After the Subject*, ed. Eduardo Cadva, Peter Connor, and Jean-Luc Nancy (New York and London: Routledge, 1991).

Derrida, Jacques and McDonald, Christie V. "Choreographies," *Diacritics*, 12/2 (1982).

Doane, Mary Ann. "Film and the Masquerade-Theorizing the Female Spectator," *Screen,* 23/3–4 (September–October, 1982).

"Veiling Over Desire," in *Feminism and Psychoanalysis*, ed. R. Felstein and J. Roof (Ithaca: Cornell University Press, 1989).

Ellison, Grace. *An Englishwoman In a Turkish Harem* (London: Methuen, 1915).

Fabian, Johannes. *Time and the Other: How Anthropology Makes Its Object* (New York: Columbia University Press, 1983).

Fanon, Frantz. *A Dying Colonialism*, trans. Haakon Chevalier (New York: Grove Press, 1965).

Black Skin, White Masks (New York: Grove Press, 1967).

Foucault, Michel. *Discipline and Punish: The Birth of the Prison*, trans. Alan Sheridan (Harmondsworth: Penguin, 1977).

Language, Counter-Memory, Practice: Selected Essays and Interviews, ed. Donald Bouchard (Oxford: Blackwell, 1977).

The History of Sexuality, vol. I, *An Introduction*, trans. Robert Hurley (New York: Vintage, 1990).

Power/Knowledge: Selected Interviews and Other Essays 1972–1977, ed. Colin Gordon (New York: Pantheon Books, 1980).

Freud, Sigmund. *Three Essays on the Theory of Sexuality*, trans. James Strachey (New York: Basic Books, 1975).

Gautier, Théophile. *Constantinople*, trans. Robert H. Gould (New York: Henry Holt and Company, 1875).

George, Rosemary Marangoly. "Homes in the Empire, Empire in the Home," *Cultural Critique* (Winter 1993–4).

Gordon, David. *Women of Algeria: An Essay on Change* (Cambridge, Mass.: Harvard Middle Eastern Monograph Series, 1968).

Gourgouris, Stathis. "Tarih ve Rüya Arasında Ulus-Biçimi," *Toplum ve Bilim*, 70 (Fall 1996).

Grosz, Elizabeth. *Sexual Subversions:Three French Feminists* (Sydney: Allen and Unwin, 1989).

Volatile Bodies: Toward a Corporeal Feminism (Bloomington: Indiana University Press, 1994).

"Experimental Desire: Rethinking Queer Subjectivity," in *Space, Time and Perversion* (New York and London: Routledge, 1995).

Harper, Mary. "Recovering the Other: Women and the Orient in Writings of Early Nineteenth-Century France," *Critical Matrix*, 1/3 (1985).

Hatem, Mervat. "Through Each Other's Eyes: The Impact on the Colonial Encounter of the Images of Egyptian, Levantine-Egyptian, and European Women, 1862–1920," in *Western Women and Imperialism: Complicity and Resistance,* ed. Nupur Chaudri and Margaret Strobel (Bloomington: Indiana University Press, 1992).

Heath, Stephen. "Joan Riviere and the Masquerade," in *Formations of Fantasy*, ed. V. Burgin, J. Donald, and C. Kaplan (London and New York: Methuen, 1986).

Irigaray, Luce. *Speculum of the Other Woman*, trans. Gillian Gill (Ithaca: Cornell University Press, 1985).

This Sex Which is Not One, trans. Catherine Porter (Ithaca: Cornell University Press, 1985).

Marine Lover, trans. Gillian Gill (New York: Columbia University Press, 1991).

JanMohamed, Abdul. "The Economy of Manichean Allegory: The Function of Racial Difference in Colonialist Literature," in *"Race", Writing, and Difference*, ed. Henry L. Gates (Chicago: University of Chicago Press, 1986).

Jay, Martin. "Scopic Regimes of Modernity" in *Modernity and Identity*, ed. Scott Lash and Jonathan Friedman (Oxford and Cambridge: Blackwell, 1992).

Jayawardena, Kumari. *Feminism and Nationalism in the Third World* (London and New Jersey: Zed Books, 1986).

Jonathan, Crary. "Modernizing Vision," in *Vision and Visuality*, ed. Hal Foster (Seattle: Bay Press, 1988).

Kabbani, Rana. *Europe's Myths of Orient* (Bloomington: Indiana University Press, 1986).

Kandiyoti, Deniz. "Women and the Turkish State: Political Actors or Symbolic Pawns?," in *Woman-Nation-State*, ed. Nira Yuval-Davis and Floya Anthias (New York: St. Martin's Press, 1989).

"Women as Metaphor: The Turkish Novel From the Tanzimat to the Republic," in *Urban Crises and Social Movements in the Middle East: Proceedings of the C.N.R.S.: E.S. R.C. Symposium*, ed. Kenneth Brown *et al.* (Paris: Harmattan, 1989).

"End of Empire: Islam, Nationalism, and Women in Turkey," in *Women, Islam and the State*, ed. Deniz Kandiyoti (Philadelphia: Temple University Press, 1991).

Keddi, Nikkie and Beck, Lois. *Women in the Muslim World* (Cambridge Mass.: Harvard University Press, 1978).

Kirby, Vicki. "Corporeal Habits: Addressing Essentialism Differently," *Hypatia*, 6/3 (Fall 1991).

Knauss, Peter. *The Persistence of Patriarchy: Class, Gender, and Ideology in Twentieth Century Algeria* (New York: Praeger, 1987).

Lacan, Jacques. *The Four Fundamental Concepts of Psychoanalysis*, trans. Alan Sheridan (New York and London: Norton & Company, 1981).

The Seminar of Jacques Lacan II: The Ego in Freud's Theory and in the Technique of Psychoanalysis 1954–1955, ed. Jacques-Alain Miller, trans. Sylvana Tomaselli (New York and London: Norton and Company, 1991).

Laclau, Ernesto. "Universalism, Particularism and the Question of Identity," *October*, 61 (Summer 1992).

Laclau, Ernesto and Mouffe, Chantal. *Hegemony and Socialist Strategy: Towards a Radical Democratic Politics* (London: Verso, 1987).

"Post-Marxism Without Apologies," in *New Reflections on the*

Revolution of Our Time, ed. Ernesto Laclau (London and New York: Verso, 1990).

Lane, Edward. *An Account of the Manners and Customs of the Modern Egyptians* (New York: Dover Publications, 1973).

Lazreg, Marnia. "Gender and Politics in Algeria: Unravelling the Religious Paradigm," *Signs*, 15/4 (Summer 1990).

Lewis, Bernard. *The Emergence of Modern Turkey* (Oxford: Oxford University Press, 1961).

Lewis, Reina. *Gendering Orientalism: Race, Femininity and Representation* (London: Routledge, 1996).

Lloyd, David. "Race Under Representation," *Oxford Literary Review*, 13/1–2 (1991).

Lowe, Lisa. *Critical Terrains: French and British Orientalisms* (Ithaca: Cornell University Press, 1991).

Mani, Lata, "The Contentious Traditions: The Debate on *Sati* in Colonial India," *Cultural Critique*, 7 (Fall 1987).

Mani, Lata and Frankenberg, Ruth. "The Challenge of Orientalism," *Economy and Society*, 14/2 (May 1985).

Miller, Jacques-Alain. "Jeremy Bentham's Panoptic Device," trans. Richard Miller, *October*, 41 (Summer 1987).

Mills, Sara. *Discourses of Difference: An Analysis of Women's Travel Writing and Colonialism* (New York and London: Routledge, 1991).

Minces, Juliet. *The House of Obedience* (London: Zed Press, 1980).

Mitchell, Timothy. *Colonizing Egypt* (Cambridge: Cambridge University Press, 1988).

Mohanty, Chandra Talpade. "Feminist Encounters: Locating the Politics of Experience," *Copyright* 1 (1998).

"Under Western Eyes: Feminist Scholarship and Colonial Discourses," *Feminist Review*, 30 (Autumn, 1988).

Mohanty, S. P. "Us and Them: On the Philosophical Bases of Political Criticism," *The Yale Journal of Criticism*, 2/2 (1989).

Moi, Toril. "Patriarchal Thought and the Drive for Knowledge," in *Between Feminism and Psychoanalysis*, ed. Teresa Brennan (London and New York: Routledge, 1989).

Montagu, Lady Mary Wortley. *The Complete Letters, 1708–1720*, vol. I, ed. Robert Halsband (Oxford: Clarendon Press, 1965).

Moore-Gilbert, B. J. in *Kipling and Orientalism* (London: Croom Helm, 1986).

Mutman, Mahmut. "Under the Sign of Orientalism: the West vs. Islam," *Cultural Critique*, 23 (Winter 1992–3).

"Under Western Eyes," in *Prosthetic Territories: Politics and*

Hypertechnology, ed. Gabriel Brahm Jr. and Mark Driscoll (Boulder, Colo.: Westview Press, 1995).

Naggar, Carole. "The Unveiled Algerian Women, 1960," *Aperture* (Summer 1990).

Nerval, Gerard de. *The Women of Cairo, Scenes of Life in the Orient*, vol. I (George Routledge and Sons: London, 1929).

Nietzsche, Friedrich. *The Will to Power*, trans. Walter Kaufmann and R. J. Hollingdale (New York: Vintage Books, 1968).

   Beyond Good and Evil, trans. Walter Kaufman (New York: Vintage Books, 1974).

   The Gay Science, trans. Walter Kaufman (New York: Vintage Books, 1974).

Norris, Christopher. *Derrida* (Cambridge, Mass.: Harvard University Press, 1987).

Nupur, Chaudri. and Margaret, Strobel (ed.). *Western Women and Imperialism: Complicity and Resistance* (Bloomington: Indiana University Press, 1992).

Olson, Emelie. "Muslim Identity and Secularism in Contemporary Turkey: 'The Headscarf Dispute,'" *Anthropological Quarterly*, 58/5 (1985).

Parker Francis., Hulme, Peter, and Iversen, Margaret (eds.). "Introduction," in *Colonial Discourse/Postcolonial Theory* (Manchester: Manchester University Press, 1994).

Parry, Benita. "Resistance Theory/ Theorizing Resistance or Two Cheers for Nativism," in *Colonial Discourse/Postcolonial Theory*, ed. Francis Parker, Peter Hulme and Margaret Iversen (Manchester: Manchester University Press, 1994).

Poole, Sophia. *EnglishWoman in Egypt*, vol. II (London: Charles Knight, 1844).

Radhakrishnan, R. "Nationalism, Gender and the Narrative of Identity," in *Nationalisms and Sexualities*, ed. Andrew Parker *et al.* (New York and London: Routledge, 1992).

Richon, Oliver. "Representation, the Despot and the Harem: Some Questions Around an Academic Orientalist Painting by Lecomte-Du-Nouy (1885)," in *Europe and its Others*, Proceedings of the Essex Conference on the Sociology of Literature, vol. I, ed. F. Barker *et al.* (Colchester: University of Essex, 1985).

Riviere, Joan. "Womanliness as Masquerade," in *Formations of Fantasy*, ed. V. Burgin, J. Donald and C. Kaplan (London and New York: Methuen, 1986).

Robbins, Bruce. "Comparative Cosmopolitanism," *Social Text*, 31/32 (1992).

Rorty, Richard. *Philosophy and the Mirror of Nature* (Princeton: Princeton University Press, 1979).

Rose, Jacqueline. "Introduction II," in *Feminine Sexuality: Jacques Lacan and The École Freudienne*, ed. Juliet Mitchell and Jacqueline Rose (London: Macmillan, 1987).

Said, Edward. *Orientalism* (Harmondsworth: Penguin, 1978).

"Orientalism Reconsidered," *Cultural Critique*, 1 (Fall 1985).

"Yeats and Decolonization," in *Nationalism, Colonialism and Literature*, A Field Day Pamphlet, 15 (1988).

"Representing the Colonized: Anthropology's Interlocutors," *Critical Inquiry*, 15 (Winter 1989).

Culture and Imperialism (New York: Alfred Knoff, 1993).

Schor, Naomi. "This Essentialism Which Is Not One: Coming to Grips with Irigaray," *differences*, 1/2 (1989).

Bad Objects: Essays Popular and Unpopular (Durhan: Duke University Press, 1995).

Scott, Joan. "Multiculturalism and the Politics of Identity," *October*, 61 (Summer 1992).

Silverman, Kaja. "Fragments of a Fashionable Discourse," in *Studies in Entertainment: Critical Approaches to Mass Culture,* ed. Tania Modleski (Bloomington: Indiana University Press, 1986).

Spivak, Gayatri Chakravorty. "Rani of Sirmur," in *Europe and Its Others*, ed. Francis Baker *et al.*, vol. I (Colchester: University of Essex, 1985).

"Imperialism and Sexual Difference," *Oxford Literary Review*, 8/1–2 (1986).

"Three Women's Texts and a Critique of Imperialism," in *"Race", Writing, and Difference*, ed. Henry Louis Gates (Chicago: University of Chicago Press, 1986).

"Displacement and the Discourse of Woman," in *Displacement: Derrida and After*, ed. Mark Krupnick (Bloomington: Indiana University Press, 1987).

"Can the Subaltern Speak," in *Marxism and the Interpretation of Culture*, ed. Cary Nelson and Lawrence Grossberg (Urbana: University of Illinois Press, 1988).

"Subaltern Studies: Deconstructing Historiography," in *In Other Worlds* (New York and London: Routledge, 1988).

"Naming Gayatri Spivak," interview with Maria Koundoura, *Stanford Humanities Review* (Spring 1989).

"Neocolonialism and the Secret Agent of Knowledge," interview with Robert Young, *Oxford Literary Review*, 13/1–2 (1991).

"French Feminism Revisited: Ethics and Politics," in *Feminist Theorize the Political*, ed. Judith Butler and Joan Scoat (New York and London: Routledge, 1992).

Starobinski, Jean. *Jean-Jacques Rousseau: Transparency and Obstruction*, trans. A. Goldhammer (Chicago: University of Chicago Press, 1988).

Szyliowich, Irene. *Pierre Loti and the Oriental Woman* (Hong Kong: Macmillan, 1988).

Thomas, Nicholas. *Colonialism's Culture: Anthropology, Travel and Government* (Cambridge: Polity Press, 1994).

Trinh, T. Minh-ha. "Introduction," *Discourse*, 8 (Winter 1986–7).

White, Hayden. *Tropics of Discourse: Essays in Cultural Criticism* (Baltimore and London: Johns Hopkins University Press, 1982).

Whitford, Margaret. "Luce Irigaray and the Female Imaginary: Speaking as a Woman," *Radical Philosophy*, 43 (1986).

Willemen, Paul. "Voyeurism, The Look and Dwoskin," *Afterimage*, 6 (Summer 1976).

Woodhull, Winifred. "Unveiling Algeria," *Genders*, 10 (Spring 1991).

Woodsmall, Ruth Frances. *Woman in the Changing Islamic System* (Delhi: BIMLA Publishing House, 1983, 1st edn 1936).

Young, Robert. *White Mythologies: Writing History and the West* (London: Routledge, 1990).

  Colonial Desire: Hybridity in Theory, Culture and Race (London and New York: Routledge, 1995), p. 9.

Zizek, Slavoj. "Looking Awry", *October*, 50 (Fall 1989).

  The Sublime Object of Ideology (London and New York: Verso, 1989).

Index

CPSIA information can be obtained
at www.ICGtesting.com
Printed in the USA
LVHW080504271222
735859LV00006B/434